THE JEW AND HIS DUTIES

THE JEW
AND HIS DUTIES

The Essence of the
KITZUR SHULHAN ARUKH
Ethically Presented

by HYMAN E. GOLDIN

HEBREW PUBLISHING COMPANY
NEW YORK

CONTENTS

Part Two: Our Holy Seasons

x *Contents*

PART ONE

OUR DUTIES TOWARDS GOD

CHAPTER I

THE DOCTRINES OF JUDAISM

I. GOD

The first and foremost doctrine of the Jewish religion is the belief that there is one God, and only One. This concept is expressed by the confession of faith, which the Jew must recite twice daily, morning and evening: "Hear, O Israel: the Lord our God, the Lord is One." This is the battle-cry of the Jewish religion.

The great Jewish master, Moses Maimonides, born in Spain, in the year 1135, formulated thirteen articles of the Jewish faith, which have since been incorporated in our Prayer Books. They are recited at the end of the morning weekday prayers.

The thirteen articles can be divided into three groups. The first group consists of five articles, as follows:

1. I believe with perfect faith that the Creator, blessed be His name, is both Creator and Ruler of all created things, and that He alone has made, does make, and ever will make all works of nature.

2. I believe with perfect faith that the Creator, blessed be His name, is One, and no unity is like His in any form, and that He alone is our God, who was, is, and ever will be.

3. I believe with perfect faith that the Creator, blessed be His name, is not a body, no corporeal relations apply to Him, and nothing exists that has any similarity to Him.

4. I believe with perfect faith that the Creator, blessed be His name, was the first and also will be the last.

5. I believe with perfect faith that the Creator, blessed be His

3

name, is alone worthy of being worshiped, and that no other being is worthy of our worship.

These five articles of faith form one fundamental doctrine of Judaism—Belief in God.

BELIEF IN THE EXISTENCE OF A CREATOR. A mortal being, whose reason and knowledge are limited, even as his other faculties are limited, cannot know what God is. The human mind cannot comprehend Him. The human eye cannot see Him. Finite minds cannot comprehend Him, for God is Infinite.

God cannot be found in any particular part of the universe, because He is the Cause of all existence and the Source of all intellect. He is, therefore, above and beyond all. We know God only by His works, and we accordingly attribute to Him qualities which He alone possesses.

This doctrine, that a Creator exists, is evidenced by the wondrous power, beauty, and order of nature. Considering this, we must arrive at the conclusion that there exists an all-mighty, all-wise Creator of the universe.

BELIEF IN HIS UNITY. We believe that there is no other God besides Him, nor is there any being that can be compared to Him or that can share in His divinity. He is not composed of parts or of persons. He is an Absolute Unity. To ascribe God-like power to any other being, or to associate any other being with Him, is to deny His very existence, and is idolatry.

Belief in an Absolute Unity, carries with it the belief in a universal religion, and in a universal brotherhood. (See, *Belief in the coming of the Messiah,* p. 8.)

BELIEF IN HIS SPIRITUALITY. He has not the limitations of a body. He is a Spiritual Being, the Spirit of all existence, permeating all and everything.

We are forbidden to worship God under any form or image, or present Him as though He had some form visible to the eye. And when the Holy Scriptures speak of God's arm, or hand, or face, as though He had human form, such anthropomorphisms are figurative. They are merely human expressions that convey ideas within human comprehension; as the Talmud frequently expresses it (Berakot 31b;

a. fr.) "Diberah Torah kileshon bene adam" (the Torah speaks according to the language of men). The Scriptures use metaphors and phrases adapted to human understanding. God, being a Spirit, has no corporal parts. Similarly, when the Holy Scriptures speak of God's anger, hatred, or vengeance, such words merely express human emotions, conveying human ideas to humans having finite minds.

BELIEF IN HIS ETERNITY. He is infinite in time and in space. He is without beginning and without end. He remains from everlasting to everlasting ever the same. He is immutable. He is not subject to change.

BELIEF THAT GOD IS THE SOLE OBJECT OF MAN'S WORSHIP. There is no other being to whom we may offer prayers, either in heaven or on earth, except the One God in heaven. We are forbidden to call any being by the name of God or worship him, except Him, the Father of all men and the Spirit of all life.

Many ancient nations were worshipers of the sun, moon, and stars. The Egyptians were worshipers of beasts and of men who represented strength. The Greeks worshiped beasts and men who represented beauty. The Persians worshiped the power of good and evil, and the Babylonians the power of destiny. The Jewish religion is the only one, even in our own day, that teaches pure Monotheism—that God is the only self-conscious Being, undivided and indivisible, dwelling in all and yet above all, the perfect Unity, who alone is worthy of being worshiped.

II. REVELATION OF GOD TO MAN

The sixth, seventh, eighth and ninth articles of faith formulated by Maimonides, form another fundamental doctrine of the Jewish faith—Revelation of God to man. They are:

6. I believe with perfect faith that all the words of the prophets are true.

7. I believe with perfect faith that the prophecy of Moses our teacher, peace be unto him, was true, and that he was the chief of the prophets, both of those that preceded him and of those who followed him.

8. I believe with perfect faith that the whole Law, now in our

possession, is the same which was given to Moses our master, peace be unto him.

9. I believe with perfect faith that this Law will not be changed, and that there will never be any other Law given by the Creator, blessed be His name.

BELIEF IN THE REVELATION OF GOD TO PROPHETS. God communicated His will to the people of Israel through the Prophets by the wondrous power of inspiration. These Prophets revealed God's truth and righteousness to the consciences of men; thus they revealed God in man and attempted to establish the true religion of humanity.

Maimonides writes regarding prophecy (Guide for the Perplexed, Part II, Ch. xxxii, 2–3): "It is impossible that an ignorant person should be a prophet; or that a person being no prophet in the evening, should unexpectedly, on the following morning, find himself a prophet, as if prophecy were a thing that could be found unintentionally. . . . There are numerous passages in Scripture as well as in the writings of the sages, which support the principle that it depends chiefly on the will of God who is to prophesy, and at what time; and that He only selects the wisest. . . . For prophecy is impossible without study and training; when these have created the possibility, then it depends on the will of God whether the possibility is to be turned into reality."

Prophecy means the attainment of that degree of spiritual development through which we can hear the word of God, perceive spiritual light, feel the Divine impulse, and be conscious of the working of the divine mind upon our own.

The ideals and admonitions of our Prophets were derived through the Spiritual Light, Divine Impulse or Mind. The Prophets attained the power of perception by reason of their spiritual development. The actual perception was permitted only in dreams or visions.

BELIEF IN THE SUPREME AUTHORITY OF MOSES. Moses is the greatest of all prophets, under whose leadership was concluded the main covenant between God and Israel. When the people were assembled at the foot of Mount Sinai to receive the Law of God, they were consecrated to be a nation of prophets and priests of God for all time to come.

All other prophets received their messages in visions or in dreams, but about Moses the Scriptures say (Ex. xxxiii, 11): "God spoke to Moses face to face"; and again (Num. xii, 8): "Mouth to mouth I will speak to Him." God is incorporeal, and no mortal can see His presence. The Biblical expressions are Hebrew idioms, meaning one directly to the other, "As one speaketh to a friend" (Ex. xxxiii, 11).

BELIEF IN THE DIVINE ORIGIN OF THE LAW. The Torah, or the Five Books of Moses, has come down to us from Moses on Mount Sinai without any addition, diminution, or change. The origin of the Torah as it is now in our possession is divine, having been given us by God in its entirety.

BELIEF IN THE IMMUTABILITY OF THE LAW OF MOSES. We, as Jews, believe in the Torah, the Law of God. It remains the covenant of God with Israel and all mankind for all time to come, never to be altered or changed even by God Himself. It will remain in force for ever, as God's revelation to man.

III. REWARD AND PUNISHMENT

The last four of Maimonides' articles of faith form another group that teach a third fundamental doctrine of the Jewish faith—Reward and Punishment. The four articles are:

10. I believe with perfect faith that the Creator, blessed be His name, knows all the actions of the children of men and all their thoughts. As it is said (Ps. xxxiii, 15): "He that fashioneth the hearts of them all, that considereth all their doings."

11. I believe with perfect faith that the Creator, blessed be His name, rewards those who keep His commandments and punishes those who transgress them.

12. I believe with perfect faith in the coming of the Messiah, and although he may tarry, I daily hope for his coming.

13. I believe with perfect faith that there will take place a resurrection of the dead at a time which will please the Creator, blessed be His name, and exalted be His remembrance forever and ever.

BELIEF THAT GOD IS ALL-KNOWING. His knowledge comprises all things, deeds and thoughts, past, present and future. He knows the thoughts of all men, even when they are not expressed by word of mouth.

BELIEF IN REWARD AND PUNISHMENT. God is just. He deals in righteousness with all men. He rewards them for their good deeds and punishes them for their sins, giving them time to repent and mend their ways. He educates and leads them, through trial and suffering, from error to truth, and from vice to virtue. By reward and punishment, by joys and sorrows, He leads them to ever higher aims.

BELIEF IN THE COMING OF THE MESSIAH. Many prophets of Judah foretold that a King, a Messiah (anointed) from the house of David, would at the end of all times establish a reign of peace over the world, and would unite all nations in the glorification of God and the brotherly love of man, while residing at Jerusalem as the holy center. This glorious future, when all men and nations shall be made one by the divine covenant of love and peace, of justice and truth, is called *the time of the Messiah*, or *the Messianic Kingdom*.

The fundamental principle underlying the prophecies of our great spiritual leaders is pure monotheism, the belief in ONE GOD. And this belief in a Divine Oneness, an Absolute Unity, carries with it the belief that some day, "at the end of time," a Messiah will come who will be identified with the Oneness of Humanity, who will establish a Unity of People and of God's Kingdom on Earth, when wars will cease, and Universal Peace, Universal Brotherhood, and Universal Happiness will become a reality.

People who believe in a multiplicity of divine powers can scarcely believe in a unity of mankind and in a world where peace and tolerance reign. Only believers in a Unified Divinity strive to achieve the unity of peoples and races by peaceful methods. It was because the Jew believed in an Undivided Divine Power that he developed the prophetic ideal of a millennium of an undivided humanity, of universal peace and happiness, the eradication of war and hatred among people.

Israel, according to the Prophet Isaiah (lii–liii), has been chosen by God as His instrument for the accomplishment of this end. Israel is not only the prophet but also the martyr of this true religion of Universal Brotherhood and Messianic Hope. It is, therefore, the sacred duty of every Jew to preach and practice the ideals of life, privately and socially, in whatever country he lives, and be loyal to God and His Law.

BELIEF IN RESURRECTION. Immortality of the soul. Man, as far as his mortal frame is concerned, shares the destiny of all animate beings. He is born, he dies, and is subject to the same laws of growth and decay as is every other earthly creature. But we, as Jews, believe that man has a soul which is a part of God Himself, a spirit of His spirit. The soul of man is immortal and shares in the eternal nature of God.

We share in the belief of our former sages that, at some future time, the body will be reunited with the soul and rise from the grave to a new life on earth. This is the hope of resurrection. We, who believe in God's immutable will as manifested in nature's laws, hold fast to the doctrine that the body is perishable; but the spirit is imperishable, and continues forever with God, the Fountain of all life.

The belief in the immortal nature of our soul, prompted our sages of old to expound the doctrine that this earthly life and all it offers us is only "Like an antechamber of the world to come" (Mishnah, Abot iv, 21). We should use our earthly span of life as a preparation for the higher life of godliness and righteousness which lasts forever, and not upon vain things. We know that eternal happiness is the reward for doing good; and everlasting misery and remorse are the consequences of evil actions.

It is true that human intellect cannot understand the transition of human souls to other spheres of activity, nor in a life hereafter. But this failure to understand does not preclude the existence of life hereafter. For that matter, we are unable to understand much that exists around us. We do not know, for instance, the real nature of the simplest physical forces, the diffusion of gases, gravitation, light, heat, sound, chemical action, electricity, magnetism, molecular action, the countless suns in the skies, the motions of the countless stellar systems, all the unaccountable phenomena of nature. But we cannot deny their existence because we fail to understand their mysteries.

CHAPTER II

PRAYERS

Man has always conceived of a deity, of a supernatural power, in one form or another. No matter how crude his concept of deity may have been, he has always sought ways in which to establish communion with his deity, either to show him gratitude and pay him homage, or to speak to him of his needs and fears.

When the Jews were in their own land, Palestine, and were able to worship God in the Holy Temple at Jerusalem, they adopted the method of sacrificing offerings to their God and chanted songs, as a means of communicating with Him. On certain occasions, the Jews offered fervent prayers, in addition to sacrifices.

After the destruction of the Temple, when sacrifices were no longer possible, the Jewish sages adopted the method of establishing communion with God by offering prayers, public or private, at certain fixed times and seasons, and on special occasions. The founders of the synagogue instituted prayers to be offered three times each day at certain fixed times and in certain formulas in the Holy Tongue, Hebrew. The Jews have accordingly established houses of prayer, synagogues, in every Jewish community in the lands where their destiny has taken them.

The custom of praying three times each day is very ancient. Daniel prayed three times daily (Daniel vi, 10), and the Psalmist sings (lv, 17): "Evening, morning and noon will I pray." Our Talmudists say (Berakot 27b) that Abraham instituted the *shaharit* (morning prayer), Isaac the *minhah* (afternoon prayer), and Jacob the *maarib* (evening prayer).

10

These public prayers are seldom offered for individuals and their needs. They are mostly national in character, calling for the restoration of Zion and the coming of the Messiah, at whose advent all peoples will recognize the existence of the true God in heaven. Thus, while scattered in foreign lands, the Jews pray for universal peace, the cessation of hostilities, and the brotherhood of men.

Prayer is the communion of one's soul with God. As the child trustfully comes to its parent with its every joy or sorrow, trouble or perplexity, so do we follow the deepest need of our nature when we pour forth our prayers to God our Father.

To Him we offer praises in adoration of His greatness; thanksgiving in recognition of all His blessings; supplication when we feel our human weakness and need. We plead for forgiveness when conscious of sin and misdoings; yearn for consolation in trouble and affliction; pray for hope and strength in anguish and perplexity, and proffer our humble submission to His will in hours of trial and tribulation.

When we pray, we do not presume to acquaint the All-knowing God with our wants, but, feeling that God is nigh when we call on Him, we derive strength and courage, comfort and inspiration from the conviction that He is our all-benign Father, who hears the prayers of all His children. We should, therefore, make it the holiest duty of our life to seek constant communion with God on high, that we may secure His help and favor at all times.

Prayer is a very important part of Jewish spiritual life, and it is the special duty of every Jew to worship God by offering prayers to Him, thereby acknowledging His sovereignty over the universe. By praying to Him, we also recognize that He is our Master in whose hands are the destinies of all men, and that nothing can be accomplished without His will. Prayers and other forms of devotion are expressions of our religious sentiments, our longing to give expression to our feeling of awe and adoration. And although we may pray for our needs at all times and in any manner we think proper, nevertheless we must follow the formulas of prayers instituted by our sages in olden times. We must also pray in the language chosen by them for praying, which is Hebrew, and pray at the times fixed by them for offering such prayers. For, by praying in the same language, in the same formulas, and at fixed times, the Jews in Diaspora will remain one people, though they speak the language and follow the customs peculiar to the lands of their adoption.

It is, therefore, our sacred duty to become familiar with the Hebrew language, and to become acquainted with the various laws and customs concerning the prayers, the most important of which are given in the pages that follow.

I. WHEN RISING IN THE MORNING

1. "I have set the Lord always before me" says the Psalmist (Ps. xvi, 8). This is a very important principle in Jewish life. For, the manner in which we behave when alone in the house, is not the same as when in the presence of a great king. Our manner of speech amid the members of our own family and friends, is not the same as when we are in the company of a king. In the latter case, we certainly would take care that our behavior and speech be properly prepared beforehand. So much the more, then, should we be cautious when we consider that the Great King, the Holy One, blessed be He, whose glory fills the universe, is always present and observing all that we do. As it is said (Jer. xxiii, 24): "Can a man hide himself in secret places that I shall not see him? saith the Lord. Do I not fill the heaven and the earth?" When we have a true feeling of awe and reverence, it will restrain us from doing or saying things which are displeasing to Him, and thus give life a solemn and earnest purpose.

God has implanted the sense of shame in our soul. We blush at unbecoming sights, words, acts and thoughts. We should do nothing, even in strictest privacy, say nothing, and read nothing that would make us ashamed of ourselves.

2. As soon as we awake in the morning, we must be mindful of the mercy of God, blessed be His name. While still in bed, we should therefore say: "I thank Thee, O living and eternal King, because Thou hast graciously restored my soul to me; great is Thy faithfulness." (Since the proper name of God is not mentioned in this prayer, we may say it immediately upon rising from our sleep, although our hands are yet unwashed.)

3. The first garment which a male must put on, is the *talit katan*

(the small four-fringed garment), commonly known as the *arba kanfot* (see p. 42), for he is not allowed to walk even as much as four cubits without having a fringed garment on. But, as his hands are still un-washed, he may not pronounce the benediction on putting it on.

4. Every human being when rising from his sleep in the morning, is like a new-born creature insofar as the worship of the Creator is concerned. Each person should therefore prepare himself for worship by purifying himself. He should wash his hands, ritually, by spilling water on them three times, even as the high priest used to do before beginning his service in the Temple at Jerusalem.

5. The ritual handwashing is performed thus: We take a full cup of water in our right hand and put it in the left; then we spill water with the left upon the right, and then we take it in the right and spill it on the left, repeating this performance three times.

6. No soap may be used while performing the ritual handwashing; but soap may be used immediately thereafter.

7. It has been ordained by our sages of old that a prayer in the form of a benediction should be pronounced on the occasion of per-forming a religious duty. In this benediction, we bless, or rather praise, the Almighty for having made us a holy people by ordering us to fulfill His commandments. The Jew thus not only expresses his willingness to obey his God, but he even expresses his gratitude to his God for having been privileged to receive His commandments.

8. The following benediction is pronounced immediately after washing the hands and before drying them: "Blessed art Thou, O Lord our God, King of the universe, who hath sanctified us with His commandments, and hath commanded us concerning the washing of the hands." We are not allowed to walk around without having our hands washed ritually, except in cases of extreme necessity. We have to wash our faces also, in honor of our Creator; because it is written (Gen. ix, 6): "For in the image of God hath He made the man." We should also rinse our mouths of all impurities, because we have to pronounce the Great Name in purity and cleanliness.

9. Before the morning hand-washing, we should not touch either our mouths, our noses, our eyes, our ears, or any kind of food.

10. Hands must be washed on the following occasions: On

awakening from sleep, on leaving the lavatory or bath, after paring one's nails, after having one's hair cut or combed, after taking off one's shoes (with bare hands), after touching any unclean thing, after touching parts of the body which are usually covered, after leaving a cemetery, after accompanying the dead, and on leaving the house where a corpse lay.

II. BEFORE PRAYING

1. Before we perform a holy deed anywhere, such as the study of the Torah, or prayer, we must be certain that the place is pure: no unclean matter should be found there and nothing unseemly be visible.

2. While the slightest doubt remains concerning the cleanliness of the place, we must take care not to utter anything that is holy.

3. From the moment the day dawns—since this is the time when prayers may be commenced—we are not permitted to begin any kind of work, or commence the transaction of any business, or start a journey before we have prayed.

4. One is not permitted to eat or drink before praying. But if one is old or feeble and cannot wait until the congregation leaves the synagogue, [especially on Sabbaths and Festivals when the services are prolonged], one may say the *shaharit* (morning prayer) at home, then say the *kiddush* (sanctification prayer), and partake of some food. Such a person should then go to the synagogue, listen attentively while the congregation prays the *shaharit*, and afterwards pray with them the *musaph* (additional prayers). However, if one is ill, or if one cannot concentrate upon the prayers without food or drink, one may eat or drink before praying.

5. Water, and tea or coffee without sugar or milk, may be taken before praying, even on Sabbaths and Festivals when the *kiddush* must be recited before eating.

6. It is written (Amos iv, 12): "Prepare to meet thy God, O Israel." In other words, we should prepare ourselves before the Holy One, blessed be He, and put on decent garments when going to pray, as a subject prepares to meet his king. Even when praying in our houses, we should be properly clothed.

7. It is proper to give charity before praying, and to resolve to abide by the command of God (Lev. xix, 18): "And thou shalt love thy neighbor as thyself."

III. MORNING BENEDICTIONS

1. The benediction "Asher natan lasekhvi binah" (who hath given the cock understanding) should not be uttered before daylight.

2. The benediction "Pokeah ivrim" (who openeth the eyes of the blind), may be said even by a blind person, for he, too, is benefited by sight in that others can show him the way.

3. After the benediction "Hamaabir shenah meenai" (who removeth sleep from my eyes), no *amen* should be responded, because this is not the end of the benediction; for "Yehi ratzon milphanekha" (may it be Thy will) is also a part of this benediction, and the end thereof is "Gomel hasadim tobim leamo yisrael" (who bestoweth kindly favors to His people Israel).

4. Even he who is awake all night must say all the morning benedictions when praying, except the benediction "Al netilat yadayim" (concerning the washing of the hands).

IV. THE TEPHILIN

1. The Almighty God commanded us to lay the *tephilin* on the arm and on the head. When we put on the *tephilin*, we must reflect that by doing this we are fulfilling the command of the Holy One, blessed be His name. The *tephilin* contain four sections of the Torah, which speak of the unity of God and of the exodus of the Israelities from the land of Egypt. The *tephilin* are put on the arm nearest the heart and on the head as a symbol of submission both of thought and feeling of the soul which resides in the brain, and of the desires and longings which spring from the heart. In so doing, we consent to fulfill that which is written (Num. xv, 39): "And that ye seek not after the inclination of your heart and the delight of your own eyes."

Thus Maimonides writes (Hilkot Tephilin iv, 25): "Great is the sanctity of the *tephilin*, for while the *tephilin* are on a man's head and about his arm, he is humble and God-fearing; he is not drawn away by levity and idle conversation, nor does his heart entertain evil thoughts; but he fills his heart with thoughts of truth and righteousness." (See p. 39.)

2. It is of extreme importance that we observe the precept regarding the *tephilin*. They who fail to put on the *tephilin* are reckoned among those transgressors in Israel who sin with their bodies, because they refuse to subjugate their bodies to the worship of the Almighty. We must see to it that the *tephilin* always be in proper condition, and that the capsules and the straps be black. If we are careful in performing the precept of *tephilin* and treat the *tephilin* with respect, our days will be prolonged, and we are certain of having a share in the world to come.

3. The *tephilin* must be put on at the morning service only on week days, but not on the Sabbath or on Festivals, because concerning the *tephilin* it is written (Ex. xiii, 9): "And it shall be for a *sign* unto thee." But such a sign is not needed on Sabbaths and Festivals, as these holy days themselves are a *sign* between God and Israel, as it is written (Ex. xxxi, 17): "It is a sign between Me and the children of Israel for ever."

4. The time for putting on the *tephilin* begins from that hour of the morning a man can recognize his neighbor, with whom he is slightly acquainted, at a distance of four cubits.

5. Because the precept of *tzitzit* (fringe) must be performed daily, including Sabbaths and Festivals, whereas the precept of *tephilin* is to be performed on week days only, the *talit* (fringed garment) must be put on before we put on the *tephilin*. This is the general rule: The precept which is more frequently observed takes precedence over that which is less frequently observed.

6. The *tephilin* of the hand should be put on the elevated part of the biceps of the left arm, and be made to incline slightly towards the side, so that when we let our arm down, the *tephilin* should be on a level with our heart. The *tephilin* of the head is put on the head midway between the eyes. And its place commences from where the hair begins to grow and continues upward to the place where the child's skull is soft; that is, the lower part of the bridge of the *tephilin* shall not be lower than the place where the hair begins to grow, and the upper end of the bridge shall not be higher than the place where

a child's skull is soft. The knot in the strap must be placed on the back of the head above the nape of the neck at the base of the skull. The strap should be fastened on the head, so that the *tephilin* should not incline either towards one side or another.

7. The *tephilin* must be put on while standing. We must not shake the *tephilin* from the bag, because we slight thereby a divine command, but we must take them out with our hand. We first put on the *tephilin* of the hand, and before tightening the knot we say the benediction, "Lehaniah tephilin" (to put on the *tephilin*). We then tighten the knot and make seven coils on our forearm, that is, between the elbow and the wrist. Thereafter we immediately put on that of the head, and before we tighten it we say the benediction, "Al mitzvat tephilin" (concerning the commandment of the *tephilin*). We then tighten it and say, "Barukh shem kebod malkhuto leolam vaed" (blessed be His name whose glorious kingdom is for ever and ever). After that we make three coils on the middle finger, one around the middle phalanx and two around the lower phalanx. While making the three coils, we recite the two verses from Hosea (ii, 21, 22): "Veerastikh li leolam," etc. (And I shall betroth thee unto Me forever, etc.). The *tephilin* are thus compared to the bridal garland, a symbol of the devotion between Israel and God. Thereafter we coil the strap around three fingers and then around the palm of our hand, making it appear like the letter *shin*.

8. If one should happen to take first from the bag the *tephilin* of the head, one should put it away, cover it, and put that of the hand first.

9. Nothing must come between the flesh and the *tephilin*, with the exception of one's hair.

10. No conversation is permitted between the putting on of the *tephilin* of the hand and that of the head. It is even forbidden to wink the eyes or make motions with the hands. Even if we hear the *kaddish* or *kedushah*, we must not interrupt by reciting it or by responding *amen*, but we must keep silent and pay attention to what the congregation is saying. If, however, we hear someone else saying the benediction, "Lehaniah tephilin" (to put on the tephilin), we may respond *amen* to it, because *amen* is a corroboration that we

believe in the precept of the *tephilin*; this therefore is not an interruption.

11. If by error we should interrupt, we must touch the *tephilin* on the hand, repeat the benediction, "Lehaniah tephilin," make the knot tight, and thereafter put the *tephilin* on the head and say the necessary benediction. If, however, the interruption has been made for the need of the *tephilin*, we need not repeat the benediction "Lehaniah tephilin."

12. The *tephilin* of the hand and of the head are two separate and distinct precepts, and the inability to observe one does not bar the observance of the other. Therefore, if we have only one of the *tephilin* available, or if by reason of some accident we are able to put on only one, we are bound to put that one on. If it is the one for the hand, only the benediction "Lehaniah tephilin" is said; but if it is the one for the head, then we must say both benedictions: "Lehaniah tephilin" and "Al mitzvat tephilin"; and we must also say: "Barukh shem kebod malkhuto leolam vaed" (blessed be His name whose glorious kingdom is for ever and ever.)

13. For the purpose of putting on *tephilin*, the hand with which a man naturally writes determines which side shall be considered his "right" side. The hand opposite the writing-hand shall be considered the "left" hand, and it is on this hand that the *tephilin* should be worn. However, a man not born left-handed, who has accustomed himself to write with his left hand but does all his other work with the right hand, is considered right-handed, as are all ambidextrous persons.

14. The prescribed width of the straps, whether belonging to the *tephilin* of the head or of the hand, is no less than the length of a barley. The prescribed length for both straps of the *tephilin* for the head is to reach down to a man's navel, or a trifle above that. The strap of the hand should be long enough to make seven coils upon the arm and three windings upon the middle finger with enough left over to tighten it. If the strap be torn, whether it be of the head or of the hand, a Rabbi should be consulted.

15. Care should be taken that the straps always be with their black side out.

16. If the *tephilin*, when not in the bag, fall to the ground, we must fast. But if they fall down while in the bag, we need not fast, but we must give charity.

17. As long as the *tephilin* are on, our attention must not be diverted from them even for a moment, except during the prayer of the *shemoneh esreh* (eighteen benedictions) and while studying the Torah. It is forbidden to eat a substantial meal while having the *tephilin* on, but casual refreshments may be taken. Sleeping, even if only for a little while, is prohibited while wearing the *tephilin*.

18. The *tephilin* should not be taken off until we say, "Yehi ratzon shenishmor hukkekha" (May it be Thy will that we keep Thy statutes) contained in the prayer "Uba letzion goel" (and a redeemer shall come to Zion).

19. The *tephilin* must be removed while standing. First we unwind the coils around the middle finger and two or three coils from around the arm, then we remove the *tephilin* of the head, and finally the *tephilin* of the hand. It is customary to kiss the *tephilin* when putting them on and when taking them off. The *talit* should not be taken off before the *tephilin* are removed.

20. The *tephilin* must be placed in their bag in such a way that we may be certain the following day of taking out the *tephilin* of the hand first. The *tephilin* may not be placed one on the top of the other, but side by side. The bag containing the *tephilin* should be placed in the bag of the *talit* so that the *talit* is uppermost.

21. It is now the prevailing custom that a boy does not put on the *tephilin* before he becomes *Bar Mitzvah* (duty bound to fulfill the precepts; see p. 222), that is, until he has completed his thirteenth year. However, he may accustom himself to the practice of performing the precept of putting on the *tephilin* by beginning to put them on about a month before *Bar Mitzvah*.

22. Women are exempt from observing the precept of putting on the *tephilin*. There is a general rule of law laid down in the Talmud, that women, because they are more occupied with their duties at home, are free from ceremonies which must be performed at a specified time. Since the *tephilin* must be put on at a specified time,

namely, on weekdays only and not on Saturdays and Holidays, this rule of law applies.

23. It is proper to have the *tephilin* examined occasionally, because at times they become imperfect on account of perspiration. If the *tephilin* are used only occasionally, they should be examined twice in seven years, because there is a possibility that they have become mouldy. If the capsules are torn, or if the *tephilin* fell into water, the parchments must be examined. However, if there is no one competent to examine them and sew them up again, one should put them on without having them examined, in order not to neglect the performance of the precept relating to the *tephilin*, but without saying the benedictions.

V. THE SANCTITY OF THE SYNAGOGUE [1]

As in ancient times, when daily sacrifices were offered by the priests every morning and evening and additional ones on holy days, the congregation of Israel was enjoined to erect a sanctuary to bring God to the people, so it has become the duty of Israelites living together in a township or city to provide for a place of divine worship and religious instruction and to keep it sacred. In fact, our Sages tell us that the inhabitants of a community may force one another to build a synagogue for divine worship.

Private devotion has its proper place in the family circle, where morning and evening and meal-time are the hours set for prayer and grace. But public service has its higher object of uniting the worshipers in prayer as brothers, children of our Father in heaven.

LAWS RELATING TO THE SANCTITY OF THE SYNAGOGUE

1. It is the duty of every man to select a synagogue where he may pray permanently, and to select therein a permanent seat for worship.

2. The sanctity of the synagogue and the house of study is very great, because of the presence of the One who dwells therein. A place where the Almighty is worshiped is designated by the Talmud as "Bet mikedash meat" (Minor Holy Temple). In the Temple we

[1] See pages 10–12.

are forbidden to engage in gossip or to make any calculations other than those concerning religious matters, such as the counting of charity money. Such places must be respected, kept perfectly clean, and well lighted.

3. It is highly meritorious to pray in a synagogue or in a house where the Law of God is expounded, even if it happens that at times the required quorum for prayer, of ten male adults (*mineyan*), is lacking.

4. Before entering such holy places, we must wipe the dust from our shoes, and we must take care that there be no dirt either on our bodies or on our garments.

5. We must not enter a holy place merely for the purpose of taking shelter from the heat or from rain. We may enter there to call a friend, but we must first read there some verses of the Torah, study some Mishnah, offer some prayer, listen to some religious discussion, or, at least, sit down for a while (for even just sitting in holy places is considered meritorious). Thereafter, we may call our friend.

6. It is forbidden to eat, drink, or to take even a short nap in places of worship. For the sake of fulfilling a religious duty, such as circumcisions, weddings, or the like, it is permissible to have a meal there in which there is no drunkenness and no frivolity.

7. Upon leaving a synagogue, we must neither run nor walk with great strides, because this would indicate that our stay at the synagogue was burdensome. However, if we are on our way to perform a religious duty at that time, it is our duty to hasten our step.

VI. PESUKE DEZIMERAH (SPECIAL VERSES OF THE PSALMS)

1. The prayers from "Hodu" (praise ye) to the end of "Az yashir" (then sang Moses), are called "Pesuke Dezimerah" (Special Verses of the Psalms). "Barukh sheamar" (blessed be He who said) is the benediction preceding them, and "Yishtabah" (praised be) is the benediction following them. The prayers from "Barukh sheamar" through the "Shemoneh Esreh" (silent prayer) must not be interrupted with conversation even when held in the Holy Tongue (Hebrew).

2. While reciting "Barukh sheamar" we take the two front fringes of the *talit* and stand up. Upon concluding the benediction with the words "Mehullal batishbahot" (extolled with praises), we kiss the fringes and release them from our hands.

3. "Mizemor letodah" (a Psalm of thanksgiving offering) should be recited while standing up and with joy, because it is in the stead of a thanksgiving offering. From "Vayebarekh david" (and David blessed) as far as "Attah hu adonai haelohim" (Thou art the Lord God), should also be recited while standing up. The "Shirah" (Song of Moses), "Az yashir," should likewise be recited while standing up, and with joy and attention. One should also stand up while reciting the benediction "Yishtabah" (praised be).

4. The Psalm "Mizemor letodah" is omitted on Sabbaths and on Festivals, because it relates to a free-will thanksgiving offering, and neither vows nor free-will sacrifices may be offered on these days. This Psalm is likewise omitted during *Hol Hamoed* (Intermediate Days) of Passover, and on the days preceding Passover and the Day of Atonement.

VII. MINEYAN (QUORUM FOR PRAYER)

King Solomon says (Prov. xix, 28): "In the multitude of people is the king's glory." Therefore it is the duty of every Israelite to make an effort to pray with the congregation. Public service not only creates a greater religious sentiment and enthusiasm, but it also has, as its higher object, the uniting of many hearts in prayer to our common Father in heaven and the awakening of loftier sentiments of faith and loyalty in the individual. According to the Talmud, public service may be conducted only in the presence of ten male-adults, which constitutes a legal quorum for the performance of any religious function.

LAWS CONCERNING THE MINEYAN

1. The inhabitants of a community may compel one another to build either a house of study or a synagogue, and to buy books for the purpose of study. In places where there is no regular "mineyan" (quorum) for public prayer, the inhabitants may compel one an-

other, by means of fines, to attend public service that the required quorum, may be made up and the regular daily prayers be not interrupted.

2. Concluding the prayer "Yishtabah" (praised be), the Reader recites half-*kaddish*. But neither *kaddish*, nor *barkhu* (bless ye the Lord), nor *kedushah* (see Section X, below) may be said, nor may the Torah be read, unless ten male-adults are present. If less than ten are present during the recital of "Yishtabah" and the quorum is thereafter completed, the Reader should not recite the half-*kaddish*, because *kaddish* is to be said only after a prayer recited in the presence of ten. The worshipers should therefore wait, but no longer than about half an hour, until ten assemble before saying "Yishtabah."

3. An adult is one who is thirteen years old and is going on his fourteenth year.

4. It is necessary that all the ten worshipers be in one place, the Reader included; but if some of them are in one room and others in another room, they do not constitute a quorum, even though the door between the rooms may be open.

5. All must listen carefully to the reciting of the *kaddish* and make all responses with due deliberation, especially when responding: "Amen, yehe shemeh rabba" (Amen, let His great name).

6. If there are nine persons present who listen to the Reader, no *kaddish* should be said, because no holy subject may be recited unless ten male adults are present; that is, one to officiate and nine to listen and respond. Nevertheless, if one of the ten is praying the "Shemoneh esreh" (silent prayer), although he may not respond with them, he may be counted in the quorum; and the same is true even if there are two, or three, or four of them praying the "Shemoneh esreh"; for so long as there remains a majority of the quorum who can respond, the minority does not render it invalid. But if one of them is asleep, he must be awakened, because a sleeping person cannot be counted in the quorum of ten.

7. After the Reader finishes the half-*kaddish* (after "Yishtabah"), he recites in a loud voice: "Barekhu et adonai hameborakh" (Bless ye the Lord who is to be blessed), and the congregation re-

sponds: "Barukh adonai hameborakh leolam vaed" (Blessed be the
Lord who is to be blessed for ever and ever); and then the Reader
repeats the last verse.

8. If there is a quorum of only ten present in the synagogue, no
one of the ten persons is allowed to leave.

9. No one should officiate without obtaining the consent of the
congregation. If a person officiates without obtaining consent, but
imposes his office upon the congregation, the congregation must not
respond "Amen" after his benedictions.

VIII. THE PRAYER "SHEMA" (HEAR)

The term "Shema" applies to the three portions of the Holy Scriptures (Deut. vi, 4–9): "Shema yisrael" (Hear, O Israel); (Deut. ix,
13–21): "Vehayah im shamoa" (And it shall come to pass if ye shall
hearken); and (Num. xv, 37–41): "Vayomer adonai" (And the Lord
spake), as is contained in all Prayer Books. Because the first portion
of the Biblical texts begins with the word "Shema," all the three
portions are designated by "Shema."

At all times pious men have assembled at sunrise and at sunset and
also at festal seasons for common worship and devotion. The founders
of the synagogue, Anshe Knesset Hagedolah (the Men of the Great
Assembly), in obedience to the command of God (Deut. vi, 4–7):
"And thou shalt speak of them . . . when thou liest down, and when
thou risest up," prescribed that every faithful son of Israel should
recite every morning and evening such prayers and parts of Scriptures, as were best fitted to express his *acknowledgment of the
sovereignty of God,* and his *willingness to serve Him and fulfill all
His commandments.*

They instituted our daily prayers for morning and evening, which
consists chiefly of: (a) "Shema," with the benedictions that precede
and follow it, having reference to either sunrise or sunset, to the love
of Israel for the light of the Law and the redemption of Israel by
God, both in the past and in the future; (b) The *Tephilah* (prayer
proper), or "Shemoneh Esreh" (see Section IX, pp. 27–29); and (c)
Readings from the Torah (see Section XXII, pp. 34–36).

The recital of the "Shema" was called "Kabbalat ol malekut

shamayim" (the acceptance of the yoke of the Kingdom of Heaven), the *confession* of the Jewish faith.

In the "Shema," we, as Jews, first proclaim the basic doctrine of the Jewish religion, the Unity of God, the belief that there is One God, and Only One, in heaven and on earth. (See Chapter I, above). Morning and evening, twice daily, we proclaim our confession of faith which is, the battle-cry of the Jewish religion: "Shema yisrael, adonai elohenu, adonai ehad" (Hear, O Israel, the Lord our God, the Lord is One). This is the basic principle of the Jewish Creed. Throughout the ages, thousands of Jewish martyrs, suffering torture and death for the sake of their God and His Law, breathed their last breath with this confession of faith on their lips.

Then we declare our highest duty towards God, which is to love God as our Father, "With all our heart, with all our soul, and with all our might." Belief in God alone is not enough, but it is necessary to love God, and this love must be translated into deed and into obedience; we must manifest our gratitude and love to God by obeying His will and by avoiding sin, both in action and in thought. The Love of God—and consequently, obedience to God—is the basis of Jewish Life: "And these words which I command thee this day shall be upon thine heart; and thou shalt teach them diligently unto thy children."

LAWS CONCERNING THE "SHEMA"

1. The time to commence the reading of the morning "Shema" is the same as the time set for putting on the *tephilin* (see Section V, p. 15), and it extends to the end of the first quarter of the day, whether the day is long or short. The length of the day is reckoned from daybreak until the stars become visible to the naked eye. The ideal fulfillment of the precept is to do as the pious men of old, who began the reading in time to finish the "Shema," together with its benedictions, by dawn. To follow their example is to merit great reward. The reading of the "Shema," however, should not be delayed past the first quarter of the day, even though it is permissible to read the "Shema" with its benedictions before a third of the day has passed. After that time it is no longer permitted to read the benedic-

tions, but one may read the "Shema" by itself at any hour of the day.

2. The three benedictions of the "Shema" are: "Yotzer or" (who formest light), "Ahabah rabbah" (with abounding love), and "Emet veyatzib" (true and firm).

3. The "Shema" may be read either sitting or standing. If the worshiper is sitting, he should remain so, for he is not permitted to rise; but he must not read it while lying down; and if he is already lying down, he should lean on his side and read. If he is ill and it is difficult for him to lie on his side, then he should merely incline a little to one side.

4. Before we begin reading this prayer, we should bear in mind that we are about to perform the precept of reading the "Shema," as the Holy One, blessed be He, has commanded us. When we say "Shema yisrael" (Hear, O Israel), we must pay heed to its meaning, namely, that the Lord who is our God, is the only One, one and alone in heaven and on earth.

5. When we say "Vahabienu leshalom" (O bring us in peace) before reading the "Shema," we take the fringes of the *talit* in our hands and hold them. It is customary to kiss the fringes whenever we mention the word "tzitzit" (fringes), and "emet" (true), and to hold them till we say the words "Veneemanim laad" (and desirable for ever), when we again kiss them and release them from our hands.

6. When we say "Ani adonai elohekhem" (I am the Lord your God), we must immediately add the word "emet" (true); no interruption may be made between these words. The Reader, too, must privately conclude the "Shema" in like manner, but he thereafter repeats aloud "Adonai elohekhem emet." Everybody must listen attentively to these three words recited by the Reader, for with these three words are completed the two hundred and forty-eight words in the "Shema" prayer, corresponding to the two hundred and forty-eight bones in a man's body. Thereafter we begin with "Veyatzib" (and firm), but we do not repeat the word "emet" again. If we pray privately, we must add before the "Shema" the three words "El melekh neeman" (God is a true King) in order to supply the three words we missed by failing to hear the Reader's repetition, and thereby complete the number of two hundred and forty-eight words.

7. If we have read the "Shema" privately and then entered the synagogue and found the congregation reading the "Shema," we must read the entire "Shema" with them, and we will receive reward therefor as though we had read a portion of the Torah.

IX. *THE SHEMONEH ESREH (EIGHTEEN)*

As has been stated before (Section VIII, above), the Men of the Great Assembly formulated prayers to be offered by every Israelite, consisting of the "Shema" and the "Tephilah" (the prayer proper), or "Shemoneh esreh" (Eighteen).

This prayer is very ancient, and is generally referred to in the Talmud as "Tephilah" (the prayer par excellence), because it is considered as the most important prayer in the morning, afternoon, and evening services.

This prayer is also known as the "Amidah" (standing), because it is to be recited while standing up. But it is most commonly known as the "Shemoneh esreh" (eighteen), because it originally had consisted of eighteen benedictions. Later on a nineteenth benediction, "Velamaleshinim" (And for slanderers), was added.

The "Shemoneh esreh" is composed of three groups of benedictions: (a) Three bendictions of praise at the beginning; (b) twelve (now thirteen) benedictions containing petitions in the middle part; (on the Sabbath and Festivals, the middle part consists of but one petition); and (c) three benedictions of thanks at the close.

LAWS CONCERNING THE SHEMONEH ESREH

1. The time for reading the morning prayers begins at sunrise; nevertheless if we say our prayers at dawn, our duty is done. The time for prayer terminates when one-third of the day has passed, and it is forbidden to delay it longer. If, however, we have delayed saying our prayers beyond this time, even if intentionally, we may pray till mid-day, although our reward in that case will be less. If we wilfully delay our prayers until mid-day, the prayers must be left unsaid.

2. On saying "Tehillot leel elyon" (praises to the most High God), before reading the "Shemoneh esreh," we rise and prepare our-

selves for the prayer of the "Shemoneh esreh;" we walk three paces backward and say "Tehillot leel elyon" up to "Gaal Yisrael" (who redeemed Israel). Then we walk three paces forward, in the manner of one nearing and approaching a king. We should make no interruption between "Gaal yisrael" and the "Shemoneh esreh," not even for saying "Amen," the "Kedushah," or "Barekhu," because we must closely connect redemption with prayer.

3. The worshiper should be mindful of the fact that the Divine Presence is before him. He should banish from his mind all other thoughts. Let him assume that if he were in the presence of a mortal king, he would surely arrange his words and concentrate well upon them lest he stumble in his speech; how much more, then, should he concentrate his thoughts when in the presence of the Supreme King of kings, because to Him, blessed be His name, thoughts are like spoken words, and He examines all thoughts.

4. The worshiper should think of the words that he pronounces with his lips. If he is unable to understand the meaning of the Hebrew words, he should at least think while praying about matters that humble the heart, and direct his thoughts toward his Father in heaven.

5. He should place his feet close together, bend his head slightly downward, and close his eyes so that his attention be not diverted; and if he reads from a prayerbook, his eyes should not be removed from the book. He should pray with heartfelt devotion inspired with awe, fear and humility, and he should pronounce the words with full attention and care.

6. He should be careful to pray the "Shemoneh esreh" in an undertone so that no one other than himself may hear what he is saying.

7. He should not lean against anything whatsoever while praying the "Shemoneh esreh;" unless he is ill, in which case he may read it sitting or even lying down, provided that he concentrate his thoughts upon the prayers. If he is too ill to articulate the words, he should meditate the prayers in his heart.

8. When praying the "Shemoneh esreh," he should stand facing Israel, and think that he is facing Jerusalem, the Holy Temple, and

the Holy of Holies. Therefore, we who dwell West of the land of Israel, turn towards the East.

9. It is necessary to bend the knees and bow four times while saying the "Shemoneh esreh:" at the beginning and the end of the first benediction, and at the beginning and the end of the benediction "Modim" (we give thanks). When we say "barukh" (blessed art) we bend the knees, and when we say "attah" (Thou) we bow and bend our heads. Before pronouncing "adonai" (O Lord), we gently raise ourselves to an erect position. So at "modim" we bend the knees and bow, and before uttering the name of God, we rise to an erect position. Old people and invalids to whom bending the knees is painful should merely incline their heads. It is forbidden to increase the occasions for bowing down when saying the other benedictions.

10. While saying the "Shemoneh esreh," the worshiper should not blink his eyes, nor grimace with his lips, nor point with his finger, nor interrupt even for the saying of "Amen," or "Kedushah," or "Barkhu," but he should remain silent and listen to what the Reader and the congregation are saying, and this will be accounted to him as if he had performed his duty by properly responding.

11. On concluding the "Shemoneh esreh," he should recite "Elohai netzor" (O my God, guard), and before saying "Oseh shalom" (He who maketh peace), he should bow and walk only three steps backward after the manner of a servant who takes leave of his master. The steps should be of average size.

12. It is forbidden to any one to sit within four cubits of one praying the "Shemoneh esreh," unless one is engaged in something which likewise belongs to the order of prayer.

13. A feeble person should not be prevented from remaining seated within four cubits of one who prays the "Shemoneh esreh."

14. If a person is intoxicated to the extent that he would not be able to speak with the deference due a great and respected personage, he is not permitted to say the "Shemoneh esreh." If such a man does say the "Shemoneh esreh," his prayer is considered an abomination, and he is obliged to repeat the prayer when he is sober.

15. During the winter, we include "Mashib haruah umorid haga-shem" (Thou causest the wind to blow and the rain to fall) in the "Shemoneh esreh." We begin saying it at the *Musaph* (additional prayer) on *Shemini atezret* (eighth day of solemn assembly). (See page 139). Before beginning the "Shemoneh esreh" the *shamesh* (beadle) announces: "Mashib haruah umorid hagashem" as a re-minder to the congregation. "Mashib haruah" is said through the *Musaph* service on the first day of *Pesah* (Passover). But when the Reader repeats the *Musaph* on that day, he no longer says "Mashib haruah."

16. We begin including "Tal umatar" (rain and dew) in the "Shemoneh esreh" at the *maarib* (evening) service of the sixteenth day after the *Tishre tekuphah* (cycle), which is about the fourth or the fifth day of December, and we say it till Passover.

X. THE READER'S REPETITION OF SHEMONEH ESREH

After the Reader completes the reading of the silent "Shemoneh esreh" with the congregation, he repeats the prayer in an audible voice, so that the congregation may respond "Barukh hu ubarukh shemo" (Blessed be He and blessed be His name) after hearing the name of God mentioned in the benedictions, and "Amen" at the end of each benediction.

When the Reader finishes reading the first group of the three benedictions of praise, ending with "Mehayeh hametim" (Who re-viveth the dead), the congregation reads the *kedushah* (holiness), in which it proclaims the holiness of God by reading: "Kadosh, kadosh, kadosh" (Holy, holy, holy), even as it was proclaimed by the angels in the prophetic vision of Isaiah (vi, 3).

God is holy. He is free from every fault and defect. He is pure and perfect in the highest degree. He loves only truth and righteous-ness. He hates falsehood and wrong. He is absolutely good. No mortal being knows what God is. He is the Absolute Being to whom all beings owe their existence. God revealed His Law to the Israelites whom He admonished to follow the commandments of morality and ethics, so that they might become a holy people.

LAWS CONCERNING THE READER'S REPETITION
OF THE SHEMONEH ESREH

1. Upon concluding the silent reading of the "Shemoneh esreh,"
the Reader walks backwards three steps and remains standing as
long as it takes one to walk four cubits. Then he returns to his place
and says in an undertone: "Adonai sephotai tiphetah" (O Lord,
open Thou my lips), and then begins in a loud tone: "Barukh attah
adonai" (Blessed art Thou, O Lord). Everyone present must be
silent and listen with attention and devotion to what the Reader is
saying, and respond "Barukh hu ubarukh shemo" (Blessed be He and
blessed be His name) and "Amen" to every benediction as required.
Even the study of the Torah is forbidden during the Reader's repetition of the "Shemoneh esreh;" and needless to say, there must be no
idle conversation.

2. Since the Reader has already said the silent "Shemoneh esreh"
for himself, he repeats it only for the sake of the listeners. It is
necessary that there be at least nine people in the congregation to
listen and respond, so that the Reader's benediction may not be said
in vain; if there be no more than an even quorum of ten, the Reader
should not begin the repetition until all of them have finished praying so that all may be able to respond.

3. While reciting the "Kedushah" every one should keep his feet
close together, and when saying, "Kadosh, kadosh, kadosh" (holy,
holy, holy), and "Barukh" (blessed be), and "Yimelokh adonai"
(the Lord shall reign), he should raise himself on his toes, and
according to custom, lift up his eyes.

4. Before the Reader says the benediction "Sim shalom" (Grant
peace), he should say the priestly blessing, "Elohenu velohe
abotenu, barekenu" (Our God and God of our fathers, bless us).
When he says "Veyishmerekha" (and keep thee), the congregation
says, "Ken yehi ratzon" (may thus be His will), but they should not
say "Amen." The same procedure is followed when he says "Vihun-
nekha" (and be gracious unto thee), and "Veyasem lekha shalom"
(and give thee peace). This benediction is said only at the *Shaharit*

(morning) and *Musaph* (additional) service, but not at the *Minhah* (afternoon) service. On a public fast day, when the benediction "Sim shalom" is said also in the *Minhah* service, then the Reader also says "Elohenu velohe abotenu." But the latter is not said in the house of a mourner, nor is it said on the Ninth Day of Ab in the morning service.

5. On a public fast day, if there are ten persons present who fast the whole day, the Reader says "Anenu" (Answer us) before the benediction "Rephaenu adonai" (Heal us, O Lord) in the morning and afternoon services.

6. The "Shemoneh esreh" is not repeated aloud by the Reader unless at least six male adults, who have just said the "Shemoneh esreh," are present, since six constitute a majority of the quorum. If fewer than these six are present, the entire "Shemoneh esreh" is not repeated aloud, but one of them reads aloud up to "Hael hakkadosh" (the holy God), and the *Kedushah* is said, and then he concludes the "Shemoneh esreh" silently.

XI. TAHANUN (PETITION FOR GRACE)

Tahanun, in Hebrew means *petition for grace.* The sages ordained that a Jew must daily offer supplication for pardon of sin. Psalm vi has been chosen for this purpose, and as an introduction to this supplication for pardon, the verse "Vayomer david" (and David said) (II Sam. xxiv, 14) was chosen.

It is told in the Scriptures (II Sam. xxiv) that when David sinned against God, by counting the Jewish people, the Prophet Gad was commissioned to rebuke him for his crime. Gad offered the king a choice: punishment by God or punishment by man. Whereupon David threw himself upon the mercy of God, uttering the immortal preference: "Let me fall, I pray thee, into the hand of the Lord, for His mercies are many; but let me not fall into the hand of man."

This *petition for grace* was known as "Nephilat appayim" (falling on the face), because it used to be recited lying face down upon the ground. But this has since been modified into an inclination of the head on the arm.

LAWS CONCERNING THE TAHANUN

1. The term *tahanun* is applied to the prayer commencing with "Vayomer david" (and David said), and includes Psalm vi, and "Shomer Yisrael" (O Guardian of Israel), and "Vaanahnu lo neda mah naaseh" (As for us, we know not what to do). This prayer is read after the "Shemoneh esreh" in the morning and afternoon services.

2. Psalm vi is recited while inclining our head on the arm.

3. At the morning services, since the *tephilin* is on the left arm, we rest the head on the right arm, but at the *Minhah* (afternoon) service, we use the left.

4. The rite of resting the head on the arm is to be performed while sitting, but if necessary, it may be done while standing.

5. This rite of inclining the head on the arm is performed only in a place where a *sepher torah* (Scroll of the Law) is found, otherwise it is omitted.

6. When praying in the house of a mourner, or in a house where a death has occurred, even if there is no mourner, the *tahanun* is omitted during the seven days of mourning, even at the *Minhah* service of the seventh day. In the synagogue, a mourner omits the *tahanun* while the rest of the congregation goes through the prayer.

7. The *tahanun* is not said in a synagogue when a circumcision takes place, or when the father of the child to be circumcised, or the *sandek* (godfather), or the *mohel* (circumciser) pray therein, even though the circumcision takes place elsewhere.

8. The *tahanun* is likewise omitted in a synagogue when a bridegroom is present, during the seven days of bridal festivity. This applies, however, only when the bridegroom or the bride has not been previously married. The period is limited to three days in the case of a widower who marries a widow.

9. The *tahanun* is omitted on *Rosh Hodesh* (New Moon), on the fifteenth day of the month of Ab, on the fifteenth day of Shebat, on Hanukkah, Purim, Shushan Purim, and the two days of Purim Katan (the small Purim, of the first Adar in a leap year), on Lag

Baomer (thirty-third day of counting the Omer), during the entire month of Nisan, on the ninth of Ab, on the days between Yom Kippur (Day of Atonement) and Sukkot (Feast of Tabernacles), from Rosh Hodesh Sivan till after the day following Shabuot (Pentecost), and on the day after Sukkot. The *tahanun* is omitted at the *Minhah* (afternoon) service preceding the days above enumerated, but it is read at the *Minhah* service preceding the day before Rosh Hashanah (New Year) and the day preceding the day before Yom Kippur.

10. On Mondays and Thursdays, we read "Vehu rahum" (and He being merciful) before the *tahanun*. These Special Supplications are designated as "Vehu rahum" because they commence with these two Hebrew words. These are to be read while standing, slowly, and with great devotion. On days when the *tahanun* is omitted, these Supplications are likewise omitted. (See following Section).

XII. READING OF THE TORAH

One of the main objects of public worship was instruction in the Law of God. For this reason the Anshe Knesset Hagedolah (the Men of the Great Assembly) ordained that portions of the Five Books of Moses be read on certain days of the week, on certain festive seasons and twice on the Sabbath, at the morning and afternoon services.

In ancient times, the villagers of Palestine used to come into the nearest town on Mondays and Thursdays to attend the Law Courts and the markets. Because many of these villagers might not hear the Torah read on Sabbaths, it became customary to read a portion of the Pentateuch on market days. For the same reason, Mondays and Thursdays have been chosen for offering the Special Supplications of "Vehu rahum."

On Mondays and Thursdays, immediately after the reading of the *tahanun,* a *sepher torah* (Scroll of the Law) is taken out of the holy ark; and three persons, a Kohen, a Levi and an Israelite, are called up to pronounce the benedictions over the Torah, while we read the first *parshah* (section) of the *sidrah* (weekly portion) which is to be read the following Sabbath.

LAWS CONCERNING THE READING OF THE TORAH

1. The person who takes out the *sepher torah* of the holy ark to carry it to the desk whereupon it is to be read, should walk with it at his right side, and when taking it back to the ark, he should walk with it at his left side. The *sepher torah* however, should always be carried on the right arm.

2. He who is called up to the reading of the Torah should wrap himself in a *talit* (fringed garment) and should take the shortest way going up to the reading desk, and the longest way going down. If the two ways are equally distant, he must ascend at his right and descend at his left. It is customary for the person called up to the Torah not to descend until after the one called up after him has said the last benediction.

3. After the Scroll is opened, the one who is called up looks at the passage to be read, and taking hold of the two handles, says: "Barekhu et adonai hameborakh" (Bless ye the Lord who is to be blessed). He should recite this aloud so that the entire congregation may hear and respond: "Barukh adonai hameborakh leolam vaed" (Blessed is the Lord who is to be blessed for ever and ever). The Reader then reads the prescribed portion and the one who is called up follows him silently.

4. It is forbidden to take hold of the Scroll itself with bare hands. It must be held either by means of the *talit,* or by its rollers.

5. Both the one called up and the Reader, must stand while the Torah is read. They are forbidden to lean against anything. But a feeble person is permitted to lean if necessary.

6. During the reading of the Torah, it is forbidden to indulge in conversation even regarding matters of the Law.

7. If there is a Kohen in the synagogue, he must be called first to the reading of the Torah, and he may not waive his right to be called first. After the Kohen, a Levi is called, and if there is no Levi, the Kohen is called again in his stead, and we say "Bimekom levi" (in the stead of the Levi). If there is no Kohen present, we call either a Levi or any Israelite in his stead. If an Israelite is called up in place of a Kohen, then a Levi should not be called after him.

8. The number of persons called to the reading of the Torah is as follows: On Mondays, Thursdays, public fasts, Sabbath afternoon, *Hanukkah,* and *Purim,* three persons; on *Rosh Hodesh* (New Moon), and *Hol Hamoed* (Intermediate Days of Festivals), four; on *Pesah, Shabuot, Sukkot,* and *Rosh Hashanah,* five, and an additional one for the *maftir;* on *Yom Kippur* morning, six and the *maftir;* on Sabbath, seven and the *maftir.* On Sabbath the number may be increased, but not on any other day. On Simehat Torah (Rejoicing of the Law), we increase the number so that everyone present may be called up to the Torah.

9. Two brothers, whether of one father or one mother, should not be called up to the Torah in succession; nor should a father, a son, or a grandson succeed one another.

10. A minor should not be a Reader of the Torah; neither should he be called up to say the benediction over the Torah.

11. After the reading of the Torah, half-*kaddish* is said. It is omitted, however, at the *Minhah* (afternoon) service of the Sabbath and on fast days, since it is to be recited before the "Shemoneh esreh."

XIII. MINHAH AND MAARIB SERVICES

The second service of the day, as instituted by the *Anshe Knesset Hagedolah* (Men of the Great Assembly), is known as *Minhah,* the afternoon service. *Minhah,* in Hebrew, means *gift,* or *gift-offering,* to God. During the existence of the Temple at Jerusalem, the *korban tamid* (the regular sacrifice) was offered twice daily, in the morning and in the afternoon. With these daily sacrifices, there was offered a sacrifice of grain or cereal which was known as the *minhah.* The term *minhah* came to designate the afternoon and not the morning service, because it was so called in the Holy Scriptures, where, in describing the contest between the Prophet Elijah and the priests of Baal at Mount Carmel, the Biblical narrative begins with the words (II Kings xviii): "And it came to pass at the time of the offering of the *minhah,* etc."

The third prayer of the day is the *Maarib* (evening service), at which the "Shema" must be recited.

LAWS CONCERNING THE MINHAH AND MAARIB SERVICES

1. The proper time for offering the *Minhah* prayer is at nine and one-half hours of the day (3:30 p. m.). However, in cases of necessity, it may be recited immediately after six and one-half hours of the day (12:30 p. m.). In many communities the custom prevails of reciting the *Minhah* prayer shortly before nightfall.

2. Before reciting the *Minhah* prayer, hands should be washed up to the wrist. If on concluding the *Minhah,* an interruption occurs before saying the *Maarib* (evening) service, or if an interruption occurs between the *Shaharit* (morning) service and the *musaph* (additional) service, the hand-washing must be repeated.

3. *Ashre* (Psalm cxlv) with which the *Minhah* commences, should be recited in the presence of ten male adults, so that the Reader may recite the *kaddish* when *Ashre* is concluded. The Reader should wrap himself in a *talit* (fringed garment) before saying *Ashre.*

4. If the time prescribed for praying *Minhah* is limited because nightfall is approaching, immediately after the *kaddish* the Reader begins reciting the "Shemoneh esreh" aloud, while the congregation listens and makes the responses until the Reader says "Hael hakkadosh" (the holy God), to which all respond "Amen," and after saying the *Kedushah,* all worshipers silently recite the "Shemoneh esreh." If, however, they are so pressed for time that, should they wait for the Reader to conclude "Hael hakkadosh," they would be unable to say the "Shemoneh esreh" while it is yet daylight, they may pray together with the Reader, saying silently, word by word with him until "Hael hakkadosh." It is nevertheless proper that there should be at least one worshiper present who can respond "Amen" to the Reader's benedictions.

5. The time for reading the "Shema" of the *Maarib* (evening) service is when three stars become visible to the naked eye.

6. It is forbidden to begin a meal or to engage in any manner of work one-half hour before the stars become visible.

XIV. THE ORDER OF THE NIGHT

1. It is proper for every God-fearing Jew to examine his deeds of the day that has passed, before going to sleep. If he finds that he has transgressed in any way, he should feel remorse, repent, and whole-heartedly resolve not to repeat the transgression. Special scrutiny is required with regard to common sins, such as lies, flattery, scorning, and slander. He should also resolve to forgive any person who has wronged him, so that no man may be punished because of him, for the Talmud says (Shabbat 149b): "He for whose sake a man suffers punishment, is not permitted to enter the domain of the Holy One, blessed be He."

2. If we have failed to read the three sections of the "Shema" at the *Maarib* service, we should recite them when we read the "Shema" before retiring at night. If we have already said the three sections at *Maarib*, we need say only the first section of the "Shema" before retiring. After that we recite the Psalms and the Biblical verses referring to God's mercy, such as we find in the regular Prayer Books.

3. We should remove our clothes before retiring for the night, and we should accustom ourselves to sleeping on our side and not on the back with our face upward, or on the stomach with our back upward.

CHAPTER III

THE JEWISH HOME

I. THE MEZUZAH

It is to be borne in mind, that in the Jewish religion there are no amulets. The *tephilin,* the *tzitzit,* the *mezuzah,* as well as all other ceremonials, are religious symbols which convey certain religious truths, facts, doctrines, or events of the past. In the Holy Scriptures they are called "testimonies" and "signs." They serve to testify to, and are the symbols of, the special relation of God to the people. They are outward expressions of the Jewish inner thoughts, of purity, holiness, and righteousness. They act as reminders to the Jews that they must understand and obey the Law of God.

The Jewish religion is unique in that it controls and regulates every phase of Jewish life. Its rules of conduct apply not only to our behavior in the synagogue, but also to our every-day dealings with our fellowmen, to the conduct of our private lives, the way we conduct our homes, and even to our mode of thinking.

The Jewish home must bear a distinctive character. God is to be found everywhere, not only in temples and synagogues. Our homes, too, can be made holy by our deeds and thoughts. If our homes have a Jewish atmosphere; if peace and harmony exists between the members of our family; if in our homes, God's word is heard and discussed; if sacred books are studied there, then our homes become shrines, holy places; and our tables become altars of God.

The very entrances to our homes must be marked with holiness. The Almighty commanded us to write His laws on the door-posts of our homes. We therefore procure a *mezuzah,* a small piece of parchment upon which are inscribed by hand two sections of the Law of God which are read by us in the "Shema" every morning and evening. (See Chapter II, Section VIII, pp. 24–27). On the reverse side of the parchment, the word *Shaddai* (Almighty) is inscribed. This parchment is encased in a metal or wooden tube and affixed to the door-post.

The inscription in the *mezuzah* begins with the words: "Shema Yisrael, Adonai Elohenu, Adonai Ehad" (Hear, O Israel, the Lord our God, the Lord is One). Thus the *mezuzah* fastened to the door-post, reminds us: (a) That those who occupy these premises believe that there is only One God in heaven and on earth; and (b) That God is present in our homes. And since our Father in heaven is always in our midst, our homes must always be holy, godly, and peaceful, and we must always abstain from doing anything evil in His sight. There must not be quarreling, nor cursing, nor hatred, nor slanderous talk.

Maimonides (Hilkot Mezuzah VI, 13) says: "It is the religious duty of every man to perform the precept of affixing the *mezuzah.* Whenever we enter or leave the house, we are confronted with the Name of the Holy One, blessed be He, and recalling His loving kindness, we are reminded that in this world nothing endures but God, that all is vanity but the love of God and His commandments."

LAWS CONCERNING THE MEZUZAH

1. The *mezuzah* must be affixed to every door of the house. Even if one occupies many rooms, and in every room there are many doors made for exit and entrance, one must affix the *mezuzah* to each one of these doors, even if only one of these doors is actually used.

2. The *mezuzah* must be affixed on the right hand side as one enters. If by error it is affixed to the left hand side, it must be removed and affixed to the right hand side, and the benediction must be repeated before refastening it.

3. The *mezuzah* must be affixed within the upper third of the

door-post, but it must be no less than one hand-breadth distant from the upper door-post. If it is affixed lower that the upper one-third, it must be removed and affixed to the proper place, and the necessary benediction must be said upon refastening it.

4. The *mezuzah* is affixed in this manner: We roll the parchment from the end of the sentence to the beginning, that is, from the last word "Ehad" (One), towards the first word "Shema" (Hear), so that the word "Shema" be on the top; then we put it in a tube, and fasten it with nails to the door-post diagonally, having the top line containing the word "Shema" towards the house, and the last word towards the outside. If the door-post is not wide enough, the *mezuzah* may be fastened to it perpendicularly. The *mezuzah* is not considered valid if it is merely suspended; it must be fastened with nails at top and bottom.

5. Before affixing the *mezuzah*, we say this benediction: "Blessed art Thou, O Lord our God, King of the universe, who hath sanctified us by His commandments, and hath commanded us to affix the mezuzah." If several *mezuzot* are to be affixed at one time, the saying of one benediction before affixing the first *mezuzah* will suffice for all. If a *mezuzah* happens to fall by itself from the door-post, the benediction must be repeated when it is affixed again.

6. A building not used for a permanent residence needs no *mezuzah*. Therefore a *sukkah* (booth) made for the feast of Tabernacles requires no *mezuzah* during the days of the feast.

7. A *mezuzah* should never be affixed to the door-post of a bathroom.

8. When we move from a house which is to be occupied by a Jew, we must not remove the *mezuzot*, but we must leave them there and the new occupant should pay for them.

9. Because the purpose of the *mezuzah* is to remind us of His name, blessed be He, therefore we should kiss the *mezuzah* upon leaving the house and upon entering it.

10. The *mezuzah* of a private dwelling should be examined twice in seven years, but that of a dwelling belonging to many should be examined only twice in a jubilee (fifty years).

II. THE TZITZIT (FRINGES)

By the command of the Almighty, through His Prophet Moses, the Jews were ordered to wear *tzitzit* (fringes) attached to the four corners of a garment. The reason for wearing the *tzitzit* is given by the Almighty (Num. xv, 39): "That ye may look upon it, and remember all the commandments of the Lord, and do them." The special garment with the four fringes attached to it, is known as *talit katan* (the smaller fringed garment), or as *arba kanfot* (the four-cornered garment). This ritual garment is "the Jewish coat-of-mail," as further told by the Almighty: "That ye seek not after your own heart and your own eyes." He who wears the *arba kanfot* will be able to ward off unworthy and immoral impulses; the garment will instill in the wearer an idealism and a determination to abide by the laws of God and abstain from doing evil.

LAWS CONCERNING THE TZITZIT

1. The precept relating to *tzitzit* (fringes) is considered a very serious one. Therefore every Jew must be careful to wear a *talit katan* all day. Upon putting on the *talit katan,* the following benediction is said: "Blessed art Thou, O Lord our God, King of the universe, who hath sanctified us by His commandments, and hath commanded us concerning the precept of the tzitzit."

2. The number of the fringes is four, one on each of the four corners of the *talit.*

3. The aperture into which the fringe is inserted must not be more than three thumb-breadths removed from the edge.

4. It is the general custom to make five double knots in the fringes between which there are four spaces. It is done in this manner: we put the four threads through the aperture and make two knots; we then take the longest thread, that is called the *shamesh* (servile), and coil it around the threads seven times, and make two knots; we coil it around again eight times, and make two knots; then we coil it around again eleven times and make two knots; and finally we coil it around thirteen times and make two knots. (Thus the number of coils adds up to thirty-nine, equalling the numerical value of the

letters spelling out God's name, Yud, He, Vav, He, and the Hebrew word "ehad".) Whereas the beauty of the fringes lies in that all the spaces be of equal dimension, we should make the threads far apart in the first space, where the number of coils is the smallest; in the second, we should make them somewhat nearer; and so, in the third and the fourth. The prescribed length of the fringe, that is, beginning with the first knot to the end of the threads, must be no less than twelve thumb-breadths. For the same reason of beauty, it is proper that all the spaces together be one-third of the prescribed length, and the loose threads two-thirds thereof; we should therefore take care that every space be the size of a thumb's breadth; then all the spaces taken together will equal four thumb-breadths and the threads that remain loose will equal eight thumb-breadths in length. If the threads are longer, we should accordingly make the spaces a little larger. It is best to be sure to make all the knots by tying together the four threads on the one side with the four threads on the other side, so that each of the four inserted threads are divided, one-half on one side and the other half on the other side.

5. Before wrapping ourselves in the *talit,* we must examine the fringes, including the threads in the apertures and the coils, to ascertain whether they are in order, and separate the threads so that they may not be entangled.

6. The benediction over the *tzitzit* should be said only during the day and not during the night time. Care should be taken not to say the benediction in the morning before one is able to distinguish between blue and white colors.

7. Women are exempt from observing the precept of wearing *tzitzit.* There is a general rule of law laid down in the Talmud, that women, because they are more occupied with their duties at home, are free from ceremonies which must be performed at a *specified* time. Since the fringed garment must be worn at a specified time, namely, during the day only and not at night, this rule of law applies.

8. If we take off the *talit* intending to put it on immediately again, we need not say the benediction upon putting it on again. But if we intend not to put it on again immediately, but thereafter change our

minds and put it on again, we must then say the benediction again upon putting it on.

9. It is permissible to borrow the *talit* belonging to someone else even without his knowledge, to pray in it and say the benediction over it, because it is presumed that a person is willing that a precept be performed with his property when there is no pecuniary loss involved. But it must not be taken out of the house where it is found, because the owner may object. If the *talit* was folded, the borrower must leave it folded.

10. If one or two of the four (doubled into eight) threads of the fringes have been torn off, and there is enough left of each torn thread to make a loop the size of four thumb-breadths, and if the other threads are perfect, such fringes are valid.

11. The threads of the fringes must be twisted, and if any thread has become untwisted, the untwisted part is then considered as entirely cut off and non-existent.

12. Severe is the punishment of anyone who neglects the performance of the precept of fringes. He who is scrupulous in its performance will be worthy of beholding the Divine Presence.

III. WASHING THE HANDS BEFORE MEALS

1. The wisdom and value of the practice of washing the hands before meals is too obvious to need comment. But Judaism, to make the practice more impressive, elevates it to the dignity of a religious ceremony.

2. But even before washing the hands for an intended meal, we must bear in mind that if we possess cattle or poultry, we are forbidden to eat before we provide them with food.

3. Nothing may be interposed between the hands and the water during the hand-washing ceremony. Therefore, before washing, the hands should be carefully examined. Nails, if they are large, must be cleaned so that no clay or dirt remains under them which might be considered an interposition. It is likewise necessary to remove the rings from the fingers before washing so that there be no interposition.

4. The hands must be washed before partaking of bread over

which the benediction "Hamotzi" (He who bringeth forth) is said. (See Section that follows.) If the bread we intend to eat is no less than the size of an egg, we must say the benediction for washing hands; but if it is less than the size of an egg, we need not say the benediction.

5. The water used for washing the hands must be poured out of a vessel which is whole, having neither a hole nor a crack through it.

6. First the right hand should be washed, and thereafter the left. The water must cover the entire hand up to the wrist, leaving no part unwashed; therefore the fingers should be slightly separated when washing.

7. After washing both hands and before drying them, we say the following benediction: "Blessed art Thou, O Lord our God, King of the universe, who hath sanctified us by His commandments and hath commanded us concerning the washing of the hands."

8. If there is no vessel available, we may dip our hands into a river or into a well and pronounce the benediction "Concerning the washing of the hands." In case of emergency, we may dip our hands in snow, provided there is enough snow on the ground to make up forty *seahs*.

9. Salt water, or foul, or bitter, or turbid, which is not fit for a dog to drink, is unfit for washing the hands.

IV. THE BREAKING OF BREAD

Our tables can be turned into altars of God, if the food we eat at them is *kosher*, by the law of God, and if God's name is mentioned at meals. According to the concepts of the Jewish religion, eating is more than just a necessary process for keeping alive. It partakes of the nature of sacrifice and is invested with the nature of holiness, when we utter the necessary benedictions over our food; when we express our gratitude to the Almighty for His abundant kindness in providing us with the necessities of life, by saying Grace after meals, and by engaging in conversation, while at the table, about serious and not frivolous things.

The Talmud (Berakot 35b) says: "It is written (Psalms xxiv, 1): "The earth is the Lord's, and the fulness thereof," which infers that everything belonging to God is sacred. Just as one is guilty of a trespass when one derives any benefit from sacred things before they are redeemed, so it is forbidden to derive *any* pleasure in this world without first thanking the Almighty by pronouncing a benediction. He who does derive benefit without a benediction is considered as if he had committed a trespass against the sanctuary of God." And Rabbi Levi adds: "According to the Psalmist, everything belongs to God, but when consecrated by a benediction, it becomes man's privilege to enjoy it."

As regards the utterance of a benediction, some products of the soil are considered as a class, and an identical benediction is pronounced over all the various kinds that compose that class. Over all the products of the tree, for instance, the benediction "Bore peri haetz" (who created the fruit of the tree) is said, whether one partakes of apples, pears, plums, or the like. And "Bore peri haadamah" (who created the fruit of the ground) is pronounced over all products which grow in or above the ground, whether it is over turnips, vegetables, beans, or the like. While other products, because of their importance and distinguished character, such as wine and olive oil, require a special benediction, although they are products of the tree. (See Sections IX and X, pp. 52–54.)

Bread, although made from the products of the soil, such as wheat, oats, rye, and the like, nevertheless requires a special benediction, known as "Hamotzi" (who bringeth forth), and not the one generally pronounced over such products of the soil. The reason advanced for the uniqueness of bread is that it is regarded as the most important of foods which is needed for the sustenance of life.

LAWS CONCERNING THE BREAKING OF BREAD

1. Before eating bread made of the five species of grain, wheat, barley, spelt, oats, or rye (see Section XII, p. 55) we say the benediction "Hamotzi," which reads: "Blessed art Thou, O Lord our God, King of the universe, who bringest forth bread from the earth," and after eating it, we say the Grace after meals (see Section that follows).

2. No interruption should be made between washing the hands

and the benediction "Hamotzi," unless it be to respond "Amen" to another's benediction.

3. We must eat immediately after pronouncing the "Hamotzi," and we may not interrupt even for the purpose of responding "Amen", before we have eaten a piece of bread the size of an olive.

4. It is proper to have salt set on the table before breaking bread, and to dip into the salt a piece of bread over which the "Hamotzi" is said, because the table represents the altar and the food symbolizes the offerings, and it is said (Lev. ii, 13): "With all thine offerings thou shalt offer salt."

5. We need not say a special benediction before or after eating any kind of food which is generally eaten in the course of the meal to satisfy hunger, such as meat, fish, relishes, crushed grain soup, pancakes, and the like, and it is immaterial whether the food is such as is generally eaten without bread. For since we usually partake of such food during a meal to satisfy our hunger, it forms a part of the meal, and is therefore blessed by the "Hamotzi" said over the bread, as well as by the Grace recited after the meal.

6. Neither do we have to say a benediction over the beverage drunk during the meal, for it is not customary to eat a meal without drinking. Wine, however, forms an exception because of its importance, and we must say a benediction over it when drinking it during the course of the meal.

V. THE GRACE AFTER MEALS

1. The Lord our God commanded us through Moses (Deut. viii, 10): "And thou shalt eat and be satisfied, and thou shalt bless the Lord thy God." Thus we are obligated by the Law of God to thank the Almighty for having provided us and the other creatures of the world with food. We are, therefore, not allowed to leave our seats at the table before saying Grace after the meal. We may not even leave to finish our meal in another room, nor may we leave with the intention of returning to finish our meal at the same table.

2. If at the time we say the "Hamotzi" we intend to go thereafter into another room to finish our meal and say the Grace there, it is permissible to do so, provided we eat there a slice of bread no

less than the size of an olive. This, however, may be done only when we wish to be present at a religious feast.

3. The tablecloth and the bread must still be upon the table when Grace after meals is said. This is to indicate the abundance of food which the Lord, blessed be His name, has supplied for us, in that He gives us enough to eat and to spare.

4. It is customary either to remove or to cover the knives left on the table, before reciting the Grace after meals. For the table is compared to the altar, and concerning the altar it is written in the Holy Scriptures (Deut. xxvii, 5): "Thou shalt not lift up any iron upon them." For iron shortens the life of man while the altar prolongs his days, and it is improper that the one that shortens life should be raised on the one that prolongs it. The table, too, prolongs the days of man and permits him to atone for his sins by having poor wayfarers at his table; for the power of hospitality is so great that it causes the Divine Presence to be in our midst.

5. Even if we have eaten only a piece of bread no larger than the size of an olive, we must say Grace thereafter.

6. The Grace after meals should be recited neither while standing nor while walking, but only while seated.

7. If three male persons have eaten together, it is their duty to unite in saying the Grace after meals.

8. The person who leads in saying the Grace should begin by inviting the other two to say the Grace, and he says: "Hab lan unebarekh" (come, let us say Grace). Or he may say it, as is the prevailing custom, in the Yiddish language: "Rabotai, mir villen bentshen" (gentlemen, let us say Grace), and the rest of the company respond: "Blessed be the name of the Lord henceforth and for ever," which is repeated by the leader. Then he continues: "With the sanction of these honored guests, we will bless Him, of whose bounty we have partaken"; those present reply: "Blessed be He of whose bounty we have partaken, and through whose goodness we live." The one who leads in saying the Grace repeats the last sentence. If there is a quorum of ten present, they add "Our God," after "Blessed be."

9. The leader then recites the Grace aloud, while the others quietly say every word with him, and at the conclusion of each benediction they should hasten to finish the benediction before him, so that they may respond "Amen."

10. If women partake of a meal together with men who are obliged to unite in saying Grace, they must listen to the recital of the Grace. It is the custom not to reckon a minor as part of a quorum for saying Grace unless he is at least thirteen years and one day old.

VI. GENERAL RULES RELATING TO BENEDICTIONS [1]

1. Before uttering any benediction, we must first ascertain which one we must say, so that when we mention God's name, which is the most important part of the benediction, we should know what we are thanking Him for. It is forbidden to do anything else while uttering the benediction; and it must not be uttered hurriedly; attention should be paid to the meaning of the words.

2. When we utter a benediction, our mouths must be free of food and even of saliva.

3. It is forbidden to utter carelessly or unnecessarily either the great name of God or any other name attributed to Him, whether in the Holy Tongue (Hebrew), or any other. When we wish to mention the name of God, let us instead say merely "Hashem" (the Name), and not as the unlearned erroneously say "Adoshem," for this is undignified.

4. Great care should be taken not to utter any benediction in vain. If by inadvertence we do utter a benediction in vain, or we mention the name of God unnecessarily, we should thereafter say: "Blessed be He and blessed be His name for ever and ever." If immediately after pronouncing the name of God (in a benediction), we remind ourselves that there is no need for us to say the benediction, we must then conclude it with (Psalms cxix, 12): "Teach me Thy statutes." As this is a complete verse in itself, it is considered as something to be studied, and the Name is consequently not mentioned unnecessarily.

[1] See Section IV, p. 45.

5. If we are in doubt whether we have uttered any one of the necessary benedictions, excepting Grace, we are not bound to repeat it.

6. Upon hearing a benediction pronounced, we must say, "Blessed be He and blessed be His name," at the utterance of the Name (adonai), and we must respond "Amen" at the conclusion of the benediction. "Amen" means *it is true,* and therefore when saying "Amen" we should remember that what the benediction says is true, and that we believe in it implicitly.

7. When we hear a benediction to which we need only listen in order to fulfill our obligation, as, for example, the benediction said over the blowing of the *shofar* or reading the *megillah,* we must not say, "Blessed be He and blessed be His name," because such a response would be considered as an interruption of the benediction.

8. We must be careful to pronounce the word "Amen" correctly, and to say it immediately upon the conclusion of the benediction—being neither too slow nor too fast; nor should we ever raise our voices louder than the Reader's.

9. We should not respond "Amen" after our own benedictions, except in the Grace after meals, when we conclude, "The builder of Jerusalem."

VII. BENEDICTIONS SAID BEFORE ENJOYING THE GIFTS OF GOD

Our Talmudic sages teach us that no man has the right to deny himself the legitimate pleasures of life. Everyone, according to the will of our Creator, must enjoy the bounties of the creation. They tell us (Jerusalem Talmud, Kiddushin, end) that a man will be called to account in the world to come for having declined to eat whatever his eyes beheld. Rabbi Eleazar, they relate, was wont to save small coins with which to buy of everything at least once a year. However, in appreciation of God's creation of such enjoyments, we are admonished never to eat, or drink anything, nor to enjoy the smell of a fragrant plant or a beautiful sight in nature, without thanking God, the Giver of all good, for it.

1. We must pronounce a benediction before we eat or drink anything, no matter how little it may be.

2. Although if we inadvertently say the benediction "Shehakol" (all things exist) over any article of food, be it even bread or wine, our religious duty is done, nevertheless this must not be done intentionally. It is therefore our duty to learn to distinguish the various benedictions and to say that which is appropriate to the kind of food about to be enjoyed.

3. No interruption should be made between the saying of the benediction over food and the swallowing of the first mouthful of food. If after saying the benediction, we make an interruption, before eating, by speaking of something irrelevant to the meal, we must repeat the benediction; but if we delay in eating by pausing silently, we need not repeat the benediction. Any delay made for the purpose of the meal, is not considered an interruption. Therefore, if we desire to partake of a large-sized fruit which we must cut before eating, we should say the benediction over the whole fruit (because it is meritorious to say a benediction over an entire article of food), and the delay caused by cutting the fruit for the purpose of eating it, is not considered an interruption. However, if we have reason to fear that the uncut food might prove not good to eat (as a single piece of fruit that might be wormy), we should open it and examine it before saying the benediction.

VIII. THE BENEDICTION "BORE MINE MEZONOT"

1. If we should eat pastry made of any of the five species of grain, baked for the purpose of being served as sweetmeats, but less than the quantity sufficient for a regular meal, we need neither wash the hands before eating it, nor say the benediction "Hamotzi" over it. But we should say a special benediction: "Bore mine mezonot" (who created various kinds of food), which reads: "Blessed art Thou, O Lord our God, King of the universe, who created various kinds of food," and

after eating we should say "Al hamiheyah" (for the sustenance). (See Section XII, p. 55.) If, however, we should eat thereof a quantity sufficient for a meal, then it is governed by the same rules of law as apply to proper bread, and we must wash our hands and say the "Hamotzi," and thereafter say the Grace after meals.

2. "Bread served as sweetmeats" is construed to mean bread which is prepared like pies filled with fruit, meat, cheese, and the like, or which is prepared like pancakes, or which is kneaded with oil, fat, honey, milk, eggs or cheese, or fruit juice, and which contains less water than other fluids.

3. The quantity of food constituting a meal, is not to be measured by each individual's own appetite, but what the majority of people usually consume at meal-time. Whether it be pastry or bread that is eaten, the same rule of law applies.

IX. THE BENEDICTION OVER WINE AND OLIVE OIL [1]

1. Before drinking wine we say the benediction "Bore peri haggaphen" (who created the fruit of the vine), and after drinking it we say "Al haggephen" (for the vine). (See Section XII, pp. 55–56.) If the wine is still bubbling, or fermenting, or if it contains honey and spices, or absinthe which is bitter, or if it gives forth the odor of vinegar, as long as it tastes like wine, it is considered as wine for the purpose of the benediction.

2. A mixture of wine and water which contains not more than one-sixth part of wine, is to be considered merely as water. If the mixture contains more than one-sixth of wine, and it is the custom of that locality to drink such a mixture as wine, it is to be considered as wine for the purposes of the benedictions.

3. Just as the benediction over bread serves to consecrate all other foods regularly eaten during the meal, so does the benediction over wine cover all other beverages, providing they were set before us when we said the benediction over the wine, and that we intended to drink them at the time we said the benediction. But if they were not set before us, nor did we intend to drink them when we said the benediction over the wine, it is doubtful whether they re-

[1] See Section IV, pp. 45–46.

quire a benediction. We should therefore avoid drinking other beverages, in such event, until we have recited the necessary benediction after drinking wine.

4. If one enjoys olive-oil so much that the utterance of a benediction is required, one says "Bore peri haetz" (who created the fruit of the tree). (See following Section.)

X. THE BENEDICTIONS "BORE PERI HAETZ"; "BORE PERI HAADAMAH"; AND "SHEHAKOL" [1]

1. Before eating fruit which grows on trees, one should say the benediction "Bore peri haetz" (who created the fruit of the tree), which reads: "Blessed art Thou . . . who created the fruit of the tree." Before partaking of the produce which grows in or above the ground, such as turnips, vegetables, beans, and herbs, one should say the benediction "Bore peri haadamah" (who created the fruit of the ground), which reads: "Blessed art Thou, O Lord our God, King of the universe, who created the fruit of the ground." A tree (for the purpose of this law) must have branches which do not perish in the winter, and which produce leaves in the spring, even though the leaves be as thin as the capsules of flax. But a plant whose branches perish in the winter and whose root alone remains, is not called a "tree" and over its fruit we say "Bore peri haadamah."

2. Before partaking of food, which is not the product of the soil, such as meat, fish, milk, and cheese, and before drinking any beverage other than wine or olive-oil (see preceding Section) we say the benediction "Shehakol" (all things exist), which reads: "Blessed art Thou, O Lord, our God, King of the universe, at whose word all things exist."

3. Although mushrooms and truffles receive their nutrition from the moisture of the earth, their growth depends not upon the soil but upon the atmosphere; therefore they cannot be called "fruit of the ground," and the benediction "Shehakol" should be said over them.

4. The benedictions "Bore peri haetz" and "Bore peri haadamah" should be said only over food that is usually eaten raw. But if it is customary to eat a certain food only when cooked, and it is never-

[1] See Section IV, pp. 45–46.

theless eaten raw, "Shehakol" should be said. Pickled foods and salted foods are considered the same as cooked food, and the benediction "Bore peri haadamah" should be said before eating them.

5. Before eating radishes, one should say the benediction "Bore peri haadamah." The same benediction is said over garlic and onions that are soft and which are usually eaten when raw, provided they are to be eaten without bread. If, however the garlic or onion has become pungent in taste, being too old to be considered fit for eating raw, and it is nevertheless so eaten, the benediction "Shehakol" should be said.

6. We say "Shehakol" over sugar. If one sucks or chews sugar-cane, cinnamon, or licorice, and only the taste thereof is enjoyed, while the chief part is ejected, then the benediction "Shehakol" is likewise said.

XI. BENEDICTIONS OVER SOUP, FRUIT, AND VEGETABLE EXTRACTS

1. Over liquids extracted from fruits and vegetables we say the benediction "Shehakol." This also applies to the honey extracted from dates, as no liquid is termed "fruit," except wine and olive-oil. For wine, which is highly regarded, a special benediction has been set, "Bore peri haggaphen." If one enjoys olive-oil, which is also highly regarded, so much that the utterance of a benediction is required, one says, "Bore peri haetz." (See Section IX, above.)

2. If we cook fruits which are usually eaten raw, we say the benediction "Shehakol" before partaking of their juice. However, if we cook an easily procurable fruit which it is customary to dry and to cook, we should say the benediction "Bore peri haetz" over the juice, whether or not we eat the fruit. If we cook pulse or vegetables, according to the general method of preparing gruel food for consumption, we should say the benediction "Bore peri haadamah" over the juice, whether or not we partake of the rest of the dish.

3. If we soak or cook fruits for the sake of their juice, we say over the juice the benediction "Shehakol"; hence, over tea, coffee, or beer, whether made from dates or from barley, the benediction to be said is "Shehakol."

4. If vegetables or fruits, such as cucumbers, beetroots, and leeks, are preserved until pickled in water, we say "Shehakol" over their juice.

5. The same applies to fruits, vegetables, pulse and the like, which are cooked in a liquid which has a taste peculiar to itself, as for instance, in vinegar, or in beetroot soup, or in milk, and the benediction "Shehakol" should be pronounced over their liquid.

XII. THE CONCLUDING BENEDICTION

1. After eating the fruit of any tree, other than those included in the seven species mentioned in the Torah (see Par. 4, below), or any fruit of the ground, or any vegetable, or any food that is not the direct produce of the soil, one should say the benediction "Bore nephashot rabbot" (who created many living things).

2. The concluding benediction, like Grace after meals (see Section V, Par. 5, above), must not be said unless one has eaten a quantity not less than the size of an olive.

3. If one drinks a hot beverage slowly, such as tea or coffee, no concluding benediction is said, since each sip, taken separately, contains less than the quantity required for the concluding benediction.

4. The land of Israel is famous for the seven species of food which it produces, as it is written (Deut. viii, 8): "A land of wheat and barley, and vines and fig-trees and pomegranates; a land of olive-trees and honey." If one eats bread made of the five species of grain, namely, wheat and barley expressly mentioned in the Torah, and also spelt, or oats, or rye, which belong to the family of wheat and barley, one must say the Grace thereafter which consists of three complete benedictions. However, after eating food which is not really bread but which is farinaceous (see Section VIII, pp. 51–52), prepared from the five species of grain mentioned above; and after drinking wine or eating grapes or raisins or figs; and after eating pomegranates, olives, or dates, these being the "honey" of which the Torah speaks, inasmuch as honey exudes therefrom; one must say the concluding benediction embodying in a brief form the three blessings of the Grace after meals.

5. The concluding benediction embodying the three blessings

which is said after eating food over which "Bore mine mezonot" is said (see Section VIII, pp. 51–52), begins thus: "Blessed art Thou, O Lord our God, King of the universe, for the sustenance and for the nourishment"; and concludes thus: "And we will give Thee thanks for the land, and for the sustenance. Blessed art Thou, O Lord, for the land, and for the sustenance, and for the nourishment."

The benediction after wine begins: "For the vine and for the fruit of the vine"; and concludes: "For the vine and for the fruit of the vine. Blessed art Thou, O Lord, for the land and for the fruit of the vine."

The benediction after fruit begins: "For the trees and for the fruit of the trees," and concludes: "For the land and for the fruits. Blessed art Thou, O Lord, for the land and for the fruits." After eating fruit which comes from Israel, the Holy Land, we conclude the Grace thus: "For the land and for its fruit."

If we have eaten various kinds of farinaceous food and fruit, and have drunk wine, we combine the three benedictions into one Grace, first mentioning "For the sustenance," and then "For the vine," and finally "For the tree."

6. On the Sabbath, or Festivals, or New Moon, we include in the concluding benediction whatever relates especially to these days; but if we have forgotten to include it, we need not repeat the benediction.

7. It is forbidden to leave the place of eating or to engage in any occupation before saying the concluding benediction, lest we forget to say it. If, nevertheless, we have left the place of eating, and if the benediction we have omitted is "Bore nephashot rabbot," we may say it wherever we are. If, however, we have omitted the blessing embodying the three benedictions, we must return to the place where we have eaten and say it there.

XIII. IMPORTANT FOODS AND ACCESSORIES

1. If we eat two articles of food, or if we eat and drink, and one of these articles is important for us while the other is merely accessory to it, so that the second would not have been eaten without the first, as, for example, eating a small piece of bread to mitigate the

pungency of brandy or of herring, we say a benediction only over the important food. For ritual purposes, the accessory food is not considered as eaten at all.

2. This rule concerning accessory foods applies only when the important food is eaten first, and provided that, when saying the benediction over it, we intended to eat the accessory food as well, and therefore mentally included the latter in our original benediction. If, however, we leave the place of eating and go into another room before eating the accessory food, we must then say a separate benediction over it.

3. If we desire to drink some wine or brandy, and in order not to drink it on an empty stomach, we wish to eat first a small piece of bread, we should first say the benediction over the wine or the brandy, and drink a little of it; then this benediction will exempt the accessory from any further benediction.

4. If we wish to partake of two articles of food—for example brandy or coffee, and dessert, such as honey-cake or preserves, we should say a separate benediction over each, first over the cake or preserves because they are considered more important, and then over the brandy or coffee.

XIV. ORDER OF PRECEDENCE RELATING TO BENEDICTIONS

1. If we have before us several varieties of fruit and we desire to partake of all of them, we should be guided by the following conditions: if they are all subject to the same benediction, we should say it over the kind we like best; if we are equally fond of all, and if there is among them one of the seven species with which the land of Israel was blessed (see Section XII, par. 4), we say the benediction over this one even if there should be only a half of that fruit, while the others are whole; but if there is none of the seven species among them, then if only one fruit is whole and the others are not whole, the benediction should be said over the whole fruit. If there are two kinds of fruit to be eaten, one of which is subject to the benediction "Bore peri haetz," and the other to the benediction "Bore peri haadamah," thus requiring the recital of both, we should first say

the benediction for that fruit which we prefer. If we have no preference, and if none of the fruits is of the seven species of Israel, and if both are equally whole, then the benediction "Bore peri haetz" takes precedence over the benediction "Bore peri haadamah."

2. When eating several kinds of food, the benedictions "Bore peri haetz" and "Bore peri haadamah" take precedence over the benediction "Shehakol," whether or not we prefer the food over which "Shehakol" is to be said.

3. The benediction "Hamotzi" (who brings forth bread) takes precedence over the benediction "Bore mine mezonot" and both take precedence over the benediction over wine, "Bore peri haggaphen."

XV. BENEDICTIONS PRONOUNCED ERRONEOUSLY

1. If by error, one says the benediction "Bore mine mezonot" over proper bread, or the "Hamotzi" over cake, he has fulfilled his obligation. If, however, he has said the "Hamotzi" over boiled food, whether or not it is prepared from the five species of grain, his obligation is not fulfilled. If by error, he says the benediction "Bore peri haggaphen" over grapes, or if he errs in saying, after eating grapes, the concluding benediction "Al haggephen," his obligation is fulfilled, as grapes are also fruit of the vine.

2. If by error one says the benediction "Bore peri haadamah" over fruit of the tree, or if by error he has given precedence to the benediction over the fruit of the ground with the intention of exempting thereby the fruit of the tree, his obligation is fulfilled, as the fruit of the tree also gets its sustenance from the ground. But if he says the benediction "Bore peri haetz" over the fruit of the ground, his obligation is not fulfilled.

3. If by error one says over wine the benediction "Bore peri haetz," his obligation is fulfilled. If, however, he immediately becomes aware of the error, he should at once add "Bore peri haggaphen."

4. If by error one says the benediction "Shehakol" over any article of food, even if it be over bread or wine, one's obligation is nevertheless fulfilled.

XVI. THE BENEDICTION OVER FRAGRANCE

1. Just as we are forbidden to enjoy any article of food or drink before pronouncing a benediction over it, so are we forbidden to enjoy any fragrant odor before saying a benediction. In this case, however, we are not required to say a concluding benediction.

2. If the fragrance be of an edible fruit, whether of a tree or of the soil, and even if the fruit be of a kind that is eaten only when mixed with other ingredients, such as the nutmeg, or the lemon, inasmuch as that fruit is used principally as food, we should say the benediction: "Blessed art Thou, O Lord our God, King of the universe, who hath given fragrance unto fruit." This benediction is said, however, only when we intentionally inhale the fragrance. If we do so unintentionally, we are not obliged to say a benediction. If we inhale the scent of roasted coffee because we find it pleasant, we should say the benediction, "Who hath given fragrance into fruit."

3. If the thing out of which the fragrance arises is a tree or a plant, we say the benediction: "Who hath created fragrant woods." Therefore over the myrtle, or the rose, or frankincense, or the like, we say the benediction: "Who hath created fragrant woods," since they are chiefly valued for their fragrance and not as a food.

4. If the fragrance arises from herbs and vegetables, we say the benediction: "Who hath created fragrant herbs." A vegetable is distinguished from a tree in the following manner: if it possesses a stem as hard as the stalk of flax, and if it grows perennially and produces leaves, it is a tree, but if the stalk is always soft, it is an odorous herb.

5. If, like musk, it is neither a tree nor a herb, on inhaling its fragrance we say the benediction: "Who hath created various kinds of spices." The same benediction is to be said on smelling dried mushrooms, if we find their odor pleasant.

6. Over balsam-oil which grows in the soil of the land of Israel, the special benediction, "Who hath created sweet-scented oil," has been instituted, on account of its special association with the land of Israel.

7. If by error we confuse the benedictions, "Who hath created fragrant herbs," and "Who hath created fragrant woods," and substitute one for the other, we may not consider our obligation fulfilled. If, however, we say the benediction, "Who hath created various kinds of spices," over any of the odorous objects, our obligation is fulfilled. Therefore, if we are in doubt of what benediction to say because we are unable to distinguish the species, we should say the benediction, "Who hath created various kinds of spices."

8. Oil or wine that has been scented with fragrant wood, is subject to the benediction, "Who hath created fragrant woods;" and if scented with fragrant plants, it is subject to the benediction, "Who hath created fragrant herbs." If scented with fragrant wood and plants, it is subject to the benediction, "Who hath created various kinds of spices." In all cases where the fragrance is due to several articles mixed together, the benediction "Who hath created various kinds of spices" is said.

9. Spices stored in a room as merchandise, and not for the special purpose of smelling them, and perfume used only to scent garments and not meant to be inhaled for its fragrance, require no benediction, even when we smell them intentionally.

10. If, however, we enter a store where various spices are sold, or a chemist's shop, and we intend to smell them, we should previously say the benediction "Who hath created various kinds of spices," as the spices are placed there for this purpose by the shopkeeper as a means of encouraging purchasers.

11. When the scent arises from an object other than its original source, as from garments which have been perfumed, or from a vessel which has absorbed the scent of spices it has held, or from hands which have retained the odor of citrons or other fruit they have handled, no benediction is required.

XVII. THE BENEDICTIONS OVER JOY AND GRIEF

Just as we owe to the Almighty thankfulness when we are prosperous and happy, for He is the Author of life and health, the Giver of all joy and success, so also must we express our blessing when affliction and trial are upon us, for these are sent to chasten and better our souls. As God, the Creator and Ruler of the world, is both Goodness and Wisdom, so does all that occurs in the world serve a good and wise purpose. Every evil in life, whether physical or moral, must, therefore, lead to some good in the end. Death and Sin are not powers of evil, but agencies of God sent to test man's power, trials that bring out the good in ways often mysterious to us. The Jew does not believe in a Devil. Satan is represented as one of the angels of God, sent to try Job and not to act as his fiend.

The duty, then, we have towards God is to have perfect faith in Him and feel confident that, whatever danger or distress may beset us, He will in the end lead us to the path of salvation.

LAWS CONCERNING THE BENEDICTIONS OVER JOY AND GRIEF

1. If we hear personal good tidings from an eye-witness whom we consider reliable, or if we ourselves witness an event fortunate to ourselves, we must say the benediction "Sheheheyanu" (who kept us in life). If, however, the good fortune benefits not only ourselves but others as well, we should say the benediction, "Hattob vehammetib" (who is good and dispenseth good), which reads: "Blessed art Thou, O Lord our God, King of the universe, who is good and dispenseth good to others," implying gratitude for us as well as for our fellowmen.

2. Upon the birth of a son, both father and mother should say the benediction "Hattob vehammetib" (who is good and dispenseth good).

3. On hearing bad tidings, we should say: "Blessed art Thou, O Lord our God, King of the universe, the just Judge." It is our duty to bless God for the misfortune with a perfect mind and a willing spirit, just as we bless Him for the good things.

4. A man should accustom himself to say always: "Whatever the All-merciful does is for our good."

5. Upon the death of a relative, or even of one who is not a relative but who was a pious man or a scholar and whose death grieves us sorely, we should say the benediction: "Blessed art Thou, O Lord our God, King of the universe, the just Judge." On the demise of

one whose death does not cause us so great a grief, we should say: "Blessed be the just Judge," omitting the Divine Name and Kingship (O Lord our God, King of the universe).

6. If we build or buy a house, or if we purchase vessels or valuable garments, although we have previously acquired similar possessions, provided we have never owned these before and we rejoice in their acquisition, we should say the benediction "Sheheheyanu" at the time the purchase is made or upon the completion of the building.

7. Upon putting on a new garment for the first time, we say the benediction "Malbish arumim" (who clothes the naked). Even if we have already said this benediction in the morning prayers, we must repeat it when putting on the new attire. If, however, we had the new garment on when we said this benediction (malbish arumim) in the morning prayer, we need not repeat it because of the new attire. If we purchase a new *talit* (fringed garment), we should say the benediction "Sheheheyanu" after we have inserted the fringes therein, but if we omit to say it at that time, we should say it when we wrap ourselves in it for the first time after having said the benedition "Lehitateph batzitzit" (to wrap ourselves in a fringed garment).

8. On purchasing articles for household use, we say the benediction "Hattob vehammetib."

9. If we are presented with a gift, we must say the benediction "Hattob vehammetib," as both the recipient and the donor derive benefit from the gift. If the recipient is poor, then the donor derives pleasure in that the Almighty has granted him the means of giving charity, and if the recipient is rich, the donor is gratified by the former's acceptance of the gift.

10. On purchasing new sacred books, we do not say the benediction "Sheheheyanu," as the things with which sacred duties are performed are not for sensual enjoyment.

11. On purchasing an article of slight value, such as a shirt, or shoes, or socks, we should not say a beendiction, even if we are poor and its acquisition gives us joy. If a rich man purchases new utensils, the acquisition of which would fill one of the middle class

with joy, but which the rich man in comparison with his wealth esteems but lightly, he should not say a benediction.

12. It is customary to say to one who puts on new apparel: "Mayest thou wear out this garment and acquire a new one." But we do not express this wish to one who wears new shoes or a new garment made of fur or leather, even if the fur or leather be sewn beneath cloth, because a new garment like this one requires the killing of a living being, and it is written (Psalms cxlv, 9): "And His mercy is upon all His works."

13. If we partake for the first time of new fruit which is reproduced each year, we should first say the benediction "Sheheheyanu" and then the benediction appropriate to the fruit. If we have neglected to say "Sheheheyanu" when we first partook of the new fruit, we should not say it when partaking of the same fruit afterwards. If we have before us several kinds of new fruit, one benediction "Sheheheyanu" will suffice for all.

14. We do not say "Sheheheyanu" over fruit which is not fully ripe.

15. We do not say "Sheheheyanu" over new vegetables or turnips, for the reason that they remain well preserved for a long time by being kept in the ground or in sand, and as they are plentiful, we do not take great joy when eating them new.

16. No "Sheheheyanu" should be said upon smelling a fragrant odor.

17. Upon seeing a friend to whom one is greatly attached, or one's father, or one's teacher after a separation of thirty days, one should say the benediction "Sheheheyanu." If the time of separation has been twelve months, one should say the benediction: "Blessed art Thou, O Lord our God, King of the universe, who reviveth the dead;" but one need not say "Sheheheyanu." But if during the twelve-month period one has received a letter or has had news of the loved one's welfare, one should not say "Who reviveth the dead," but "Sheheheyanu." This law applies to both male and female: if a man sees his wife, or his mother, or his daughter, or his sister, or if a woman sees her husband, or son, or brother, the appropriate benediction should be said.

18. Upon meeting a friend with whom one has corresponded but never met, one need not say the benediction, as in this case the joy of meeting is not likely to be as great.

XVIII. BENEDICTIONS OVER SIGHTS IN NATURE

1. We are not permitted to enjoy a beautiful sight in nature, without thanking the Almighty for it. On seeing fruit trees in blossom, we must say the benediction: "Blessed art Thou, O Lord our God, King of the universe, who hath made the world wanting in nought, but hath produced therein goodly creatures and goodly trees wherewith to give delight to the children of men." This benediction should be said only once a year. If we have delayed saying the benediction past blossom time, we should not say it at all.

2. On seeing shooting stars which dart across the sky from place to place with a transient light, or a comet, or a meteor, or on witnessing an earthquake, or a hurricane, or lightning, we say the benediction: "Blessed art Thou, O Lord our God, King of the universe, who hath made the creation." (This benediction should be said over a shooting star but once during the night, even if we should see more than one. Over a comet we say a benediction but once in thirty days.) On hearing thunder after the lightning has passed, we say the benediction: "Blessed art Thou, O Lord our God, King of the universe, whose strength and might fill the world." If we see lightning and hear thunder simultaneously, we say only the benediction "Who hath made the creation." If upon seeing lightning, we have said the benediction "Who hath made the creation" and hear the thunder at that instant or immediately after that, it is not necessary to say a benediction over the thunder, for the benediction said over the lightning covers both. The benedictions over the thunder and the lightning should be said directly when they happen, and if an interruption occurs, the benediction should not be said.

3. So long as the clouds have not passed by, one benediction exempts all the lightnings and thunders that may be seen or heard. But if the clouds have disappeared and the sky has cleared between one lightning and the other or between one peal of thunder and another, we must repeat the benediction. A flash of lightning due

to the heat and unaccompanied by thunder, is not of the same nature as (storm) lightning, and does not require the saying of a benediction.

4. On seeing the rainbow, we say the benediction: "Blessed art Thou, O Lord our God, King of the universe, who remembereth His covenant, is faithful to His covenant, and keepeth His promise." We must not gaze too much at the rainbow.

5. At the sight of seas, or mountains famous for their great height, we say the benediction: "Who hath made the creation."

6. If the Holy One, blessed be He, has wrought a miracle for someone, having helped him in a supernatural manner, then on seeing the place where the miracle occurred, he should say the benediction: "Blessed art Thou, O Lord our God, King of the universe, who hath wrought a miracle for me in this place."

7. On seeing a great Jewish scholar distinguished for his knowledge of the Torah, we say the benediction: "Blessed art Thou, O Lord our God, King of the universe, who hath imparted of His wisdom to them that fear Him." On seeing man versed in secular science, we say: "Blessed art Thou, O Lord our God, King of the universe, who hath given of His wisdom to flesh and blood."

8. On seeing graves of Israelites, we say: "Blessed art Thou, O Lord our God, King of the universe, who formed you in judgment," etc.

9. Thirty days must elapse between repetitions of any of the above benedictions when they are applied to the same individual person or object. New benedictions must be said upon seeing different graves or different persons, without regard to time intervals.

XIX. THE BENEDICTION "HAGGOMEL"

1. Four classes of people must thank God for special mercy, that is, they must say the benediction "Haggomel:" (a) He who has crossed the ocean safely and has reached his desired destination; (b) he who has passed safely through a desert or a dangerous road, or has been saved from any peril or dangerous accident; (c) he who has recovered from a serious illness, or from a serious wound, or from an illness which has confined him to bed for at least three

days; and (d) he who has been released from prison, even if the imprisonment was due to civil matters. All these should say the benediction known as "Haggomel" (who vouchsafeth benefits), which reads: "Blessed art Thou, O Lord our God, King of the universe, who vouchsafeth benefits unto the undeserving, who hath vouchsafed all good unto me;" to which the listeners should respond: "He who hath vouchsafed all good unto thee, may He vouchsafe all good unto thee for ever."

2. The benediction "Haggomel" should be said in the presence of no less than ten male adults, in addition to the one saying the benediction. It is customary to say "Haggomel" on being called up to say the benediction over the Torah. We must not, however, deliberately delay saying the benediction "Haggomel" longer than three days. Consquently, if the event calling for the benediction should take place on a Monday after the Torah has been read, "Haggomel" should be said immediately before ten male adults and not be postponed until the next reading of the Torah on Thursday. If one is a mourner who may not be called up to the Torah, he should say "Haggomel" immediately after the event, before ten male adults. If, by error, one delays saying "Haggomel" longer than three days, one may still say it thereafter.

3. He who has been blessed by a miracle is in duty bound to set aside for charity as much as his means will allow, and he should divide this sum among those who are occupied in the study of the Torah, and say: "Behold, I give this money to charity, and may it be the Divine Will to consider this as if I had brought a thanksgiving offering." It is also fitting that he should institute some public improvement in the city where he resides, and every year on the anniversary he should set that day apart to thank God and to recall the miracle.

XX. FORBIDDEN FOODS

Another law ordained by the Almighty for the purpose of distinguishing Israel as a holy people from the rest of mankind, is that regarding unclean meat. This distinction betwen clean and unclean meat was observed by priests of many ancient nations in Asia and

Africa. But that which, among other nations, only the priests and saints observed as a means of sanctification and distinction, the whole Jewish people were ordered to observe as "a kingdom of priests and a holy nation" (Ex. xix, 6).

According to the Holy Scriptures (Lev. xi; Deut. xiv, 3–22), the Almighty forbade the use of certain classes of animals as food. Any meat of animals that have cloven hoofs and do not chew the cud, or of those that do chew the cud but have no cloven hoofs, is unfit for use by the Jewish people. An animal to be considered *kosher* (fit for use) must have cloven hoofs and chew the cud. Concerning ham, bacon, and other hog meat, there is a specific commandment in the Law of Moses (Lev. xi, 7; Deut. xiv, 8): "And the swine, though it has cloven hoofs, but since it cheweth not the cud, it shall be unclean to you; of their flesh ye shall not eat."

The Holy Scripture forbids the use of all kinds of shellfish such as lobsters, oysters, clams, and crabs, as well as all creeping things. The general rule regarding fish is (Lev. xi, 9–10; Deut. xiv, 9–10) that "fish that do not have scales and fins" are forbidden.

The Law of Moses enumerates twenty-four kinds of fowl, the meat of which is forbidden to Jews (Lev. xi, 13–19; Deut. xiv, 12–18). The most common among them are: The vulture, eagle, raven, ostrich, owl and bat.

LAWS CONCERNING FORBIDDEN FOODS

1. The Law of Moses forbids the use of the hindquarter part of even clean (kosher) animals (Gen. xxxii, 33), unless the forbidden parts and bloodvessels are properly removed. Most butchers know how to purge only the forequarters of *kosher* animals, but not the hindquarters. We therefore use the forequarter meat only, and abstain from using the hindquarter meat.

2. Any product made of unclean fish is forbidden. Therefore when buying oil and fish roe, great care should be exercised to obtain only that which comes from clean (kosher) fish. Caviar prepared of the roe of sturgeon is forbidden.

3. Eggs of forbidden birds may not be used. It is therefore our duty to abstain from buying liquid eggs unless we know their origin.

The general shape of *kosher* eggs is broadly rounded at one end and tapers at the other.

4. The prohibition against eating blood (see Section that follows) has been extended even to eggs, and the blood found in them is forbidden. Occasionally it is prohibited to eat the entire egg because of blood-specks; therefore the egg should be examined well before using it in the preparation of food.

5. The blood of all animals is forbidden, except that of fish, but even fish-blood should not be collected into a single vessel, because people might be under the impression that it is blood which is forbidden. If, however, it is evident that it is the blood of fish, as when it contains scales, then its use is permitted.

6. The sages prohibit the eating of the bread of a non-Jew. There are localities where people are not strict and do purchase bread of a non-Jewish baker, either because it is better or because there is no Jewish baker at all in that place. However, regarding the bread of a non-Jewish private person, they are more strict and would permit the use of it only in cases of extreme necessity. There is one authority who holds that in places where a baker cannot be found, it is even permissible to partake of the bread of a non-Jewish private person, and one need not wait for *kosher* bread; and the prevailing custom is in accordance with that authority.

7. Meat and dairy products may not be eaten or boiled together. In certain instances, it is not even permissible to derive any benefit from meat mixed with dairy products. Whenever therefore, meat and dairy products happen to become mixed together, a Rabbi should be consulted.

8. It is customary to mark all utensils used for dairy foods, so that they may not be interchanged with those used for meat.

9. After eating meat or a dish prepared with meat, one should wait six hours before eating dairy food.

10. If one has eaten food which has been prepared neither with meat nor with meat-fat, but which has been cooked in a pot used for boiling meat, even if the pot was not cleansed beforehand, it is permissible for him to eat dairy food immediately thereafter.

11. After eating dairy food, we may immediately partake of meat.

But after eating cheese, we should carefully examine our hands to make sure that no particles of cheese cling to them; we should also cleanse our teeth and rinse our mouths. If the cheese was stale and hard, we must wait six hours before eating meat.

12. It is not customary ritually to purify utensils used for dairy food so that they may be fit for the use of meat. Neither should meat utensils be purified for use of dairy food.

13. It is strictly forbidden to eat or drink anything that contains worms or mites. Hence it is forbidden to drink the water from rivers or wells known to be infested with worms before it has been filtered; and if one has inadvertently used such unfiltered water for soaking, washing, or cooking any food, the food should be forbidden.

14. The water should be filtered through a finely spun cloth capable of excluding even the smallest insect.

15. Vinegar which contains worms, is unfit for use even if it has been filtered, because it is believed the smallest worm in vinegar will pass through any cloth.

16. The black spots, sometimes found in fruit and in such vegetables as beans, peas, and lentils, are the breeding places of worms and may not be eaten. When such spots are found in fruit, they may be cut out and the rest of the fruit may be eaten; but when found in a bean, pea, or lentil, the whole must be discarded.

17. All fruits, as a rule, may contain worms, and therefore require examination before being eaten or cooked. Before cooking, or before preserving them in honey or sugar, or when making jam, the fruit must be opened one by one and the stones removed, in order that the examination may be thorough.

18. Flour and cereals containing large worms, may be rendered fit for use by being sifted through a sieve, through which the worms cannot pass. But flour and cereals containing mites, must be entirely discarded, as mites will also pass through the sieve.

19. Worms are often found in the interior of fish, especially in the brain, liver, intestines, mouth and ears. Haddock is most susceptible to worms. The places where worms are likely to be found, must be thoroughly examined before using the fish.

20. If in cutting fruit or vegetables, we happen to cut up a worm,

we must wipe the knife well, and cut out and discard that part of the fruit or vegetable where the worm has been cut.

21. To determine whether a given food contains mites, we spread some of the food on a slightly warmed plate. If mites are present, they will creep to the surface.

XXI. SALTING MEAT

1. The Almighty was very emphatic in His command that we abstain from eating the blood of animals and fowl. He repeated this command several times in His Law (Gen. ix, 4; Lev. xvii, 14; Deut. xii, 16, 23–24; xv, 23). Our Talmudic sages have accordingly laid down the law that, in order to remove the blood from the meat effectively, the meat must be first soaked in water to open the pores, and then salted to draw the blood out.

2. Before the meat is salted it must be thoroughly washed in water. The meat should be soaked and entirely submerged in water for half an hour. Wherever a particle of blood is visible it must be thoroughly washed with the water in which it is soaked. In the case of fowl, the place where the incision was made in killing it, should also be thoroughly washed, and the blood visible inside the fowl must be washed off. If the water is very cold, it should be put in a warm place before the meat is soaked in it, because meat becomes hardened in cold water and the blood does not easily emerge.

3. Before the approach of the Sabbath, or on any other occasion when one is pressed for time, one may wash the meat thoroughly and then let it soak in water for a short time; when the water no longer becomes reddened by the blood, the meat may be salted.

4. If a piece of meat is cut up again after soaking, the new surfaces produced by the cut must be washed clean of surface-blood before being salted.

5. Frozen meat must be allowed to thaw out before being soaked, but it must not be placed near a hot stove nor put in hot water, lest the blood become hardened. In cases of emergency, the frozen meat may be soaked in tepid water.

6. The vessel used for the purpose of soaking meat may not be

used for the preparation of any other food. Therefore a special vessel should be set aside for soaking meat.

7. After the meat has been soaked, some of the water must be allowed to drain off, so that the salt may not dissolve at once and become ineffective in drawing out the blood. The meat should not be allowed to become thoroughly dry, for then the salt would not adhere to it at all, and would fail to drain the blood from it.

8. The salt should be coarser than flour so that it may not dissolve too quickly, and yet not too coarse for then it would entirely drop from the meat. The best salt is of medium size, like that used for cooking, and should be kept dry enough to be easily sprinkled.

9. The salt must be sprinkled on all sides of the meat, so that no part of the surface is left unsalted. Care should be taken to open poultry properly so that it may be well salted within.

10. The meat that has been salted must be placed where the blood can easily drain off. The salting board must be placed in an oblique position, so that the blood may flow down freely. A hollow receptacle, or a board with a hollow part or cavity where the brine may accumulate, should never be used. Meat or poultry, having a cavity, must be turned with the hollow part downward when placed on the board after salting, in order that the blood may drain freely.

11. The meat should remain in the salt for one hour; but in case of emergency, twenty-four minutes will suffice.

12. After the meat has remained in salt for the proper length of time, the salt should be thoroughly shaken off and the meat washed three times. The meat should never be put immediately after salting into a dry vessel before it is ritually purged.

13. The heads of poultry must be severed before the poultry is salted.

14. Bones which contain marrow and have meat clinging to them may be salted together with other meat; but if the bones are bare, they should be salted separately, and should not even be placed near the other meat while in the salt.

15. Liver, because it contains a large quantity of blood, may not be made *kosher* (fit for use) in the same manner as ordinary meat.

It must first be rent asunder, and then broiled over a fire, with the open parts kept in a downward position so that the blood may drain from them. Before the liver is placed on the flame, it must be purged, and while being broiled it must be lightly sprinkled with salt. It should be broiled until it is fit to be eaten as is. After broiling, it should be purged three times of the blood which has been discharged. It may then be either eaten as is or broiled.

16. Liver must be broiled either over a flame or over hot coals. When being broiled it must not be wrapped in any kind of paper.

17. Eggs found in poultry, no matter what their stage of development, must be soaked, salted and purged as if they were meat. They must not, however, be salted together with meat, and they must not be placed in a position where meat blood can drain on them. Such eggs must not be eaten or broiled together with milk or any other dairy products, because they are considered as meat.

18. The head and the brains must be salted separately from other meat. The head may be salted while it still has the hair on. Before soaking the head, it must be split open, the brain removed, and the membrane upon it rent.

19. The tips of the hoofs of animals must be cut before soaking the legs in water, so that the blood can flow out. It is permissible to salt the legs before removing the hair. While in the salt, the legs must be placed hoof-downward, so that the blood can drain out easily.

20. It is customary to cut open the heart of an animal before soaking it in water, so that the blood may issue from it.

21. It is also customary, before soaking the lungs of an animal, to cut them and lay open the large tubes.

22. Unsalted and unsoaked meat must not be put in a place where salt is sometimes kept. A special vessel in which to keep un-*koshered* (unsoaked and unsalted) meat must be set aside. Food which is generally eaten without first being washed must not be put in this vessel, lest it become contaminated with the blood of the un-*koshered* meat.

23. Meat that remains unsoaked and unsalted for three full days after the animal has been ritually slaughtered, may not be used.

If, however, the meat has been either soaked in water or purged before the three days are over, it may be soaked and salted and then boiled.

24. Before soaking the spleen, the surrounding membrane and the spleenic vein must be removed. The spleenic vein should be pulled out by its head along with the three cords that are contained in it. If any of the three cords happens to become severed, it is necessary to remove it from its root.

25. When singeing the feathers of poultry, care should be taken to use a small flame. The poultry should be constantly moved to and fro over the flame, so that the heat may not harden the blood.

XXII. IMMERSION OF VESSELS

1. New vessels and dishes, made of glass or metal, which are to be used in a Jewish home, must be sanctified for this purpose by immersing them in running water. Before the immersion, the following benediction is pronounced: "Blessed art Thou, O Lord our God, King of the universe, who hath sanctified us by His commandments, and hath commanded us concerning the immersion of vessels."

2. Wooden, clay and porcelain vessels need not be immersed; but if they have hoops of metal, or if they are glazed on the inside, they should be immersed without pronouncing the benediction.

3. Only vessels used to hold food ready to be eaten without any further preparation, need be immersed. Thus, metal vessels used for kneading or cutting dough, or the like, need not be immersed. A metal spit used for roasting meat, however, must be immersed after pronouncing the benediction. Also, trays upon which *matzot* or other food are placed, and glass bottles in which liquids are kept for pouring into drinking glasses, and pepper and coffee grinders should be immersed, but without saying the benediction.

4. Before immersing the vessel, it must be thoroughly cleansed. The whole vessel, including the handle, must be submerged in the water at one time. If the vessel is to be held in the hand during immersion, the hand should first be dipped into the water, and the vessel should then be held not tightly, but with an ordinary grip.

If the vessel is immersed by means of a cord attached to it, the cord should be knotted loosely so that the water may reach every part of the vessel.

5. A vessel with a narrow opening, must be kept in the water until the water fills it entirely.

6. A minor, whether male or female, may not be entrusted with performing the ritual of immersing vessels.

7. It is forbidden to immerse vessels either on the Sabbath or on a Festival.

XXIII. THE SEPARATION OF HALLAH (FIRST OF THE DOUGH)

Many of the Jewish ceremonies are connected with the cherished memories of the Jewish past. They go back to a time when the Jew practiced his impressive rites in the Temple at Jerusalem.

The following divine command is contained in the Holy Scriptures (Num. xv, 21): "Of the first of your dough ye shall give unto the Lord a portion for a gift throughout your generations." When the Temple was in existence, this gift, known as *hallah,* was given to the priest. The Jewish concept was that all our possessions belong to the Almighty and therefore must be consecrated to His service. Since we must make use of our possessions, the Almighty decreed that the dedication of a part of them serves to release the remainder for our own use.

Ever since the destruction of the Temple, the fulfillment of the precept to set aside the first of the dough, *hallah,* was practiced by the Jews, according to the rules of law laid down below.

LAWS CONCERNING THE SEPARATION OF HALLAH

1. From the dough made of one of the five species of grain, wheat, barley, spelt, rye, and oats, the *hallah* portion must be separated. Immediately before separating the *hallah,* the following benediction is recited: "Blessed art Thou, O Lord our God, King of the universe, who hath sanctified us by His commandments, and hath commanded us to separate *hallah.*" Then dough no less than the size

of an olive is separated and burned. The custom is to burn it in the oven with the baking bread.

2. The quantity of flour kneaded into dough which becomes subject to the law of separating *hallah*, is no less than the equivalent of the weight of forty-three and one-fifth eggs, (two and a half quarts, or three and one-half pounds).

3. Only dough kneaded for the purpose of baking requires the separation of *hallah* with the recitation of a benediction. If dough is prepared for cooking, or frying, or for any purpose other than baking, the *hallah* should be separated without saying the benediction. If, however, any part of such dough is intended to be used for baking, the benediction must be said.

4. If one intends to knead the dough with eggs or with any kind of fruit-juice, it is best to add a little water, milk, wine, honey, or olive oil to it while kneading the dough, so that the *hallah* may be separated from it and the proper benediction recited.

5. The precept concerning the separation of *hallah* applies especially to the mistress of the house; but if she is not at home and there is a likelihood that the dough may spoil before she returns, then any other person may separate the *hallah*.

6. No *hallah* may be separated on the Sabbath. Therefore, if no *hallah* is separated on Friday from the bread to be eaten on the Sabbath, a piece of each loaf used during the Sabbath must be left over. The portion thus left over must be large enough for the *hallah* to be separated and still have something left over. At the conclusion of the Sabbath, the *hallah*-portion is separated from these pieces and burned.

CHAPTER IV

HONORING THE TORAH

I. STUDY OF THE TORAH

The Jewish religion has from time immemorial not tolerated ignorance. Great emphasis has been laid by the Jewish spiritual leaders on the importance of studying and acquiring knowledge, even the knowledge of God. The philosophy of the Jewish religion has been that man should know and understand God as He is manifested through His works. Hillel the Elder who lived in the first century before the common era, used to say (Mishnah, Abot II, 6): "A man void of intelligence cannot be sensitive to sin, nor can an ignorant person be pious."

The Jewish religion teaches that it is the duty of man endowed with reason to learn the ways of God, observe His works in nature and in history, and study His revelations through the sacred books in order to arrive at an ever higher conception of His greatness and of His will, and thereby grow ever wiser and better.

LAWS CONCERNING THE STUDY OF THE TORAH

1. Every Israelite, whether he is poor or rich, healthy or suffering, young or old, must study the Torah (Law of God). If a person is unable to study the Torah, because he lacks either knowledge or time, he should at least help support others who devote their time to study, and this will be accounted to him as though he himself had studied. Nevertheless, every person should make an endeavor to study the Torah by himself, be it ever so little, every day and every

night, as it is written (Josh. i, 8): "And thou shalt meditate in it day and night."

2. He who is unable to devote all his time to the study of the Torah, but fixes certain hours of the day for study, should occupy those fixed hours with the study of the ordinary rules of law which every Israelite must know.

3. When a person interrupts his studies, he should not leave his book open.

II. SCROLL OF THE LAW AND HOLY BOOKS

1. It is a religious duty devolving upon every Israelite to write for himself a *sefer torah* (Scroll of the Law). Even if a person has inherited a Scroll from his father, he must nevertheless write another one for himself.

2. It is also the duty of every Jew to buy for himself other holy books of study, such as the Holy Scriptures, the Mishnah, the Talmud, and other law books, which he should study himself and let others study. If one cannot afford to buy both the Scroll of the Law and the other books for study, then the latter should have preference.

3. We must treat the Scroll of Law with the utmost respect, and we must assign to it a special place which must be treated with reverence and beautifully decorated. We must not handle a bare Scroll without its cover or mantle, and when we see a Scroll being carried, we must rise and remain standing until it is either brought to its place or until it is out of sight.

4. Other sacred books must also be treated with respect: if they are placed on a bench, it is forbidden to sit on this bench unless they are placed on something which is at least one hand-breadth in height. Needless to say, it is forbidden to place sacred books on the floor.

5. A Scroll of Law or any sacred book that has become worn out must not be burned, but hidden away.

6. Sacred books should not be mishandled, nor placed wrong side up; should we find them inverted, we must put them back in the proper position.

7. If one should drop a Scroll, even if it is covered by a mantle, one must fast; and it is customary that those who see it fall also fast.

III. THE TEACHER, SCHOLAR, AGED AND PRIEST

1. What parents are to our bodily life, teachers and spiritual leaders are to our moral and intellectual life. The Talmud tells us (Mishnah, Baba Mezia ii, 11) that a person must honor and reverence his teacher even more than his parents, for the reason that his parents have given him earthly existence, while his teacher has given him a share of the soul's immortal life.

2. It is written (Lev. xix, 32): "Thou shalt rise before the hoary head, and honor the face of the old man." By the expression "Old man" is meant a man versed in the Law of God. Therefore it is mandatory to reverence and honor a man learned in the Torah even if he is not advanced in years and even if he is not our teacher. It is also mandatory to respect and honor a person of seventy years or more, even though he is neither our teacher nor well-versed in the Law, provided he is not an evil-doer. Even a heathen who is old should be shown the respect of kind words and a supporting hand.

3. It is a grave sin to hate or to despise men versed in the Law of God.

4. It is a Biblical ordinance to give the Kohen (priest) certain prerogatives: He should be called first to pronounce the benediction over the reading of the Torah; he should be the first speaker at every public gathering; at a meal, he should be first to say the "Hamotzi" (the benediction over breaking bread), and to lead in the Grace after meals.

CHAPTER V

DIVERSE KINDS

Some of the Laws of Moses contain certain prohibitions known as "Hukkim" (statutes), because the reason for their observance has not been divulged. Maimonides, however, tells us that some of these laws are prohibitions against heathen practices, such as in Leviticus xix, 19 and Deuteronomy xxii 11, the crossbreeding of animals, the mixing of seeds, the wearing of *shatnez* (a garment mixed of wool and linen), and the grafting of trees. Idolatry corrupted the morals, the homes, and the welfare of society and it undermined the very foundation of the Jewish religion. Therefore the Mosaic Law strictly forbade any custom resembling the customs of the idolaters.

GRAFTING TREES

1. It is forbidden to graft a branch of one variety of tree upon another, as for example, the branch of an apple-tree upon a tree bearing citrous-fruit. Such grafting is forbidden even between closely related species as between cultivated and wild apple-trees, inasmuch as they produce two different kinds of apple. An Israelite must not allow a non-Jew to graft for him two diverse kinds of trees.

2. The law of Moses forbidding the mixing of seeds has no application to countries outside the Holy Land.

DIVERSE KINDS OF CATTLE

1. It is forbidden, either directly or indirectly, to cross-breed one's cattle or fowl with a diverse kind.

2. It is forbidden to yoke together animals of diverse kinds for ploughing or transportation or any other kind of work.

SHATNEZ

1. It is forbidden to make use of a garment mixed of wool of lambs or rams together with flax, as it is a violation of the Mosaic Law prohibiting "shatnez," a garment of wool and linen (Deut. xxii, 11).

2. It is permissible to sew garments made of lamb's skins with linen threads, as the woolen hairs are not used as threads and may be disregarded.

3. Even if ten mattresses lie one on top of the other, and the bottom one is "shatnez" (a mixture of wool and linen), it is forbidden to sit on the top mattress.

4. If a big garment contains "shatnez" at one end, it is forbidden to cover oneself with the other end, even if the forbidden part is resting on the ground.

5. If a handkerchief, or a towel, or a tablecloth, or even the covering of the desk in the synagogue upon which the Torah is read, contains "shatnez," its use is forbidden. It is also forbidden to make curtains of "shatnez," but the curtain covering the Holy Ark in the synagogue may be made of "shatnez."

PART TWO

OUR HOLY SEASONS:
SABBATH, FESTIVALS, FASTS

CHAPTER I

SABBATH

I. THE HOLINESS OF THE SABBATH

The Almighty ordained that after six days of work, we should set aside the seventh day of the week as a day of rest consecrated to God and the higher purposes of life. "Remember the Sabbath day to keep it holy," is God's command (Ex. xx, 8). The main object of the Sabbath, then, is to keep it holy. While abstaining from work, we should devote the Sabbath solely to those things which draw us nearer to God.

The Sabbath is to remind man of his higher destiny as child and co-worker of God. On that day he should lay aside the cares and labors for his bodily life, and concern himself more with the things that elevate and enrich his mind and heart, and provide for his spiritual needs.

The Sabbath is to sanctify life, and therefore it has been instituted as a day of common devotion and religious instruction. We are duty bound to attend divine service at the synagogue and listen to the word of God read and expounded, so that our lives may be improved.

Religious sentiments can best be awakened by means of observing the holy seasons, which commemorate the great events of the past and hold before us lofty visions of the future. Besides the Sabbath, which has become the corner-stone of the Jewish religion, there are the three Festivals of joy: Pesah (Passover), Shabuot (Feast of Weeks), Sukkot (Feast of Tabernacles), and the two

83

Festivals of solemn reflection: Rosh Hashanah (New Year's Day), and Yom Kippur (the Day of Atonement).

There are also minor festivals and fasts observed by Jews. They are: Hanukkah (Feast of Lights), Purim (lots), Rosh Hodesh (New Moon), Lag Baomer (thirty-third day in the counting of the Omer), Hamishah Asar Bishebat (the fifteenth day of the month of Shebat, or Arbor Day); and the four public fast days: Asarah Betebet (the tenth day of Tebet), Shibea Asar Betammuz (the seventeenth day of Tammuz), Tishea Beab (the ninth day of Ab), and Tzom Gedaliah (the fast of Gedaliah, on the third of Tishri).

LAWS CONCERNING THE HOLINESS OF THE SABBATH

1. The holy Sabbath is the great sign and covenant which the Holy One, blessed be He, has given to us to convey the great religious truth—that God is the Creator of the universe: "That in six days God made the heavens and the earth and all that is in them, and He rested on the seventh day." This belief is the foundation of our faith; for the Rabbis, of blessed memory, said that the Sabbath is equal in importance to *all* the other commandments; observing the Sabbath is equivalent to observing the whole Torah, and the desecration of the Sabbath is like denying the whole Torah.

2. All of us, even those who have many domestics, must do something in honor of the Sabbath, as it was the habit of the Rabbis of old. Rab Hisda, for instance, used to cut the vegetables very fine in honor of the Sabbath. Rabbah and Rab Joseph used to chop wood for cooking. Rab Zera was in the habit of lighting the fire over which the Sabbath food was cooked. Rab Nahman put the house in order, bringing in all the utensils needed for the Sabbath and putting away the things used during the weekdays. We should emulate their example by doing something in honor of the Sabbath and not regard it as undignified; for, if we honor the Sabbath, it redounds to our glory.

3. We should procure choice meat, fish, dessert, and good wine in honor of the Sabbath, in accordance with our means. It is proper to eat fish at every Sabbath meal provided it is not harmful to us; but if it does not agree with us, we should not eat it, because the

Sabbath is given us for pleasure and not for suffering. Fresh coverings should be put on the beds, and the table should be covered with a fresh cloth, which should remain on the table to the end of the Sabbath, and we should rejoice with the coming of the Sabbath. The mere expectation of a disinguished guest would make us active in setting our house in order; how much more so when that guest is Queen Sabbath!

4. Even a poor man should economize the whole week in order to save enough money to buy special food in honor of the Sabbath. If necessary, one should even borrow and even pledge one's personal property, in order to provide for the Sabbath. However, one who is in dire need, should be guided by the maxim of the great Talmudic sage Rabbi Akiba (Babli, Shabbat 118a): "Rather make thy Sabbath a week-day (as regards festive meals) then be dependent on men."

5. On Friday one must wash one's face and hands and bathe one's feet in warm water; and if one possesses the facilities, one should bathe the whole body in warm water.

6. On Friday we should examine our deeds of the past week, and repent for all the misdeeds we have committed, and wholeheartedly resolve not to repeat them.

7. One should try to wear fine clothes especially set aside for the Sabbath; for it is written (Is. lviii, 13): "And thou shalt honor it;" this is explained by our Rabbis as meaning, if possible one should not wear the same clothes on the Sabbath as on week-days.

II. THE LIGHTING OF THE SABBATH CANDLES

The lighting of Sababth candles is a very ancient custom in Israel. The Sabbath is a day of joy, and light is the natural concomitant of joy. (Esther vii, 16.) The Sabbath lights symbolize the serenity and cheerfulness which distinguish the Jewish day of rest; they beautify and adorn the Sabbath and make it appear more restful and holy. Light in the Jewish concept is symbolic of the Divine Commands and of the Torah. Says King Solomon (Prov. vi, 23): "For the commandment is a lamp, and the teaching (Torah) is light."

LAWS CONCERNING THE LIGHTING OF THE SABBATH CANDLES

1. The Sabbath candles should be lit about one-half hour before sundown.

2. It is meritorious to light as many candles as possible in honor of the Sabbath. Some people are accustomed to light ten, others seven. In no event should less than two candles be lit, symbolizing the two commands: "Remember the Sabbath day" (Ex. xx, 8), and, "Observe the Sabbath day" (Deut. v, 12); one candle is permissible in case of necessity only. The candles should be big enough to burn at least till after the meal. A beautiful custom is observed by many women of giving some charity before lighting the Sabbath candles.

3. It is a well-known law that a benediction must be said immediately before a precept is performed. This, however, is impossible in the case of lighting the Sabbath candles, since by pronouncing the benediction one assumes the holiness of the Sabbath, after which one is no longer allowed to light the candles. To comply with the law requiring a benediction before the performance of a precept—in this case the lighting of the candles—one first lights the candles, shuts out their light by putting one's hands before one's face while pronouncing the benediction, and immediately after saying the benediction, one removes one's hands and gazes at the light, which act is considered as if one said the benediction before kindling the light of the candles.

4. Men as well as women are obliged to light the Sabbath candles. However, the fulfillment of this duty was left to the woman, because she is always at home and attends to household duties.

5. The candles should be lit in the room and on the table where meals are generally served, in order that it may be apparent that the candles were lit in honor of the Sabbath. The candles should not be lit in one place and then transferred to another, except in an emergency.

6. It is well to place two *hallot* (white loaves of bread) upon the table before the candles are lit.

7. If a woman has once neglected to light the Sabbath candles, she should, all her lifetime, add one extra candle every Friday to

the number she previously used to light. This procedure should be repeated each time she neglects to light the candles. This rule of law does not apply if she is prevented from lighting the candles by an accident or by illness.

III. EVENING PRAYERS ON SABBATH AND FESTIVALS

1. On Friday evening it is customary to hold the *Maarib* (evening) service earlier than on week-days, in order to inaugurate the Sabbath as early as possible.

2. On concluding "Hashkibenu" (cause us, O Lord, to lie down), on the Sabbath and Festivals, we do not say as we do on weekdays, "Shomer ammo yisrael laad" (who guardeth His people Israel for ever); but we say instead, "Upheros alenu" (yea, spread over us) and conclude with, "Barukh attah adonai, hapores sukkat shalom" (blessed art Thou, O Lord, who spreadeth the tabernacle of peace), etc.

3. Concluding the "Shemoneh esreh" (silent prayer) on Friday evening, the congregation says, "Vayekhulu hashamyim vehaaretz" (and the heavens and the earth were finished), etc. This prayer must be recited while standing, in order to signify that we are witnesses to the Almighty's creation of the world.

4. After this the Reader says one benediction which contains the substance of seven: "Barukh attah adonai, elohenu velohe abotenu" (blessed art Thou, O Lord, who spreadeth the tabernacle of peace), then "Magen abot" (He was a shield), and concludes with, "Mekaddesh hashabbat" (who halloweth the Sabbath). The congregation must stand and listen attentively while the Reader is saying this benediction, and it is customary to say with him "Magen abot" until "Zekher lemaaseh bereshit" (in remembrance of the creation).

5. The above benediction is recited even on a Sabbath which occurs on a Festival or at the close of a Festival, but it is omitted on a Sabbath which occurs on either of the first two days of Passover.

6. This benediction should be said only at a regular place of worship in the presence of ten male adults; but it should not be said in a place where the male adults assemble casually to hold services, as at the house of a bridegroom, or at the house of a

mourner, unless it be their intention to pray there for several weeks.

7. It is customary for the Reader to recite the *kiddush* (see Section that follows) at the synagogue on Sabbath and Festival evenings, for the sake of those who have no families and cannot say it at home. On the first two nights of Passover, however, the *kiddush* is not chanted by the Reader at the synagogue, because persons who have no families must be given the opportunity to participate in the *seder* ceremonies. But inasmuch as, by saying the *kiddush* at the synagogue, the Reader is not exempt from saying it at home, and, as he is forbidden to partake of anything before saying the *kiddush* at home, in order that the benediction said over the wine may not be in vain, the wine is given to a child who has reached the age where he is being trained in the observances.

IV. KIDDUSH AND SABBATH MEALS

1. The Law of Moses bids us (Ex. xx, 18): "Remember the Sabbath day to keep it holy." And, as among the Jews the night ushers in the day and the Sabbath and Festivals begin with sunset, they are therefore inaugurated by solemnizing the evening meal with the recital of the *kiddush* (the sanctification of the day), and at their conclusion they are solemnized by reciting the *habdalah*. (See Section XVIII, pp. 109–110.) The Sages, of blessed memory, instituted the ceremony of the *kiddush* and the *habdalah* by saying a prayer on both occasions over a cup of wine.

2. The *kiddush* may be said and the evening meal may be eaten although it is not yet night. Before saying the *kiddush*, it is forbidden to partake of anything, even water.

3. It is meritorious to choose for the *kiddush* good, old, and preferably red wine. If suitable grape wine cannot be obtained, the *kiddush* may be recited over raisin wine. If wine cannot be obtained, one may say the *kiddush* over two whole *hallot* (white loaves of bread), but not over any other beverage. While saying "Vayekhulu hashamayim vehaaretz" (and the heavens and the earth were finished), one should stand and gaze at the candles; thereafter one may sit down, gaze at the goblet of wine, and say the benedictions "Bore peri haggaphen" (who created the fruit of the vine), and "Asher kideshanu" (who hath hallowed us).

4. Women, too, are obliged to participate in the *kiddush*. They should therefore listen attentively to the recital of the *kiddush* and respond "Amen," but they should not respond "Barugh hu ubarukh shemo" (blessed be He and blessed be His name).[1]

5. The *kiddush* should not be recited over wine which has turned sour or has a disagreeable odor. Foamy wine should be strained, but if this is impossible, the *kiddush* may be said over it as it is; but if it is covered with a white film, no *kiddush* may be recited over it, for it has presumably lost its taste.

6. The *kiddush* may, if necessary, be said over wine that has been boiled, or which contains some honey.

7. The goblet used for the recital of the *kiddush* should be in perfect condition and thoroughly clean.

8. The *hallot* should be covered whether the *kiddush* is recited over wine or over the *hallot* themselves. This is commemorative of the dew which covered the *manna* every morning from above and from beneath. (See Par. 14, p. 90.)

9. No concluding benediction should be said after drinking the wine of the *kiddush*, for inasmuch as it is one of the essentials of the meal, it is exempted by the Grace said after the meal.

10. No benediction need be said over the wine drunk during the meal, because it is exempted by the benediction "Bore peri haggaphen" (who createth the fruit of the vine) contained in the *kiddush*.

11. The *kiddush* should also be recited over a goblet of wine at the morning meal. This *kiddush* consists in simply saying the benediction "Bore peri haggaphen." Women are obliged to participate in this *kiddush* as well. It is best to recite the morning *kiddush*, too, over wine. However, if a person prefers, brandy may be substituted for wine.

12. The *kiddush*, both in the evening and in the day-time, must be recited in the room where the meal is served. The meal must be started immediately after the *kiddush*, and if one does not eat immediately thereafter, one does not fulfill the obligation concerning the recital of *kiddush*. He who does not care to eat a regular meal immediately after the *kiddush* recited in the day-time, may

[1] For the reason of this rule, see p. 5, par. 7.

say the *kiddush* and partake of some pastry; but in that event he must drink no less than a quarter of a *lug* of wine, so that he may thereafter say the concluding benediction "Al hammiheyah" (for the sustenance) and "Veal peri haggaphen" (and for the fruit of the vine). (See Chapter III, Section XII, pp. 55–56.)

13. Everybody, man or woman, is in duty bound to eat three meals on the Sabbath, one on Sabbath-eve, and two during the day. At each of the three meals it is obligatory to eat bread. The time for eating the third meal begins at one half hour past noon.

14. On the Sabbath we must say the "Hamotzi" over two whole loaves of bread at every meal. While saying the "Hamotzi" we hold both loaves in our hands, and we break one of them.

The two loaves, or *hallot*, are known as "Lehem mishneh" (in Hebrew: double bread). They recall how the Israelites, while in the wilderness on their way to the promised land, gathered on Friday a double portion of the *manna* (heavenly food) to last them for two days, because on the Sabbath they were not permitted to gather the food that descended for them from the skies. (See Ex. xvi, 11–36.)

15. If only one of those seated at table is provided with double loaves, then that one should say the "Hamotzi" and exempt the others. Before saying the "Hamotzi" he should say, "Bireshut morai verabotai" (with the sanction of my instructors and teachers), and after he has eaten some of the bread over which he has said the benediction, he should give to each one present a slice of the bread which they should eat without saying the "Hamotzi" over it.

16. On the Sabbath it is forbidden to abstain from eating even for a short time for the purpose of fasting. And it is forbidden to abstain from eating until noontime even if fasting is not intended.

17. It is forbidden to grieve over any distress on the Sabbath, but one should pray for mercy to the merciful God.

18. On the Sabbath it is meritorious to partake of fruits and delicacies, and to enjoy everything that provides one with pleasure, as it is written (Is. lviii, 13): "And thou shalt call the Sabbath pleasure."

19. On the Sabbath and Festivals, a time should be set aside to

study the Torah privately as well as for public study in an assembly. Sabbath and Festivals are given to Israel for the purpose of studying the Torah, since many are too occupied with their daily tasks during the week to study the Torah regularly. Hence, those who are unable to study the Torah during the week, are the more obliged to study on the Sabbath, each man according to his knowledge and ability.

V. THE READING OF THE TORAH AND MAFTIR

1. Concluding the "Shaharit" (morning prayer) on the Sabbath, a Scroll of the Law is taken from the ark, and seven or more male adults are called up to say the benedictions over the reading of the portion of the Torah assigned for that week. (See Chapter II, Section XII, pp. 34–36.) An eighth person is called up for the reading of the "Maftir" (the last few verses of the portion of the Torah, and the portion from the Prophets assigned for that week).

2. Between readings, the Scroll should be rolled together, but it need not be covered. However, before *maftir*, when there is a long interval during which the *kaddish* is chanted, the Scroll should be covered with its mantle. Similarly, on any occasion where there is a long interval betwen readings—for instance during the singing, when they call up a bridegroom, or while saying "Mi sheberakh" (He who blessed, etc.), the Scroll must be covered.

3. Before calling up the *maftir*, half-*kaddish* should be said. During the saying of the *kaddish*, if two Scrolls of the Law are to be used, both Scrolls should be on the table. When three Scrolls of the Torah are used, it is not necessary to place the first one on the table.

4. At the conclusion of the second benediction over the Torah by the *maftir*, one person is called up for "hagbah" (to raise the Scroll) and another for "gelilah" (to roll the Scroll together). The one called up for *maftir* should not begin saying the benedictions of the *haftorah* until the Scroll is rolled together and wrapped in its mantle.

5. After the words "Haneemarim beemet" (that were said in truth) in the first benediction over the "Haftorah," no "Amen"

should be said because it is all one benediction up to the word "Vatzedek" (and righteousness). Nor should "Amen" be answered after the words "Emet vatzedek" (truth and righteousness), in the first of the concluding benedictions after the "Haftorah," because the paragraph beginning with the words "Neeman attah" (faithful art Thou), is also a part of that benediction.

6. It is forbidden to indulge in conversation when the "Haftorah" is read.

7. In addition to the regular daily morning and afternoon sacrifices (korban tamid) that were offered in the Temple at Jerusalem,[1] the Law of Moses ordained that additional offerings be made on Sabbaths, Festivals and New Moons. These additional offerings (musaphim) were brought after the regular morning sacrifices. An additional prayer, known as "Musaph," was introduced on these days to correspond with the additional offerings.

8. The "Musaph" service is read immediately after the reading of the "Haftorah." It is a transgression to postpone this service beyond the end of the seventh hour of the day (1 p.m.); nevertheless, it may be read at any time before the end of the day, and one's obligation is considered fulfilled.

VI. THE THIRTY-NINE CHIEF LABORS FORBIDDEN ON THE SABBATH

The Talmud enumerates thirty-nine kinds of labor forbidden to be performed on the Sabbath, which are known as "Ab melakhot" (chief *or* principal labors). There are also "Toledot" (derivatives), forms of labor derived from the former, which are likewise forbidden on the Sabbath. The Talmud lays down the principle, that whatever labor was required for the building of the "Mishkan" (Tabernacle) in the wilderness, is forbidden on the Sabbath. For the reason that when God ordained through Moses (Ex. xx, 10): "Thou shalt not do any manner of work" on the Sabbath, it had reference to the types of labor required for the building of the Tabernacle.

The thirty-nine chief labors are:

1. Ploughing, or digging in the soil.

[1] See pages 10 and 36.

2. Sowing, or any manner of work done with the intention of making things grow. Hence, it is forbidden to plant, graft, cut branches of a tree, or to spill any liquid on the soil, where anything is apt to grow, because the liquid causes the soil to reproduce.

3. Reaping, or detaching anything from its place or growth, whether by hand or with an instrument.

4. Binding sheaves, or gathering and heaping severed ears of corn, or fruit, or saplings, in the place where they grow.

5. Threshing. It is not permissible to thresh anything that grows in the soil, as wheat, corn, and the like.

It is permissible to remove peas and the like from their pods, if the pods are still green and can also be eaten, because this is like separating one kind of food from another; but if the pods are dry and no longer suitable for eating, to remove the peas from them is forbidden, because of the law prohibiting "threshing."

6. Winnowing. It is forbidden to scatter anything to the winds.

7. Separating. While it is permissible to separate food from worthless matter, it is forbidden to pick out the worthless matter from the food. One may peel foods that are to be eaten immediately, but to peel foods such as garlic and onions in order to put them away is forbidden.

The law concerning "separation" applies also to nonedibles, such as utensils; whatever one desires for immediate use is considered as food, and the balance is considered worthless matter.

8. Grinding. It is forbidden to grind spices, drugs, or the like, in a mortar.

Pepper or salt needed for seasoning food may be crushed at the table with the handle of a knife or in any other convenient manner, but may not be ground in a mortar.

9. Sifting is forbidden, when the purpose is to remove the worthless matter.

10. Kneading. This includes the mixing together of flour, bran, clay, or earth.

11. Baking. This includes cooking, roasting over a fire, or by heat derived from a fire.

12. Shearing. It is forbidden to shear the fleece or fur from the

skin of an animal, whether dead or alive, or to pare the nails, or to remove hair either by hand or with an instrument.

Shreds of skin, which are like thin strips that become separated from the skin around the finger nails, should not be removed either by means of an instrument, nor by hand, nor with the teeth. A nail, most of which was torn off and causes pain, may be removed by hand but not with an instrument; but if less than half of it has become separated, it should not be removed even by hand.

13. Cleansing, that is, washing, removing clods, etc., from wool, flax, or the like is forbidden. This includes washing or wringing clothes.

Hot water should not be poured upon dishes to wash them; but the water should be poured into a vessel into which the dishes may thereafter be placed.

One may wipe off dirt, as from a garment, with a rag, but no water may be spilled on the soiled object, because the spilling of water is equivalent to washing.

14. Beating. This refers to the beating and combing of flax or wool, which is forbidden.

15. Dyeing. It is especially forbidden to dye or color anything permanently. However, even the use of a non-permanent dye is prohibited; therefore a woman is not allowed to use rouge on the Sabbath.

It is not permitted to put saffron into soup, because it colors it.

16. Spinning is forbidden on the Sabbath whether by hand or by machine.

17. Braiding, that is, any crossing of threads in a woof, constitutes a work forbidden on the Sabbath.

18. Starting a web, by making two meshes, attaching them either to the cross-pieces or to the slips.

19. Weaving two threads to a width of two fingers.

20. Separating two threads, that is, separating warp and woof.

21. Knotting, that is, making two knots one on top of the other, thus making it permanent.

It is forbidden to make one knot at the end of one thread or one cord, or to take the two ends of a thread or a cord, place them together and make one knot on both together, for in this case even one knot will make it permanent. It is permissible to take the two ends and make first one knot and on the top of it make one loop, if this is a knot which is generally made and untied every day. It is permitted to make two or more loops one on top of the other, even if this is done with the intention that it hold for many days.

22. Unknotting. It is forbidden to untie any knot that may not be tied on the Sabbath.

If a knot causes pain, it may be loosened by a non-Jew.

23. Sewing. It is not allowed to sew two stitches, if such stitches and the knot are visible on one side. The sewing of three stitches even without a knot, constitutes the act of sewing.

Sometimes when a seam becomes loose and the parts become separated, the thread is pulled together and the loose parts are made tight temporarily. This act constitutes sewing, and may not be done on the Sabbath.

24. Rending or tearing anything is forbidden, even when there is no intention of using the pieces to form a vessel.

It is forbidden to tear apart two sheets of paper that have been intentionally pasted together. If, however, the pages of a book should be accidentally stuck together by wax or by the dye used by the bookbinder, it is permissible to separate them.

25. Snaring any animal is forbidden.

It is not permissible to catch or cause to be caught any living thing on the Sabbath. But if an insect stings a person, it may be removed from the body and thrown away, although one is not permitted to kill it.

26. Slaughtering or killing anything that possesses life is forbidden on the Sabbath.

27. Flaying, or stripping the skin off the flesh is impermissible.

28. Tanning, salting, or dressing the hide of an animal in any manner is forbidden.

It is prohibited to smear anything on one's shoes, even if the intention is only to polish them.

Salting, or making a quantity of brine for pickling purposes or for preserving butter, is forbidden. One may make just enough to satisfy the requirements of the meal.

It is forbidden to salt any substance which is affected by the salting in such a way as to become soft or less pungent. Therefore it is forbidden to salt raw cucumbers, radishes or onions even if the quantity is limited to that which is needed for a particular meal. Instead, one may dip each piece in salt as one eats them, one at a time. Boiled eggs, meat, and other foods, upon which the salt has only the effect of imparting a salty flavor, may be salted, but only if they are intended to be consumed at that particular meal.

A large quantity of boiled beans may not be salted together, even if they are to be eaten immediately, because the salt serves to make them softer.

Salads made of lettuce or cucumbers, and other relishes made of onions or the like, may be salted immediately before the meal, because oil and vinegar are added, and at once weaken the effect of the salt.

If meat has not been salted for three days after the slaughter, and the third day occurs on the Sabbath, a non-Jew may rinse such meat on the Sabbath, so that it should not become forbidden food; but it may not be rinsed by a Jew.

29. Ruling or marking leather, paper or any substance at the place one desires to cut, is forbidden; and it is immaterial whether the mark is made with a dye, with one's nails, or with anything else.

30. Scraping or removing hair or wool from the skin to make the skin smooth, or peeling the skin, is forbidden.

31. Cutting or breaking anything that is not food is forbidden. Food, even that meant for beasts, may be cut and broken.

32. Writing. It is forbidden to write two letters or make two marks with ink or with any other substance upon parchment, paper, or anything else.

It is forbidden to write or to draw a picture, even with the finger, out of the liquid spilled on the table, or in the vapor on the panes of glass, or anything similar thereto, however ephemeral the design may be. It is even forbidden to make marks upon a sheet of paper with one's finger nails.

33. Erasing. It is forbidden to erase any writing of the type that may not be written on the Sabbath.

Wax found on a book, even if it be only on one letter of the book, must not be removed.

It is permissible to break and to eat on the Sabbath those tarts upon which letters or figures have been made.

34. Building, that is the erection of any structure, whether permanent or temporary, is forbidden.

It is forbidden to reset or remove windows or doors, even when they hang on iron hinges and are easily removed or reset, because he who resets them is guilty of building, and he who removes them is guilty of demolition.

It is forbidden to make a partition, however temporary, on the Sabbath or on a Festival, if it is made for the purpose of dividing something. It is, however, permissible to make a temporary partition to serve as a shield from the sun, rain, or the like.

It is forbidden to make a tent on the Sabbath, whatever its purpose. It is therefore not permissible to carry an open umbrella as a protection from the sun or from the rain, because it is considered as making a tent.

It is forbidden to replace the leg of a chair that has become loose.

35. The demolition of a structure of the type that may not be built on the Sabbath is forbidden.

A partition or a tent, which may not be made on the Sabbath, must not be removed on the Sabbath.

36. Kindling any fire, no matter how slight, is forbidden.

37. Extinguishing a fire is forbidden, unless there is danger that the fire may cause loss of life.

It is prohibited to open a door or a window opposite a burning candle lest the flame be extinguished, but one may close the window or door. It is forbidden to open or to close the door of an oven in which a fire is burning, for by so doing, one either kindles or extinguishes it.

38. Beating with the hammer, is a term used to denote the finishing touches applied to any manner of work. Thus, the removal of bastings with which the tailor has temporarily pieced a garment

together, or the removal of loose threads from a garment, constitutes "beating with the hammer."

An article of food which cannot be eaten at all without first being purged with water, must not be purged on the Sabbath even with cold water. It is permitted, however, to soak herring in cold water, as it was fit for food before soaking.

39. Carrying from one domain into another is forbidden on the Sabbath. (See Section that follows.)

VII. CARRYING FROM ONE DOMAIN INTO ANOTHER

1. There are four classes of territory with regard to the Sabbath law: (a) The private territory; (b) the public territory; (c) the territory which cannot be classified either as private or as public; and (d) the territory which is exempt.

2. A private territory is any place which measures no less than four hand-breadths square, and is surrounded either by partitions no less than ten hand-breadths high (even if they are not altogether solid), or by a trench ten hand-breadths deep and four hand-breadths wide. The open spaces of a private territory are considered private even to the very sky. The tops of the partitions surrounding private territory are also subject to the law governing private territory.

3. Streets and marketplaces which measure sixteen cubits square, are public territories, for such was the width of the road in the Levites' camp in the wilderness; highways which are sixteen cubits wide are also public territories. Anything in the public territory, measuring less than three hand-breadths high above the ground, is considered as part of such territory.

4. The following are territories which are regarded as neither public nor private: Any place which is not a public thoroughfare and is not properly surrounded by partitions, such as fields; a stream which is at least ten hand-breadths deep and four hand-breadths wide; and alleys which are partitioned off on three sides.

5. These are exempted territories: Any place in a public territory which does not measure four hand-breadths square, and is either

three or more hand-breadths in height, or which is surrounded by partitions of three or more hand-breadths high; an excavation which does not measure four hand-breadths square and is three or more hand-breadths deep. These places are considered exempt only when they are in a public territory; but when they are in a territory which is neither public nor private, they are considered as part of such territory.

6. In a public territory and in a territory which is neither private nor public, it is forbidden to carry, throw, or hand over anything a distance of four cubits. This prohibition applies even if the transfer is accomplished by a series of small movements, provided that the sum of the movements equals four cubits.

7. It is forbidden to transfer anything from one type of territory to another, except when one of the two territories is exempt. Thus an article may be passed from an exempt territory to any other territory, or from any territory to an exempt territory, provided that the aticle is not carried four or more cubits within the territory which is either public or which is neither public nor private.

8. One must not walk out with any article, other than a garment or an ornament, in a public territory or in a territory which is neither public nor private.

VIII. WASHING ON THE SABBATH

1. It is forbidden to wash one's body, or the greater part of one's body, in warm water even if the water was warmed before the Sabbath. This prohibition applies even if the washing is accomplished little by little, that is, by washing a small part of the body at a time. It is forbidden to enter a place for the purpose of perspiring there. It is, however, permissible to wash one's hands and bathe one's feet with water made warm before the Sabbath.

2. It is permissible to immerse the whole body in cold water.

3. He who bathes must be careful not to squeeze the water from his hair and not to wring any clothes. He should likewise take care not to swim, because swimming is forbidden on the Sabbath and on Festivals.

IX. CATTLE TO REST ON THE SABBATH

1. It is written (Ex. xxiii, 12): "That thy ox and thy ass may repose." Thus the Torah admonished us that our cattle and our animale must rest on the Sabbath. Hence we are forbidden to suffer our beasts to carry a burden on the Sabbath.

2. Neither a horse nor any other animal should be suffered to go out on the Sabbath with a saddle cushion tied to his back.

3. It is permitted to bid a non-Jew to milk the cows on the Sabbath, in order to relieve the animals' suffering, as the milk causes them pain. The milk, however, may not be handled on that day, therefore the non-Jew should put it away where it can retain its freshness.

4. It is forbidden to lend or to hire out a beast to a non-Jew, unless the owner stipulates with him that he must return it to him before the Sabbath.

5. It is permissible to feed one's cattle and poultry on the Sabbath, because it is our duty to provide them with food. But one is not allowed to measure out the feed to be given to them other than by estimate.

6. One should not cast grain to poultry on moist ground, as some may possibly remain there and afterwards sprout forth.

X. "MUKTZEH," THINGS FORBIDDEN TO BE HANDLED ON THE SABBATH

1. Food which has intentionally been set apart as not to be eaten on the Sabbath, either because it would be considered unfit to eat in its present state except in an emergency, or because it is to be later sold as merchandise, may be handled on the Sabbath. Parts of broken vessels which are still usable may also be handled.

2. Raw food which cannot be made fit for human consumption even in an emergency without cooking, may not be handled on the Sabbath. Likewise, it is forbidden to handle anything which is unfit for any use on the Sabbath, such as wood, feathers, skins, wool, flax, living animals, and fragments of broken vessels which are not fit for any further use. Nevertheless it is permitted to remove fragments of broken glass from any place where they may cause injury.

3. A thing "newly born," that is, something which originated on the Sabbath, such as ashes from a fire kindled on the Sabbath by a non-Jew, or an egg laid on the Sabbath, and even that which has not originated on the Sabbath, but was the result of labor which may not be performed on the Sabbath, such as fruit which a non-Jew has plucked or milk that has been milked by a non-Jew on the Sabbath, may not be handled.

4. Utensils ordinarily used for work that may not be done on the Sabbath, such as a mortar, a grinder, a hammer, an axe, or a needle, may be handled if they are to be used for permissible purposes, as, for example, cracking nuts with a hammer or cleaving provisions with an axe. However, such utensils may not be moved or handled for their own sake, as for example, in order to prevent their being stolen or damaged. It is forbidden to handle *tephilin* on the Sabbath, except to remove them from an unseemly place.

5. Articles which are purposely set apart so that they should not be used, must not be handled on the Sabbath. This applies to articles stored against spoilage, to precious utensils which the owner does not use at all, and to vessels left in one's shop for sale. They may not be handled even if they themselves or the places they occupy are needed.

6. That which is not designated as a vessel, such as wood, stones, or pieces of metal, may not be handled even when the object itself or the place it occupies is needed, unless it was designated for permanent use on the day before the Sabbath.

7. The Holy Scriptures and food may be handled on the Sabbath, even if there is no necessity therefor.

8. Boards belonging to a householder which are not for sale may be handled on the Sabbath, but if they belong to an artisan, they may not be handled unless it was his intention on Friday to make use of them on the Sabbath.

9. All things that may not be handled on the Sabbath, may be touched if they are not moved by the touch. Hence it is permissible to touch candlesticks even if the candles burn therein. But it is forbidden to touch a hanging chandelier, as this may be shaken by a mere touch.

10. If one has inadvertently left a thing, which may not be han-

dled, upon a vessel which is needed or which occupies a space which is needed, one is permitted to shake it off, or one may carry both to another place and there shake it off. This law applies if a purse with money is left in a garment which is needed.

XI. WEEKDAY MATTERS FORBIDDEN ON THE SABBATH —DOING WORK THROUGH A NON-JEW

1. On the Sabbath, it is forbidden to walk to the end of the Sabbath boundary (see Section XV, pp. 106–108), or even a lesser distance, if this is part of a journey and is taken for the purpose of hastening that journey at the close of the Sabbath.

2. On the Sabbath, it is forbidden to make a gift to any one, unless the latter needs to use the article on the Sababth. It is also forbidden to give anything as a pledge, unless it is necessary for the fulfillment of a religious duty or is requisite for the Sabbath; but even in this event, the pledge should be given in silence and should not be referred to as a pledge.

3. On the Sabbath it is forbidden to look over bills, accounts, or personal letters. If a letter is received on the Sabbath and its contents unknown, it is permitted to look at it, because it may affect our personal welfare. If, however, we know that the letter relates only to business matters, we are not allowed to look at it.

4. It is forbidden to measure anything that we may need during the Sabbath, unless it is essential to the performance of a religious duty.

5. Whatever we ourselves are forbidden to do on the Sabbath, we may not ask a non-Jew to do for us. We are forbidden even to hint to a non-Jew that we desire such a service performed, whether we do so before the Sabbath with the intention that the work be done on the Sabbath, or whether we do so on the Sabbath with the intention that the work be done for us after the Sabbath.

6. If a non-Jew, of his own accord, wishes to perform some work for us on the Sabbath, we must prevent him from doing it.

7. If we are about to sustain a loss, we may call in a non-Jew, if we are certain that he will repair the damage, as long as we avoid saying anything that might be construed as a command; but we may

say in his presence, "Whoever will save me from this loss, will suffer no loss by it."

XII. LAW CONCERNING ONE CRITICALLY ILL

1. If human life is in danger, that life must be saved even if it means the Sabbath be violated. All Divine Law is superseded by the exigency arising from danger to human life. Hence, it is a religious duty to desecrate the Sabbath for the sake of a person who is critically ill, even if that person is only an infant one day old. If the sick person will not allow the desecration of the Sabbath for his sake, he should be compelled to do so, for it is sinful to carry piety to the point of idiocy. To refuse a cure, because the cure would violate a Divine Prohibition, is not piety but fanaticism. Indeed, he who is zealous in disregarding the Sabbath for the sake of one who is critically ill, deserves praise. Even if a non-Jew happens to be present, such work should be done preferably by an Israelite. He who disregards the Sabbath for the sake of one who is critically ill, even if his exertions prove unnecessary or fruitless, is sure to receive a reward from the Lord, blessed be His name. Even when it is doubtful whether or not human life is endangered, it is mandatory to disregard the Sabbath laws and perform any work forbidden by the Law of God that is deemed needful. There is nothing that supersedes the saving of a human life, as it is said (Lev. xviii, 5): "That he may live with them," and not die on account of them.

2. If any one should declare that a person *is* or *may be* critically ill, and no competent physician is present to contradict the statement, the bare statement alone is sufficient cause for violation of the Sabbath. If two physicians disagree as to whether the invalid is critically ill, or if the invalid himself, in contradiction to the physician, claims that he is not critically ill, we must consider the invalid sufficiently ill to violate the Sabbath for his sake. If the sick person says that he requires a certain remedy, and the physician says that he does not require it, we must heed the sick person. If, however, the physician says that the remedy will harm the patient, then we must heed the physician.

3. If an experienced physician or any other competent person says that although the sick person is in no immediate danger, but that the illness may become critical unless a certain remedy is applied, even if the invalid himself says that he does not require it, the physician should be heeded and the Sabbath laws should be disregarded.

4. If a person who is critically ill requires meat and only forbidden meat is obtainable, and if the patient might be nauseated by the very thought of eating such meat, an animal should be ritually slaughtered for his sake on the Sabbath. If, however, there is no fear of causing nausea, as in the case of a child, or of one whose mind is distracted, the forbidden meat should be used and no animal slaughtered on the Sabbath.

5. A healthy person is not allowed to eat food that is cooked on the Sabbath for an invalid, but he may eat it immediately on the close of the Sabbath, if it was cooked by an Israelite.

XIII. LAWS CONCERNING CHILD-BIRTH

1. As soon as a woman begins to feel the symptoms of childbirth, whether or not she is certain of them, a physician should be brought to her immediately, even from a place many miles away.

2. A woman at child-birth is considered as one critically ill; therefore the Sabbath should be disregarded for her sake in providing all that she requires. If, however, a non-Jew is available, his or her services should be sought.

3. During the first three days of a woman's confinement, the Sabbath should be disregarded for her sake, even if she does not consider it necessary. Thereafter, until the seventh day, if she have no other pains than the regular after-pains of childbirth, the Sabbath should be disregarded for her sake only when she says that she requires it.

4. After the seven days, the Sabbath should not be disregarded for her sake even if she says that she requires it. But until the thirtieth day she is considered as a person who is ill but not critically, and all necessary work should be done by a non-Jew if such a person is available. If a non-Jew is not available, a Jew may make a fire

in a stove for her even in the month of Tammuz (approximately, July), inasmuch as a woman in confinement is in danger from cold for thirty days.

5. It is permissible to bathe a newly-born infant, cut its navel-string, straighten out its limbs, and do everything that is required.

XIV. INTER-COMMUNITY OF COURTS

1. Two or more Israelites who dwell in one court, each in a room by himself, may not carry anything from the house to the court, or from the court into the house, or from one house into another, unless they establish an "Erub" (inter-community of courts).

2. If two tenants occupy separate apartments in a house with a common vestibule serving as the entrance to both apartments, they are forbidden to carry anything into the vestibule from their apartments or from any other part of the house. If tenants share an apartment which is so divided that the occupant of the inner room has no other exit than the door of the outer room which leads into the court, nothing may be carried from one of these rooms to the other until an "Erub" has been established.

3. An "Erub" is established as follows: On Friday, towards evening, one of the tenants takes one whole loaf of his own bread, presents it to another tenant, saying the following words in whatever language they understand best: "Take this loaf and acquire a share therein on behalf of all the Israelites who dwell in this court (*or* in these courts)." The latter then takes the loaf and raises it a hand-breadth. The former takes it from him and says the benediction: "Blessed art Thou, O Lord our God, King of the universe, who hath sanctified us by His commandments, and hath commanded us concerning the precept of erub"; adding: "By virtue of this erub it shall be permissible for us to take out and carry from the houses to the court and from the court to the houses and from one house to another, for us and for all the Israelites who dwell in the houses of this court." By this act, all the dwellings are considered as common to all tenants, as one domain, and the carrying of objects from one dwelling to the other is permissible.

4. The inter-community of courts should be established every

Friday, and the loaf of bread used in this ceremony may be cut up on the Sabbath and eaten (since the loaf needs only to be whole at the inauguration of the Sabbath). If need be, the "Erub" may be made with one loaf of bread to apply to every Sabbath until the Passover, and when saying: "By virtue of this erub," etc., one should conclude thus: "For every Sabbath until the Passover which comes to us for good." In this event, it is necessary that the loaf be thin and well baked so that it will not become spoiled before the Passover. For the Sabbath during the Passover, the "Erub" should be made with *matzah* (unleavened bread) prepared according to the law.

5. The ceremony of establishing an "Erub" should not be performed on a Festival. Hence, if a Festival occurs on a Friday, it should be performed on the Thursday before the Festival.

XV. INTER-COMMUNITY OF BOUNDARIES

1. If, on the eve of a Sabbath or a Festival, one happens to be in an open field outside the limits of a city, one is forbidden to walk during the Sabbath or Festival a distance greater than two thousand cubits. If, on the other hand, he is in a city, the entire city is considered his abode, including the outskirts of the city, which is an area of seventy and two-thirds square cubits, whether or not there are buildings in that area; and it is from the periphery of that area that we measure the Sabbath boundary line.

2. A walled city, no matter how large it may be, may be traversed on the Sabbath throughout, including the outskirts, and from there we begin to measure the Sabbath boundary line. A city not surrounded by a wall but whose buildings are not separated by large vacant spaces for a distance greater than seventy and two-thirds cubits, is considered as one city, no matter how many days it may take to traverse it, and it is from the last house that the city-enclosure and the Sabbath boundary should be measured.

3. There are many laws concerning the measuring of a Sabbath boundary, and only one well versed in these laws should be entrusted with such measurements.

4. If a person must walk further than the Sabbath boundary on a Sabbath or a Festival, he is required to put down an "Erub" (inter-

community of boundaries) before the Sabbath or the Festival. He should put the "Erub" within the Sabbath boundary lines of the city, in a place to which he would be allowed to walk on the Sabbath. This place is then considered his abode, and he thereby acquires the right to walk from there two thousand cubits in any direction.

5. One establishes the "Erub" as follows: One takes bread sufficient for two meals, or a relish which is eaten with bread, such as onions, or radishes; but not salt and water, sufficient for two meals if eaten with bread, and going to the place where the "Erub" is to be put, one pronounces the benediction: "Blessed art Thou, O Lord our God, King of the universe, who hath sanctified us by His commandments, and hath commanded us concerning the precept of the erub"; adding: "By virtue of this erub it shall be permissible for me to walk from this place two thousand cubits in each direction"; after which one returns home. The "Erub" may be left to lie there for many Sabbaths, but it should be put in a safe place lest it be lost or spoiled.

6. One may delegate another to place the "Erub" for him and to pronounce the necessary benediction, adding: "By virtue of this erub it shall be permissible for (naming the principal) to walk," etc. It is essential that the one so delegated be an intelligent adult, so that even if he does not return to say he has fulfilled his mission, it may be taken for granted that he has and the "Erub" may be relied upon.

7. A group of people may obtain dispensation by means of one "Erub," if it comprises a quanity of food sufficient for all. If one person puts down one "Erub" for a group, he should make the others acquire a share in it through some one else, as is done with the "Erub" of courts (see preceding Section). An "Erub" for boundaries should not be made for anyone without his knowledge. The one who puts down an "Erub" as an agent for many, should say: "It shall be permissible for such a one, and for such a one" (mentioning all names). If he puts it down for himself as well, he should say: "For me and for such a one, and for such a one."

8. An "Erub" for boundaries should be made only for the purpose

of walking beyond the boundary line to perform there a religious precept, such as to pray in an assembly of ten; to meet one's Rabbi or friend who has returned from a journey; to attend a feast which is part of the performance of a religious act; to attend to matters in the public interest; or to complete a homeward journey.

9. The "Erub" for boundaries may not be established on a Sabbath or a Festival. If, therefore, a Festival occurs on a Friday and one desires to walk (beyond the boundary line) on the Sabbath, he is required to put the "Erub" down on the Thursday before the Festival. If a Festival occurs on a Sunday and he desires to pass beyond the boundary line on that day, he should place the "Erub" on Friday.

XVI. MINHAH (AFTERNOON) SERVICE

1. At the Minhah (afternoon) service on the Sabbath, a *sefer torah* (Scroll of the Law) is taken from the Ark, and we read the first section of the *sidrah* (portion of the Torah) which is to be read on the following Sabbath. Three persons, a Kohen, a Levi, and an Israelite (see Chapter II, Section XII, pages 34–36), are called up to say the benedictions over the reading of the Torah. No half-*kaddish* is said after reading the Torah, because we depend on the half-*kaddish* said before the "Shemoneh esreh" (silent prayer).

2. Before reading the Torah, we say "Vaani tephilati" (as for me, may my prayer). If the service is held in a place where there is no Scroll of the Law, "Vaani tephilati" is said before the half-*kaddish* in order that there be no interruption between the *kaddish* and the "Shemoneh esreh."

3. After the repetition of the "Shemoneh esreh" by the Reader, we say "Tzidkatkha tzedek" (Thy righteousness). These verses serve as an acceptance of the Divine Judgment in bringing about the death of the great pious three, Joseph, Moses and David, who died on Sabbath afternoons. These verses are omitted if the Sabbath occurs on a date whereon the "Tahanun" (petition for Grace) would not have been said if it had occurred on a weekday. (See Chapter II, Section XI, pp. 32–34.)

XVII. MAARIB (EVENING) SERVICE

1. On Saturday night, the "Maarib" (evening) service should be said at a later hour than on weekdays. In the "Shemoneh esreh" we include "Attah honantanu" (Thou hast favored us). If, having forgotten to say it, we recollect it before pronouncing the Divine Name of the benediction "Honen haddaat" (gracious Giver of knowledge), we should say "Attah honantanu" and then "Honenu" (Oh favor us). If, however, we become aware of the omission only after we have pronounced the Divine Name, we should conclude the benediction "Honen haddaat" and we need not repeat the "Shemoneh esreh," since we will afterwards recite the "Habdalah" (see Section that follows). But we should not do any manner of work or taste any food before reciting the "Habdalah."

2. After the "Shemoneh esreh," half-*kaddish* is recited, followed by "Vihi noam" (and let the pleasantness of the Lord). This must be recited while standing, and its last verse, "Orekh yamim" (with length of days), is repeated twice; thereafter "Veattah kadosh" (but Thou art holy) is said. If a Festival occurs during the week that follows, even if it occurs on a Friday, "Vihi noam" and "Veattah kadosh" are omitted. Concluding "Veattah kadosh," the whole *kaddish* is recited, followed by the recital of "Veyitten lekha" (and may God give thee).

XVIII. HABDALAH

1. It is a religious duty to sanctify the Sabbath and Festivals on their conclusion by performing the *habdalah*-ritual over a cup of wine. The word *habdalah* means *separation* or *division*. It is a term used for the ceremony and prayers by means of which a formal division is made betwen holy and profane times, as well as between the degrees of holiness of the Sabbath and the Festivals. The Jew takes solemn leave of the Sabbath, reciting the benediction containing thanksgiving to God for having distinguished the holy Sabbath from the days of the week, as He distinguished Israel as a holy nation from the rest of mankind.

2. In addition to the benediction over the wine, benedictions are

said over spices and over freshly kindled lights. Women, too, must observe the *Habdalah* ceremony. They should, therefore, listen attentively to the recital of the benedictions and respond "Amen." When wine cannot be procured, the *Habdalah* may be recited over any other beverage except water.

3. As soon as the sun sets on the Sabbath, it is forbidden to eat or drink anything except water before reciting the *Habdalah*. If, however, we prolong the third Sabbath-meal until after sunset, we are permitted to eat and drink since we began the meal when it was permissible.

4. No work may be resumed after the Sabbath, or a Festival, before the *Habdalah* is recited. Women who need to light the home before the *Habdalah* is recited, should first say: "Blessed be He who makes a distinction betwen holy and profane, between light and darkness, betweeen Israel and the other nations, between the seventh day and the six working days. Blessed be He who makes a distinction between holy and profane." If a Festival occurs on Saturday night, the blessing should be concluded thus: "Who makes a distinction between holy and holy" (that is, between the degrees of holiness of the Sabbath and the Festivals).

5. The *Habdalah* ritual is performed thus: We take the filled cup in our right hand and the spice-box in our left, and hold them thus until after we have recited the benediction, "Bore peri haggaphen" (the Creator of the fruit of the vine); then we transfer the cup to the left hand and the spice-box to the right and pronounce the benedictions "Bore mine besamim" (the Creator of divers kinds of spices) and "Bore meore haesh" (the Creator of the light of the fire). Thereafter, we again take the cup in our right hand and pronounce the benediction "Hmabdil" (who maketh a distinction). On concluding the benediction, we sit down and drink the whole contents of the cup.

6. The light for the *Habdalah* must be made out of wax and must consist of several strands twisted together like a torch; but if we have no such light, we may pronounce the benediction over two candles which should be held together so that both flames merge in one like a torch.

CHAPTER II

THE THREE PILGRIM FESTIVALS

1. LAWS CONCERNING FESTIVALS

The Almighty commanded us (Deut. XVI, 16): "Three times in a year shall all thy males appear before the Lord thy God in the place which He shall choose: on the feast of unleavened bread, and on the feast of weeks, and on the feast of tabernacles." Accordingly, during the existence of the Temple at Jerusalem, the Holy City, the people of the land of Israel, from far and near, travelled in gala procession to Jerusalem three times during the year.

While near the Temple of God at Jerusalem, the Jews observed certain ceremonies appropriate to the occasion of each Festival. They celebrated the festive events not as individuals alone, but as a group in the company of their people. Israel, as a nation—one entity—celebrated the joyous or solemn occasions. Every Jew then felt that he was an integral part of the nation, the holy people chosen by God to worship Him and to follow in His ways of purity, virtue, love, and justice. The assembling of the Jews in Jerusalem during the festive seasons, was a national reunion, whereby the people not only strengthened the bond of union among themselves, but also affirmed their bond or covenant with their Father in heaven. Thus, on the Festivals, the Jews again confirmed their intention of conducting themselves as children of Israel and as children of God, intent upon living a virtuous life, giving no cause for offense either to their neighbors, to their nation, or to their God.

Before Pesah (Passover), the first pilgrim festival, the Jews made their pilgrimage to Jerusalem, so that they might eat of the paschal lamb, the Passover-offering, near the Temple of God.

Before Shabuot (Feast of Weeks), the second pilgrim Festival, the Jews made their pilgrimage to Jerusalem to present their baskets, containing the first ripe fruits, to the priest, as an offering to God to express their gratitude to the Almighty for His bounty.

Before Sukkot (Feast of Tabernacles), the third pilgrim Festival, the Jews made their pilgrimage to Jerusalem to celebrate the Festival of Thanksgiving. They thanked the Almighty for the harvest which ended at this time of the year, and they rejoiced before the Lord by offering sacrifices, and they joined the gay processions, carrying the four species (see Section IV, below) in their hands, while the Levites played harps and other musical instruments.

Concerning the performance of manual labor on the Festivals, the Holy Scriptures provide (Ex. XII, 16): "No manner of work shall be done in them, save that which every man must eat, that only may be done by you."

I. WHAT MAY AND MAY NOT BE DONE ON A FESTIVAL

1. Any kind of work which is forbidden on the Sabbath, is also forbidden on a Festival. The Sabbath prohibition with regard to employing a non-Jew to perform forbidden work applies also to a Festival. On a Festival, as on a Sabbath, one's cattle must be allowed to rest. The rules covering the observance of a Festival differ from those of the Sabbath only with regard to the preparation of food for human beings. Kneading, baking, slaughtering, and cooking are permitted, as is the kindling of a fire, under certain conditions, even when it is not required for cooking; and the Sabbath restrictions with regard to *carrying* also do not apply on a Festival.

2. It is forbidden to split wood or even to break it by hand. It is also forbidden to collect wood that is scattered about.

3. An animal should not be slaughtered on a Festival except in case of absolute necessity. It is forbidden to sell meat by weight and at a fixed price, but one may give to another any quantity of meat which may be paid for after the Festival.

4. It is permissible to salt meat in order to purify it of its blood, even if it could have been salted on the day before the Festival, provided that it is needed on that day. If we have more meat than we need for that day, and we fear that it might spoil, we may salt it no matter how large the quantity may be, since it is all included in the same labor.

5. It is forbidden to quench a fire on a Festival, even indirectly. Consequently, it is forbidden to place a lighted candle where a wind might blow it out, even, if at the time it is placed there, no wind is blowing. It is likewise forbidden to open a door or a window opposite a lighted candle.

6. It is permissible to cover a fire with a vessel or with ashes that have been previously prepared, even though this may have a quenching effect.

7. It is forbidden to make a fire in order to heat the house, unless the cold is so intense that the food congeals, for in that event the heating is considered as related to the preparation of food.

8. We are allowed to heat water for the purpose of washing our hands, but not for bathing the whole body.

9. It is not permissible to draw fire either from a flint, or a piece of glass, or a match.

10. It is forbidden to scatter spices upon coals, either for the purpose of inhaling the odor or for perfuming the house or vessels.

II. THE BENEDICTION OF THE PRIESTS (BIRKAT KOHANIM)

1. According to the the Law of Moses (Num. vi, 22–27), *kohanim* (priests) must bless the people. In our countries, the *kohanim* bless the people at the "Musaph" (additional) services of the three pilgrim Festivals and of *Yom Kippur* (Day of Atonement). The custom prevails in some communities that if a Festival other than the Day of Atonement occurs on the Sabbath, the *kohanim* do not bless the people.

2. The *kohanim* should bless the people only in a congregation of at least ten male adults, themselves included.

3. Before going up to bless the people, the *kohanim* should drink

neither wine nor any other intoxicating beverage. A *kohen*, who because of faintness desires to eat some sweets before the "Musaph," should first listen to someone else recite the *kiddush*.

4. Before pronouncing the benediction, the *kohanim* should wash their hands up to the wrist.

5. The Levites should pour the water upon the hands of the *kohanim*. If no Levite be present, any first-born son (of the mother) should pour the water instead; and if there be no first-born present, the water should be poured by the *kohen* himself, and not by an Israelite.

6. The *kohanim* must remove their shoes before washing their hands. The *kohanim* while blessing the people should take care, out of respect to the public, that their shoes be hidden under a bench where they cannot be seen.

7. When the *hazan* (reader) begins the prayer "Retzeh" (accept), all the *kohanim* should leave their seats and go up to pronounce the benediction. They should, therefore, if possible, wash their hands before "Retzeh" is said.

8. After they go up to pronounce the benediction, they remain standing facing the Holy Ark, and after saying "Modim" (we give thanks) with the congregation, they say: "May it be Thy will, O Lord our God, that this blessing wherewith Thou hast commanded us to bless Thy people Israel be complete without offense and hindrance from now and foreever." The *hazan* (reader) says: "Our God and God of our fathers, bless us," in an undertone, but the word "kohanim" he says aloud, as this is a call to the *kohanim* to pronounce the benediction. Then he resumes in an undertone: "Thy holy people, as it is said." After the *hazan* has called "kohanim," the *kohanim* begin the benediction, all saying in unison: "Blessed art Thou, O Lord our God, King of the universe, who hath sanctified us by the holiness of Aaron;" then turning their faces toward the people, they conclude: "And He commanded us in love to bless His people Israel," to which the congregation responds "Amen," but the *hazan* should not respond "Amen."

9. They raise their hands toward their shoulders, and separate

their fingers in such a way that on each hand the fingers are paired, with a space between the thumb and forefinger and a second space between the third and fourth fingers. Between the thumbs of each hand there is another space, the right hand being held slightly above the left so that the thumbs are one above the other. Thus in all there are five spaces.

10. When the *kohanim* bless the people, they should neither look around nor divert their thoughts, but their eyes should be directed downward as when praying. The people should pay attention to the benediction and face the *kohanim*, but they should not gaze at them, nor should the kohanim gaze at their own hands. It is for this reason that the *kohanim* have made it a custom to let the folds of their *talit* (fringed garment) drop over their faces and hands.

11. Those standing behind the *kohanim* are not included in the benediction, unless they are compelled to stand there, but those standing on the sides and facing the *kohanim* are included in the benediction. Therefore those standing near the eastern wall, in the area where the Holy Ark projects from the wall, should leave their places and stand where they can be at least at the sides which face the *kohanim*.

12. The *hazan* recites the priestly benediction word for word, and the kohanim repeat each word. The congregation responds "Amen" at the conclusion of the first, second and third verses. The *hazan* should not recite the priestly benediction from memory but from a prayer-book, in order to be sure that he will not become confused.

13. While the *kohanim* repeat the words of the benediction, the congregation should be silent and listen attentively to each word pronounced by the priests.

14. Thereafter the *hazan* begins reciting "Sim shalom" (grant peace), and the *kohanim* turn their faces towards the Holy Ark and say: "Ribbono shel olam" (Master of the universe). The *kohanim* are not allowed to descend on concluding the benediction until the congregation has responded "Amen" to the blessing: "Et ammo yisrael bashalom" (His people Israel with peace).

III. PREPARATION OF FOODS ON FESTIVALS
FOR ANOTHER DAY

1. It is permissible to do work on a Festival only for the purpose of preparing food needed for that day, but it is forbidden to prepare food on the first day of a Festival for the second day, and this prohibition applies even to Rosh Hashanah (New Year's Day), although both days of *Rosh Hashanah* are considered as one. Especially is it forbidden to prepare food on a Festival for a day which is not part of the Festival. If, however, we find it necessary to cook food on the first day of a Festival for use on that day, we are allowed to cook more than may be required in a large pot so that some is left over for the evening or the following day. This is permitted only in the case of food which is cooked, because its taste is improved when a large quantity, such as meat, is boiled in one pot. Uncooked foods must not be prepared in quantities in excess of what is required for that day, no matter how little additional labor is entailed.

2. Even if actual work is not involved, as the bringing in of water, or wine for *kiddush* or *habdalah*, the act is forbidden if it does not apply to the needs of that day. It is even forbidden to put the candles in candle-sticks on the first day of the Festival when they are to be lit in the nighttime, unless they are also intended for use before the night.

3. On a Festival which occurs on a Friday, it is forbidden to bake or to cook in a separate pan or pot for the Sabbath unless the ceremony of "Erub tabshilin" (combination of dishes) has been performed on the afternoon before the Festival. This ceremony is carried out as follows: Take some bread and some food, either boiled or roasted, which is generally eaten with bread, and pronounce the benediction: "Blessed art Thou, O Lord our God, King of the universe, who hath sanctified us by His commandments, and hath commanded us concerning the precept of erub." Then we say the following formula: "By virtue of this erub be it permitted us to bake, cook, keep the food warm, light the candles, and do all work that is necessary on the Festival for the Sabbath." By this act, all the cooking for the Sabbath, which is done on Friday, merely continues

the preparation already begun on Thursday. If one does not understand the Aramaic—the language in which this formula is written— one should say it in the language one understands best.

4. Unless the food used for the "Erub" is such as is generally eaten with bread, like fish, meat, or eggs, the "Erub" is invalid. The food should be no less than the size of an olive, and the bread no less than the size of an egg. One should select the choicest food in honor of the performance of this precept. The bread should be a whole loaf, and it should be laid on the table on the Sabbath as the second loaf for the "Lehem mishneh" (double loaves of bread); and at the third meal, it should be divided and the blessing said thereon.

5. Only on Friday may food be prepared for the Sabbath by means of the "Erub tabshilin" ceremony. If a Festival occurs on Thursday and Friday, no food may be prepared on Thursday to be used for the Sabbath.

IV. REJOICING ON A FESTIVAL

1. It is our duty to honor all the Festivals and take delight in them, just as we honor and take delight in the Sabbath.

2. On the day before a Festival we must cut our hair, in order not to inaugurate the Festival with an untidy appearance. We should also bathe in warm water, comb our hair, and pare our nails on the day before the Festival, just as we do on the day before the Sabbath. We should also bake *hallot* (white loaves of bread) in our homes in honor of the Festival, just as we do on the day before the Sabbath. And, similarly, we are forbidden to eat on the day before the Festival, after the time set for the "Minhah" (afternoon) service, so that we may eat and enjoy the Festival meal with a good appetite. If the day before the Festival occurs on the Sabbath, the third meal should be eaten before the latest time set for the Minhah service (3:30 P.M.).

3. On each day of a Festival, we must have two meals, one at night and one during the day, but no third meal is necessary. We should recite the *kiddush* over a cup of wine before the meal, and distribute the portions of two *hallot* (white loaves of bread), as we

do on the Sabbath. We should be as lavish with meat, wine, and confectionery as our means permit.

4. On concluding the *kiddush* at night on every Festival, we say the benediction "Sheheheyanu" (who kept us in life), except that on the seventh and eighth nights of Passover this benediction is not said, because these two days are not a distinct festival in themselves.

5. Every man is obliged to cheer his wife, his children, and all those who are dependent upon him, in the manner appropriate to each. Thus, we should give nuts and candy to the little children, new apparel and ornaments to the women and girls, and meat and wine to the men. It is the custom to fare more sumptuously on a Festival than on the Sabbath, because concerning the Festival the Torah mentions "rejoicing" (Deut. XVI, 14), but it is not mentioned concerning the Sabbath. The Festival garments should also be costlier than those of the Sabbath.

6. Although by eating and drinking on a Festival we comply with a positive command of God, yet we should not spend the entire day in eating and drinking. We should devote half of the time to the service of God and to the study of His Torah, and half to our own pleasure.

7. When we enjoy eating and drinking on a Festival, it is our duty to feed also the orphan and the widow as well as others who are in need. He who locks the doors of his house in order to eat and drink alone with his wife and children, and gives neither food nor drink to the poor or to those whose souls are embittered, is not rejoicing in the performance of a precept, but merely indulging in gluttony.

8. When rejoicing on a Festival, one should not spend too much time in wine-drinking, jesting and levity, for these constitute not rejoicing but vanity and mere foolishness, and do not accord with the spirit of the command of God. The rejoicing should be consistent with the worship of the Creator of the universe.

9. At the conclusion of a Festival, when it is followed by a week-day or by the intermediate days of a Festival, one should say "Attah honantanu" (Thou hast favored us) in the "Shemoneh esreh" (silent prayer) of the "Maarib" (evening) service, and recite

the "Habdalah" over a cup of wine, but one should not say the benedictions over the light and over the spices.

V. HOL HAMMOED (INTERMEDIATE DAYS OF A FESTIVAL)

1. The four days that intervene between the first two days and the seventh and eighth days of Passover, and the five days between the first two days of Sukkot and Shemini Atzeret (see p. 139), are known as *hol hammoed* (Intermediate Days of Festivals).

2. On *hol hammoed* certain kinds of work may be performed. For instance, we may perform all work essential to the preparation of food for those days and for the Festival, as well as any work that may prevent our sustaining a loss.

3. It is forbidden to pluck out or cut off anything that grows, other than what is required for food for the Festival, unless the failure to do so might cause it to be spoiled. Thus we may pluck fruit or chop wood for the fire, and it is immaterial whether we pluck or cut a larger quantity than we need for the day.

4. It is forbidden to wash any clothes during *hol hammoed* even when needed for the Festival, unless it has been impossible to have them washed before the Festival. Infants' diapers may be washed during *hol hammoed*, because they are constantly needed. However, all washing, even when allowable, must be done privately.

5. Whatever is required medicinally, either for human beings or for beasts, may be done during *hol hammoed*.

6. No marriage should take place during *hol hammoed*, because we are not allowed to mix one rejoicing with another; but it is permissible to make a feast for the celebration of a circumcision, the redemption of the first-born, and engagements.

7. We are permitted to hire laborers during *hol hammoed* to do work for us after the Festival.

8. We are allowed to walk outside the Sabbath boundary line, either on foot, or in a vehicle, or on horseback.

9. On *hol hammoed*, in some communities no *tephilin* at all are put on, while in others they are put on without saying the bene-

dictions. Care should be taken that among those who worship in one synagogue there should not be some who do put on the *tephilin* and others who do not. All worshipers in the same place must abide by the custom which prevails there.

10. During *hol hammoed* the "Shaharit" (morning), "Minhah" (afternoon), and "Maarib" (evening) services, are the same as those on weekdays, except that "Yaaleh veyabo" (may our remembrance rise, come, etc.) is included in the "Shemoneh esreh" and in the Grace after meals. After "Shaharit" we say the whole "Hallel" during the Intermediate Days of Sukkot, and half "Hallel" during the Intermediate Days of Passover. On Sukkot the *tephilin* should be taken off before the "Hallel;" but on Passover the congregation should take off the *tephilin* before the "Hallel" and the *hazan* (Reader) after the "Hallel." Thereafter a *sefer toran* is taken from the Holy Ark, in which we read the portion appropriate to the occasion, and four persons are called upon to say the benedictions over the Torah. After that, we recite the Festival "Musaph" (additional) service.

2. PESAH (PASSOVER)

The feast of *Pesah* (Passover) begins on the evening of the fifteenth day, and ends on the twenty-second day of the month of Nisan. Of these eight days, the first two and the last two are holy, no manual labor being permitted. *Pesah* is primarily the Festival of Spring, a Festival in which man, in common with nature, celebrates the renewal of life; and it is the Feast of Freedom, commemorating the great event of Israel's deliverance from Egypt and holding forth the promise of mankind's future redemption from all oppression. *Pesah* is thus a festival of joy and thanksgiving, of liberty and of hope.

Pesah is the name for the paschal sacrifice. When the Angel of Death went from house to house in Egypt to slay the first-born, God passed over the threshold of the houses of the Israelites as their Protector and Saviour. The lamb sacrifice was eaten in every Jewish home, and the blood thereof was sprinkled on the doorpost as the token of the covenant by which each Israelite was rendered a priest in the sanctuary of his home and each house was dedicated to the service of God. The first night of Passover was, therefore, kept sacred at all times as a night of God's watchfulness over Israel, and celebrated in each Jewish household with song and recitations of Psalms and prayers over blessed cups of wine in gratitude to God, who has redeemed Israel from so many perils and persecutions in the past, and in joyful hope that He will bring about the great Messianic redemption in the future.

Only *matzah* (unleavened bread) must be eaten throughout the Passover festival. The *matzah* reminds us of the readiness with which the Israelites in Egypt followed the bidding of God and His servant Moses, when they were told to leave Egypt without waiting for the dough to be leavened and baked. The Israelites trusted in God, and the dough which they bore on their shoulders, was baked as *matzot*, or unleavened cakes. Thus the *matzah* offers us a lesson of perfect confidence in God and willingness to do His bidding.

The bitter herbs eaten together with the *matzah* at the Passover eve meal remind us of the bitter lot of the Israelites in Egypt.

The Passover teaches us: (a) To be forever thankful to God our Redeemer for the liberty we enjoy, and for the kindness and mercy with which He watched over us and our fathers in past days; (b) to trust in Him at all times and hope for the redemption of every oppressed nation and individual; (c) to do whatever is in our power to relieve the oppressed and give assistance to the unprotected.

Pesah is the first of the three pilgrim festivals when Jews, during the days of the existence of the Temple, marched from every corner of the land to celebrate the Festival at the Temple in Jerusalem.

I. THE MONTH OF NISAN

1. During the entire month of Nisan, we do not say "Tahanun" (petition for grace); we do not hold funeral services; and we do not say "Tzidkatkha tzedek" at the "Minhah" (afternoon) service on the Sabbath.

2. During the month of Nisan we are not allowed to fast even on the "Yahrzeit" (anniversary of the departed). The first-born sons should fast on the day before the Passover. A groom and a bride may fast during this month, even on "Rosh hodesh" (new moon) of Nisan.

3. The Sabbath before the Passover is known as "Shabbat haggadol" (the great Sabbath). On this Sabbath it is customary to recite a portion of the "Haggadah" (special prayer book arranged for Passover evening), beginning with "Abadim hayinu" (we were slaves, etc.), because on this Sabbath the redemption from Egypt and the miracles began.

II. THE SEARCH FOR LEAVEN

1. On the evening before Passover, immediately after nightfall, a search for leavened food is made. It is forbidden to begin eating or doing any manner of work one hour before nightfall. The purpose of this search is to remove from our dwellings all traces of leavened food, in obedience to the command of God (Ex. xii, 19): "Seven days there shall be no leaven found in your houses."

2. The search should be made by means of *only one* wax candle, and not by several woven together, for then it is torch. If we have no wax candle, we may make the search with a candle of tallow.

3. All the rooms into which food might be should be searched.

4. Before beginning the search, we say the benediction: "Blessed art Thou, O Lord our God, King of the universe, who hath sanctified us by His commandments, and hath commanded us concerning the cleaning away of the leaven." We are not allowed to make any interruption between the saying of the benediction and the beginning of the search. It is well not to interrupt the search until it is completed. One benediction may serve for the search of many houses.

5. Before making the search, it is customary to deposit a few crumbs of bread in noticeable places, generally on the window-sills in each room, because, should no leaven be found, the benediction for removing the leaven would have been said in vain. It is obvious, however, that if we do not make a proper search for leaven but

simply gather up these crumbs, we do not fulfill the commandment of searching, and we have recited the benediction in vain.

6. Before making the search, we put away, in a safe place, all the leaven we possess, whether it be for food or for sale. The leaven we find in our search, we likewise put away in a safe place. First, we carefully tie it up. Then, we put it in a noticeable place, where it can be easily seen in the morning, so that we may be sure to burn it.

7. Immediately after the search, we must "nullify" the leaven. The essential in "nullification" is our firm resolve to consider all leaven in our domain as non-existent, entirely valueless and comparable to dust, and as something for which we have absolutely no use. Our sages have furthermore ordained that we must give expression to these thoughts by saying the formula, "Kal hamira" (all the leaven, etc.), and if we do not understand the Aramaic words in which it is written, we should say it in the language we understand best.

8. Having nullified the leaven at night after the search, we should nullify it again in the morning after we have burnt it, and say the formula "'Kal hamira," etc.

9. All vessels, which have not been made valid for the use of the Passover, should be thoroughly scoured and washed before noon of the day before Passover, in such a manner that no leaven whatever may be found on them. They should then be put away, in a secluded place, where one does not ordinarily go. It is best to lock them up in a separate room or closet and hide the key until after Passover.

III. THE DAY BEFORE PASSOVER

1. On the day before Passover, neither "Mizemor letodah" (A Psalm of Thanks) nor "Lamentzeah" (For the Chief Musician) should be said.

2. It is forbidden to eat "hametz" (leavened food) after ten o'clock in the morning, but we may derive a benefit from it until eleven o'clock; hence, we may sell it until then to a non-Jew; but after that time, no benefit at all may be derived from it. We must

burn the leaven and nullify it while we are still permitted to derive a benefit from it; that is, before eleven o'clock.

3. In the afterneen we are not allowed to perform any work, except that type of work which is permissible on "Hol hammoed" (Intermediate Days of a Festival). (See p. 119.) We are permitted to have our work done for us by a non-Jew.

4. We are not permitted to eat *matzah* (unleavened bread) at any time during the day before Passover. We are even forbidden to give *matzah* to children who are capable of understanding the story of the exodus from Egypt. We are permitted, however, to eat foods made of *matzah* meal until the beginning of the last quarter of the day (three o'clock in the afternoon). In case of necessity only, we may eat fruit, meat, or fish after that hour, but we must eat sparingly so that we may eat with a good appetite the *matzah* served at night.

5. The first-born, either of his father or of his mother must fast on the day before Passover, even if it occurs on a Friday. However, if the first-born is invited to a feast in the honor of the performance of a religious duty, he need not then observe the fast but may partake of food in celebration of the occasion.

6. An Israelite who keeps leavened food in his possession during the Passover is transgressing the Mosaic Law which prohibits such possession. Out of such leaven he may derive no benefit, even if he nullified it before the Passover. Therefore, if we have in our possession much leaven, which we are unable to clean away, we are required to sell it to a non-Jew before Passover, while it is still permitted to derive a benefit from it.

7. If the day before Passover occurs on the Sabbath, the search for leaven should be made on Thursday night. On concluding the search we nullify the leaven by saying, "Kal hamira" (all the leaven, etc.), and on Friday morning before eleven o'clock we burn it, but without saying, "Kal hamira." On the Sabbath after the morning meal, we nullify it, and say, "Kal hamira."

8. The first-born sons fast on Thursday, and if it is difficult for them to fast until after the search for leaven is concluded, they may take some refreshment before the search, or else appoint some one,

as their agent, to search for them, and then they may eat before the search.

9. On the Sabbath, the morning service should be held at an early hour so that the breakfast may be completed while it is still permissible to eat leaven. It is proper to divide the meal thus: eat a little; say Grace; pause for a short time, during which one may walk or discuss some religious topic; then wash the hands again, eat again, and repeat the Grace; thus fulfilling the precept regarding the third meal eaten on the Sabbath.

IV. PREPARING FOR THE SEDER (PROGRAM FOR PASSOVER NIGHTS)

1. We should do our best to acquire choice wine with which to perform the precept of drinking four cups of wine.

2. For the first dipping, termed "karpas," it is best to use radishes, although celery, which has a good taste when raw, is generally used for this purpose.

3. For the bitter herbs, it is customary to use horse-radish, which, since it is very pungent, may be grated; but we must take care that it is not rendered entirely tasteless. Therefore, it should not be grated until we return from the synagogue.

4. The "haroset" (a paste-like mixture) should be made thick to symbolize the clay with which our forefathers were forced to make bricks while in Egypt. But before dipping the horse-radish into it, we add a little wine or vinegar to soften and thin it, thus making it fit for the dipping, and symbolic as well of the Jewish blood shed by the Egyptians. It is proper to prepare the "haroset" from figs, nuts, dates, pomegranates, apples and almonds.

5. From the time the Temple was destroyed, the sages have ordained that during the recital of the "Haggadah" (a book containing the special services for the *seder* nights) it is necessary that there be two special dishes on the table: a piece of shoulder-meat, roasted on coal, in memory of the paschal lamb; and an egg, in memory of the "Haggigah" offering which was sacrificed during the existence of the Temple at Jerusalem.

6. We should arrange the seats at the table while it is still day-

light, placing them in such manner that all may be able to recline on their left sides. Even a left-handed person should recline on the side which is his right and everybody else's left. The table spread should be the best we can afford to buy. The *seder*-platter, too, should be set while it is yet day, in order that on our arrival from the synagogue we may proceed without delay with the ceremony of the *seder*.

7. On the night of Passover it is good to be as lavish as possible with our finest table-ware. Even vessels not used for the meal should be placed on the table, for beauty's sake and to symbolize freedom.

8. The *seder*-platter should be arranged thus: Three whole *matzot* are placed on a platter and covered with a fine cloth; the shank bone is placed to the right of the *matzot*, and the egg to the left; the bitter herbs, which are to be eaten with the *matzah* and those over which the benediction is pronounced, are placed in the centre; the *haroset* should be put below the shank bone, and the *karpas* below the egg.

9. The cups used for wine-drinking must be without flaw, thoroughly washed, and they must hold no less than one and a half egg-shells.

V. THE SEDER ON PASSOVER NIGHT

1. Both precepts, that which concerns the eating of *matzah,* and that which concerns the drinking of four cups of wine, are to be performed only at night. Hence the *kiddush* should not be recited until it is unmistakably night, because the cup of wine over which the *kiddush* is recited is considered one of the four cups which must be drunk during the *seder*-night. After the *kiddush*, the person conducting the ceremony takes his seat to arrange the *seder*. Nuts, almonds, and the like should be distributed among the children in order to stimulate their curiosity, so that they may ask the reasons for all that they see, including the reasons for having *matzah*, bitter herbs, and for reclining. Children who are able to understand the importance of the Festival and the exodus from Egypt should be provided with four cups of wine.

The four cups of wine are symbolic of the four Biblical expressions used by the Almighty in promising the Jews redemption from the Egyptian bondage (Ex. vi, 6–7): "*Vehotzeti*, and I will bring you out; *vehitzalti*, and I will deliver you; *vegaalti*, and I will redeem you; *velakahti*, and I will take you out to Me for a people."

2. It is customary to fill one extra cup of wine, which is known as the "Cup of Elijah." The Prophet Elijah is invited to our homes for the following reasons: In the Biblical text there is a fifth divine promise which follows the above four, and that is (Ex. vi, 8): "*Vehebeti*, and I will bring you to the promised land." Some Jewish legal authorities would, therefore, have it that a fifth cup of wine is required in the *seder*, because there are five divine promises. Talmudic authorities left the decision of all moot points of law to the Prophet Elijah, who, in time to come would decide them, and the question of the fifth cup, too, was left to the same judge.

Moreover, this prophet, who was taken up to heaven alive in a fiery chariot drawn by fiery horses (II Kings ii, 11), is believed to have become immortal and to have become the heavenly guardian of the Jewish people. Elijah is the great champion of righteousness and the pure worship of God, who will appear, in the end of days to announce the arrival of the Messiah. At that time, this messenger of God will announce to the dwellers on earth the good tidings of peace and salvation, comfort for the sorrowing, the resurrection of the dead, and the establishment of the Divine Kingdom upon the earth.

On Passover night, at the celebration of the Feast of Freedom, the Jews invite Elijah to their homes, thereby indicating their implicit faith in the belief that some day the Almighty will send this immortal Prophet to announce their deliverance from the hands of modern Pharaohs.

3. To symbolize mastery and freedom, the cups should be filled by a domestic or by some one other than the person conducting the ceremony. Every participant should drink at least the greater part of each cup, and of the fourth cup no less than one and a half eggshells. In doing so, each should bear in mind that he or she is thus performing the precepts of drinking four cups, of recounting the exodus from Egypt, and of eating *matzah* and bitter herbs. All these

precepts, with the exception of the custom of reclining, apply to women as well as men. The *kiddush* should be recited as it is written in the *Haggadah*, and while drinking the wine, each man should recline on his left side.

4. After that, the person conducing the ceremony should wash his hands without saying the benediction, dry them, and cut up the *karpas* giving a portion smaller than the size of an olive to each participant, including himself. Each dips his portion in salt water and says the benediction, "Bore peri haadamah" (who created the fruit of the ground), bearing in mind that this benediction applies as well to the bitter herbs over which no benediction will be said. All then eat the *karpas*, the men reclining on their left sides. The person conducting the ceremony then takes the middle *matzah* and divides it in two unequal parts, putting the larger part on his seat for the *aphikoman*, and replacing the smaller part upon the platter. The participants then recite from the *Haggadah*, "Ho lahma anya" (this is as the bread of affliction), to "Leshanah habaah bene horin" (next year we shall be free men).

5. The cups are then filled a second time, and a child—or in the absence of a child—the person conducting the ceremony himself, or his wife, asks: "Mah nishtanah hallailah hazzeh" (wherefore is this night different), after which all begin reciting the *Haggadah*: "Abadim hayinu" (slaves we were), etc. It is proper for the person conducting the ceremony to explain the contents of the *Haggadah* to the participants in a language they all understand. If he himself does not understand the Holy Language (Hebrew), he should recite the *Haggadah* together with the translation in the vernacular, particularly the section: "Rabban gamliel hayah omer" (Rabban Gamaliel said), for it is essential that he understands the reasons given there for the paschal lamb, the unleavened bread and the bitter herbs. At "Vehi sheamdah" (and it is that promise), he should cover the *matzah*, and the participants should take the cups in their hands and say "Vehi sheamdah" to "Miyadam" (out of their hands), after which he again uncovers the *matzah*. When saying, "Matzah zu") (this unleavened bread), he should take the half *matzah* from the

platter and show it to the participants. When saying, "Maror zeh" (these bitter herbs), he should raise the bitter herbs; but when saying, "Pesah shehayah" (the paschal lamb), he should not raise the shank bone which is commemorative of the paschal lamb. When saying, "Lephikakh" (we therefore), he should cover the *matzah,* and the participants should take their cups and hold them aloft until they say, "Gaal yisrael" (Thou hast redeemed Isreal). All should then say the benediction, "Bore peri haggaphen" (who hath created the fruit of the vine), and drink the second cup of wine.

6. After that all participants wash their hands, saying the benediction, "Al netilat yadayim" (concerning the washing of the hands). The person conducting the ceremony should then take the two whole *matzot,* and placing the broken one betwen them, he should pronounce the benediction, "Hamotzi" (who bringeth forth bread); then putting the lower *matzah* down and retaining only the upper and the broken *matzah,* he should pronounce the benediction, "Al akhilat matzah" (to eat unleavened bread). Then from each of the *matzot* in his hand, he should break off pieces no less than the size of an olive, and distribute them among the participants, himself included. He should then eat both pieces while reclining on his left side. It is the custom not to dip in salt the *matzah* over which the benedictions have been pronounced.

7. He then distributes portions of the bitter herbs, each portion the size of an olive, and they all dip their portions in the "Haroset," shaking off the excess so that the bitter herbs should not lose their taste, and say the proper benediction without reclining. After that, all participants take two pieces of the lower *matzah,* each no smaller than the size of an olive, and place between them bitter herbs about the size of an olive, and say, "Ken asah Hillel" (thus did Hillel), and this, too, they eat without reclining. A person who is indisposed and is unable to eat the bitter herbs, should nevertheless chew a little of any bitter herb until he feels a bitter taste in his mouth, simply as a commemoration, without saying a benediction thereon.

8. One should now enjoy the feast, and recline while eating. Neither roast meat, nor roast chicken, nor roasted poultry of any

kind should be eaten on the first two nights of Passover, not even if it has been boiled before roasting. At the conclusion of the feast, the *aphikoman* (the half-*matzah* put away on the seat of the one conducting the ceremony) should be eaten in commemoration of the paschal lamb that was eaten at the end of the meal. One should eat of it no less than the size of an olive, and while eating it one should be in a reclining posture. After eating the *aphikoman*, one is forbidden to eat any kind of food. The third cup for the Grace is then filled, and after Grace a benediction is said over the third cup of wine which one drinks while reclining.

9. Thereafter the cup is filled for the fourth time. The door is opened, according to custom, and all recite, "Shephokh hamatkha" (O pour out Thy wrath). The door is opened for two reasons: to symbolize that this has been a watchful night, and to signify our eagerness to welcome the Prophet Elijah, the long expected messenger of God, who will proclaim the final redemption of mankind from oppression. (See p. 127.) After "Shephokh hamatkha," they recite, "Lo lanu" (not unto us, etc.). From the fourth cup of wine a full quarter (one egg and a half) should be drunk, and then the concluding benediction (see Chapter II, Section xii, page 55) is recited. The "Haggadah" is then read to the end. After the four cups, it is forbidden to drink any beverage except water.

10. A person who abstains from drinking wine the whole year because of ill-health, may either dilute the wine with water, or drink raisin wine, or mead.

11. It is customary to read the scroll containing *Shir Hashirim* (Song of Songs) in the synagogue, when one of the days of "Hol hammoed" occurs on the Sabbath (if not, on the seventh day of Passover), before reading the portion of the Torah.

12. On the eighth day of Passover, during the morning services at the synagogue, Memorial Services (yizkor) are held for the departed. If one is unable to attend the synagogue services, one may recite the Memorial Services at home.

13. In lands outside Israel, it is not permitted to partake of leavened food on the eighth day of Passover before the stars become visible.

VI. SEPHIRAH (COUNTING OF THE OMER)

1. By the command of the Almighty, we count forty-nine days from the time the *omer*-offering was brought, which was on the second day of Passover. This precept should be performed at night soon after the stars become visible; yet it is proper to count the *omer* at any time during the night. On the Sabbath or a Festival, the *omer* is counted in the synagogue after the *kiddush* has been recited. At the conclusion of the Sabbath or a Festival, it is counted before the *habdalah* is recited. When the last day of a Festival occurs on Saturday night, the *omer* should be counted before the recital of the *kiddush* and the *habdalah,* so that the *habdalah* may be said at the last.

2. If a person has forgotten to count the *omer* during the night, he should do so in the daytime, without saying the benediction, but when counting it on the following nights, he should say the benediction. If he has neglected to count the *omer* for one entire day, he should count every night thereafter without saying the benediction. If he is in doubt whether he has counted the previous night, and if he has counted on the following day, he may nevertheless say the benediction when counting on the remaining nights.

3. If we are asked at twilight or thereafter, before counting the *omer*, how many days are to be counted on that day, we should tell the inquirer the number of days that were counted on the previous day, for if we mention the number of days to be counted on that day, we are forbidden to pronounce the benediction when counting the *omer*.

4. Before we pronounce the benediction, we should know the exact number of days to be counted.

5. Because many disciples of Rabbi Akiba died during the first thirty-three days of the counting of the *omer*, certain rules of mourning are observed during those days—no one is allowed to marry, and no one is permitted to have his hair cut. On the thirty-third day of the *omer*, Akiba's disciples ceased to die, and so, on that day, a semi-holiday is observed, and the "Tahanun" (petition for grace) is not said. However, not until after dawn of the thirty-third day may the

restrictions against marriage and the cutting of hair be lifted. But if the thirty-third day of the *omer* occurs on Sunday, the hair may be cut on the preceding Friday in honor of the Sabbath.

6. It is permissible to celebrate engagements during all the *sephirah* days, even by means of feasting, but it is forbidden to dance.

7. No *tahanun* is said beginning with the "Minhah" (afternoon) service before the New Moon of the month of Sivan, until after the day following the Festival of Shabuot. (See the following section.)

3. SHABUOT (FEAST OF WEEKS)

Shabuot (Feast of Weeks), the second pilgrim festival, is celebrated on the sixth and seventh days of the third month, Sivan. This Festival is called "Feast of Weeks," because it is celebrated seven weeks after the bringing of the *omer*-offering on the second day of Passover. As a farmer's Festival, it celebrated the conclusion of the seven weeks of the cereal harvest, at which time praise and thanks were given to the Almighty. Two loaves of bread, baked of the new wheat, were brought upon the altar as a thanks-offering. As the Festival also marked the beginning of the fruit harvest, *hag habikkurim,* each Israelite brought to the Temple in Jerusalem the first ripe fruit of his orchard as an offering of thanks.

Shabuot also commemorates the significant beginning of Israel's spiritual life, as the Jews received the Law on Mount Sinai at this time of the year. Thus, Shabuot is celebrated as the day when the freedom, which the Israelites obtained through the departure from Egypt on Passover, was crowned with self-consecration to the great task of being a "Kingdom of priests and a holy nation" (Ex. XIX, 6) among the people of the earth.

Shabuot teaches us: (a) To be thankful to the Almighty for the blossoming and ripening of life in nature, so rich in blessing and hope for mankind; (b) to be thankful for the great boon of the

Law which the Almighty in His wisdom entrusted to us; and (c) that we should vow and resolve every year anew our loyalty to our great mission and to God's covenant with our fathers on Sinai.

I. LAWS AND CUSTOMS

1. On the first night of Shabuot, the *maarib* (evening) service should be put off until the stars become visible.

2. Pious Jews spend the whole night of Shabuot in studying the Law. A special book has been prepared for this occasion, called *Tikkun Lel Shabuot*. It contains excerpts from every book of the Holy Scriptures and of the Mishnah, and is read from cover to cover by religious Jews on the first night of Shabuot. People who are learned in the Law do not read from this special book. They read directly from the Talmud and other sacred books.

3. On the first day of Shabuot, it is customary to partake of food prepared with milk, and also to taste some honey, because the Law of God, which was given to the Israelites on this day in the wilderness of Sinai, is likened to "Honey and milk" (Song of Songs iv, 11); but there should also be one meal consisting of meat dishes. These two meals represent the two loaves of bread which were used in the *bikkurim* offering in the Temple at Jerusalem.

4. Because Shabuot is a Festival of the harvest and of the Law, the scroll containing the story of Ruth is read in the synagogue, because this story describes harvesting in Palestine and tells how Ruth embraced Judaism.

5. On Shabuot it is customary to cover the floors with greens and to decorate the house and the synagogue with plants, flowers, and even with trees. The greens serve to remind one of the green mountains of Sinai; they also commemorate the harvest festival of olden times.

6. On the second day of Shabuot, during the morning services at the synagogue, Memorial Services (yizkor) are held for the departed. If one is unable to attend the services at the synagogue, one may recite the Memorial Services at home.

7. See "Laws Concerning Festivals," pp. 111–120.

4. SUKKOT (FEAST OF TABERNACLES)

Sukkot (Feast of Tabernacles) begins with the fifteenth day and ends with the twenty-third day of the seventh month, Tishri, the last two days bearing special names: "Shemini Atzeret" (Eighth Day of Solemn Assembly), and "Simehat Torah" (Rejoicing with the Law).

The Almighty commanded the children of Israel (Lev. xxiii, 34): "On the fifteenth day of the seventh month is the feast of tabernacles for seven days unto the Lord." And in verse 42, He ordered: "Ye shall dwell in booths seven days." The reason for dwelling in booths is given in verse 43: "That your generations may know that I made the children of Israel to dwell in booths, when I brought them out of the land of Egypt." Thus, the dwelling in booths is a token of gratitude for God's protection of the Israelites when He shielded them in their frail tents from the storms and dangers that beset them during their forty-years journey in the wilderness.

There is another Divine Command concerning this Festival (Lev. xxiii, 39–40): "Howbeit on the fifteenth day of the seventh month, when ye have gathered in the fruits of the land, ye shall keep the feast of the Lord seven days . . . And ye shall take you on the first day the fruit of goodly trees, branches of palm-trees, and boughs of thick trees, and willows of the brook, and ye shall rejoice before the Lord your God Seven days."

Accordingly, we take the four species on *Sukkot,* consisting of the *lulab* (palm branch), the *etrog* (citron-like fruit), *hadasim* (myrtle boughs), and *arabot* (willow branches), and wave them during the festal processions while singing psalms and hymns. The waving of the *lulab* is the expression of our gratitude and joyful worship of God, the Giver of all good, Giver of the *hag heasiph,* Season of Harvest Joy and Thanksgiving, by which name this festal season is also designated. This festival marked the end of the ingathering of the last ripe fruits, ending the year's blessing.

The waving of the *lulab* was interpreted by our sages as a symbolic representation of the different types of people included in the Jewish nation. The most noted of these interpretations is the one given in the Midrash (Lev. Rabbah xxx, 11): "The four species represent the Jewish people: just as the *etrog* has both taste and fragrance, so do some Jews possess both a knowledge of the Torah and good deeds; just as the date-palm has taste but no fragrance, so do some Jews possess a knowledge of the Torah but no good deeds; just as the myrtle has fragrance but no taste, so do some Jews possess good deeds but no knowledge of the Torah; and just as the willows of the brook have neither taste nor fragrance, so do some Jews possess neither a knowledge of the Torah nor good deeds. And what did the Holy One, blessed be He, do? To destroy them all was impossible. So the Almighty said: 'Let them all be tied together with one band of brotherhood, and let one procure forgiveness for the other."

On the eighth day of *Sukkot*, we celebrate a special Festival, known as "Shemini Atzeret" (Eighth Day of Solemn Assembly), in compliance with the Divine Command (Num. xxix, 35): "On the eighth day ye shall have a solemn assembly: ye shall do no manner of servile work."

This Festival is solemnized by a prayer for "Geshem" (rain) during the "Musaph" (additional) service at the synagogue, beseeching the Almighty to give abundant rain in the Land of Israel during the rainy season which is approaching, so that the Israelites may accumulate sufficient water in their reservoirs to last them during the dry summer months. On this day we also hold Memorial Services for the departed (yizkor).

This festive season concludes with "Simehat Torah" (Rejoicing with the Law), when we read in the synagogue the closing chapters of the Torah and solemnly begin anew the reading of the Torah from Genesis. Thus, while celebrating the material harvest of Israel, we at the same time celebrate its spiritual harvest, the completion of the annual reading of the Law of God.

The Sukkot Festival thus teaches us: (a) To express our gratitude to the Almighty for His merciful guidance which He provided for our forefathers; (b) to be thankful to Him for the year's blessings; and (c) to be ever faithful to the teachings of the Torah, Israel's spiritual possession.

I. THE SUKKAH [1]

1. The building of the *sukkah* should be started immediately after *Yom Kippur* (Day of Atonement), even if it is started on a Friday. A clean place should be chosen for its site. Every Jew should personally take part in the building of the *sukkah* and the laying of its covering. Even an eminent person should consider it an honor to attend personally to the fulfillment of a precept. We must do our best to embellish the *sukkah* and to adorn it by placing in it fine furniture and beautiful coverings according to our means.

2. Enough coverings should be placed on the roof of the *sukkah* in such a fashion as to make it more shady than sunny, for otherwise it is invalid. While open spaces must be left in the roof so that the stars may be visible overhead, no single space should be more than three hand-breadths square.

3. It is permissible to build a *sukkah* during "Hol hammoed" (Intermediate Days of the Festival).

4. When dismantling the *sukkah* after the Festival, one should not step upon the boards, nor make any degrading use of the materials of which the *sukkah* was constructed.

5. During the afternoon of the day before *Sukkot*, we should not eat any bread, so that we may eat with relish the meal served in the *sukkah* at night. It is proper to dispense as much charity as possible on the day before *Sukkot*.

II. DWELLING IN THE SUKKAH

1. During the seven days of *Sukkot*, we must dwell in the *sukkah* even as we dwell in our house during the whole year. We should make the *sukkah* our principal dwelling: there we should bring our fine furniture; there we should eat, drink, study, amuse ourselves, and sleep.

2. The *sukkah* should be maintained in honor. After the meals,

[1] See Laws Concerning Festivals, pp. 111–120.

the dishes should be removed from the *sukkah*, but the drinking glasses may remain there. It is forbidden to wash the dishes in the *sukkah*, but the glasses may be rinsed there.

3. On the first night of *Sukkot*, we must eat in the *sukkah* a quantity of bread of no less than the size of an olive, even if we are made uncomfortable by cold or by rain.

4. On the second night of *Sukkot*, we should also eat in the *sukkah*, even if we suffer discomfort.

5. In the evening, when we return home from the synagogue, we enter the *sukkah* and immediately recite the *kiddush*, but before reciting the *kiddush* we must be sure that it is night. On the first night, we say the benediction "Lesheb basukkah" (to sit in the *sukkah*), and then the benediction "Sheheheyanu" (who kept us in life), so that the latter benediction may also apply to the *sukkah*; but on the second night, we say the benediction "Sheheheyanu" before saying the benediction "Lesheb basukkah."

6. If it rains so hard that the food might be spoiled by the rain, or if it is so cold that the food congeals, we are exempt from staying in the *sukkah*, and we may eat our meals in the house.

7. When we are asleep, even a little rain causes discomfort, and we are therefore permitted to leave the *sukkah* when it rains in the evening, and sleep in the house for the rest of night, whether or not the rain ceased thereafter.

8. He who is exempt from remaining in the *sukkah* and refuses to leave it, is called an ignorant person, and he obtains no reward for remaining there. He is not permitted to say a benediction, as it would be a benediction said in vain.

9. Women are exempt from performing the precept of dwelling in the *sukkah*, yet they are permitted to say a benediction when they do comply with the precept. Children are also exempt from dwelling in the *sukkah*; nevertheless it is obligatory for the father of a boy of five or more to train the boy to eat in the *sukkah*.

10. He who suffers discomfort because of intense cold, or wind, or bad odor, is exempt from dwelling in the *sukkah* after the first two days. If on the Sabbath the lights of the *sukkah* should go out

and it is difficult for one to go to a friend's *sukkah*, one may return to one's house.

III. THE FOUR SPECIES

1. We take the *lulab* in our right hand, and the *etrog* in our left. Since the benediction must always precede the performance of the precept to which it applies, and since the precept requires that the *etrog* be held in the position in which it grows—that is, with the stamen where it has been cut downward and the apex upward—therefore when we first take the *etrog* before pronouncing the benediction, we must hold it in the reverse position, with the stamen upward and the apex downward. Then we must say the benediction "Al netilat lulab" (concerning the taking of the *lulab*) while standing. On the first day of *Sukkot*, we also say the benediction "Sheheheyanu" (who kept us in life). If the first day of *Sukkot* occurs on the Sabbath when no *lulab* is taken, the benediction "Sheheheyanu" should be said on the second day. After the benediction "Al netilat lulab," we turn the *etrog* over, and holding it close to the *lulab*, wave it.

2. A left-handed person should take the *lulab* in the hand which is his right and everybody else's left, and the *etrog* in the hand which is his left.

3. Before taking the *lulab* on "Hol hammoed," it is proper to remove the *tephilin*, or at least remove the strap from the hand, so that nothing may intervene between the hand and the *etrog*. It is also proper to remove one's rings from one's fingers.

4. It is forbidden to partake of any food before saying the benediction over the *lulab*.

5. During the first six days of *Sukkot*, after concluding the "Musaph" (additional) service, it is customary to take a *sefer torah* (Scroll of the Law) up to the *hazan's* desk, and all those possessing a *lulab* and an *etrog* walk in a procession once around the *hazan's* desk, while the Holy Ark is left open until after the "Hoshanot" is said, when the *sefer torah* is returned to the Ark. On the seventh day, which is *Hoshanah Rabbah*, every *sefer torah* is taken from the Holy Ark and brought up to the *hazan's* desk, and the proces-

sion around the desk is repeated seven times, commemorative of the ceremonial observed in the Temple at Jerusalem where the altar was encircled once daily and seven times on the seventh day.

6. No procession takes place on the Sabbath, therefore no *sefer torah* is brought up to the *hazan's* desk, but the Holy Ark is left open until after the "Hoshanot" have been said.

IV. HOSHANAH RABBAH; SHEMINI ATZERET; SIMEHAT TORAH

1. The fifth day of "Hol Hammoed" (Intermediate Days of the Festival) is "Hoshanah Rabbah." It is customary to stay awake the whole of the preceding night and to study the Torah because, according to tradition, the season of judgment, which began with "Rosh Hashanah," ends on "Hoshanah Rabbah."

2. It is a custom instituted by the Prophets for each person to take on that day a special *arabah* (willow branch), besides the one which is on the *lulab*.

3. Concluding the "Hoshanot," the *arabah* is waved and then beaten against the ground five times. After the beating, the *arabah* should not be cast upon the ground, lest the precept appear to be treated with contempt.

4. We eat in the *sukkah* on "Shemini atzeret" (the Eighth day of Solemn Assembly), but we do not say the benediction "Lesheb basukkah" (to dwell in the sukkah).

5. The last day of Sukkot, which is also "Shemini atzeret," is called "Simehat torah" (Rejoicing with the Law), because on this day we conclude the reading of the Torah. In the evening after the "Maarib" (evening) service, all the Scrolls are taken out of the Holy Ark. The Torah Scrolls are given to male adults, and the Prophet Scrolls are given to boys. The *hazan* marches in front, followed by the men carrying the Scrolls and the boys carrying the *nebiim* (prophet scrolls). The *hazan* chants, as he marches, certain verses imploring the Almighty to help the Jewish people, and these are repeated by the congregation. They march through the aisles or around the *hazan's* desk. When they return to the starting point, in front of the Ark, another group takes the Scrolls, and then still another, until

the ceremony is repeated seven times. Each round is concluded by singing and dancing. After the *hakaphot* (processional), they replace the Scrolls in the Ark, keeping out only one Scroll from which the Law is read. Three people are called up to the reading of the portion "Vezot haberakhah" (and this is the blessing). After the reading of the Torah, half-*kaddish* is recited; the last *sefer torah* is now replaced in the Ark, and "Alenu" (it is our duty) is said.

6. The *hakafot* ceremony is repeated at the morning service on "Simehat torah," after which three Scrolls are kept on the desk, and many male-adults are called up to say the benedictions over the reading of the section beginning "Vezot haberakhah" up to "Meonah" (Thy refuge). This reading is repeated many times, so that all male-adults present may have a chance to say the benedictions over the torah. After this, all minors are called up. It is proper for the eldest among them to recite the benedictions, and for the rest to listen. Then the section "Hamaleakh haggoel" (the angel who redeemed) is read for them. After that the "Hatan torah" (the groom of the Torah) is called up, for whom the portion from "Meonah" to the end of the Torah is read. Then the "Hatan bereshit" (the groom of Genesis) is called up, and a portion of "Bereshit" in the second Scroll is read for him. After the saying of half-*kaddish*, the *maftir* is called up, and a portion is read for him in the third *sefer torah*.

CHAPTER III

HIGH HOLIDAYS

1. ROSH HASHANAH (NEW YEAR'S DAY)

I. SIN AND REPENTANCE

The Holy Scriptures say (Gen. i, 27): "And God created man in His own image, in the image of God created He him;" that is, man alone is God's child. Man has a dual personality: he is partly animal, and partly a god-like being. He is motivated in his actions and thoughts either by his higher, god-like nature, whence arise his good desires and inclinations, or by his lower, animal or sensual nature, whence arise the evil desires and inclinations of his heart.

Man is superior to all earthly creatures in many respects: in his bodily appearance, his upright stature, the dexterity of his fingers, his expressive countenance, and, above all, in his power of speech. But man's body is merely the temple in which the soul, the divine spirit, dwells. It is this divine possession which lends man his dignity and makes him king and master of the earth, in accordance with the Divine Will (Gen. i, 28): "And God blessed them; and God said to them: 'Be fruitful and multiply, and replenish the earth, and subdue it; and have dominion over the fish of the sea, and over the fowl of the air, and over every living thing that creepeth upon the earth.'"

The soul of man is endowed with free-will, or the power by which he is able to differentiate between good and evil, right and wrong, and determine his own actions. And this power to choose makes man responsible for his actions, whereas the animal and the infant

141

are impelled by mere instinct, and thus are not responsible for their actions.

As a free personality, man is called upon to serve God of his own accord and fulfill His will by overcoming evil and doing what is right and good. Since man is capable of developing all his intellectual and moral faculties, he is duty-bound so to live and act that he may attain the highest perfection in knowledge, virtue and character, and thereby obtain the highest reward of happiness without end.

The Jewish religious concept is that sin is the power which merely *induces* man to do wrong, but does not *compel* him to do so and that man's god-like nature consists in his mastery over sin. This is the great truth of the Jewish religion laid down by the Almighty Himself in His denunciation of Cain's behavior (Gen. iv, 6–7): "And the Lord said unto Cain: 'Why art thou wroth? and why is thy countenance fallen? If thou doest well, shall it not be lifted up? and if thou doest not well, sin croucheth at the door; and unto thee is its desire, but thou mayest rule over it.'" So the Almighty expressly said that the conduct of man is not predestined, and sin is not an evil power which *forces* man to do evil. Man can control and conquer this evil power and be good of his own free-will, thus rising above the very angels.

But God is all-kind. He loves His creatures, and provides for all their needs. He grants each being all the pleasure that is helpful to its development in the design of creation. He bestows mercy and compassion on man by giving the sinner time to repent and improve his ways. Thus the sinner still remains God's child and may obtain God's forgiveness if he repents, forsakes his evil ways, and turns to the right path.

Repentance is a feeling of sorrow and pain for having done wrong, mingled with shame and self-reproach. Repentance leads to a change of heart, if with self-humiliation, fasting and praying, we invoke God's pardon and solemnly promise to improve our ways. We are, then, no longer the same sin-laden creatures with hearts torn by bitter remorse. We try to undo our sins. Repentance means atonement and reconciliation with God, our Heavenly Father.

God alone is holy. He is the ideal of perfection and purity. Before Him we feel ashamed of our sinful acts and thoughts. It is He whom we offend in doing or planning evil, and He alone can forgive our trespass. No priest and no other power either in heaven or on earth stands between man and his Maker to mediate the atonement for our sins.

"Rosh Hashanah" (New Year's Day) ushers in for the Jew a period of penitence, and is devoted to prayer and serious thought. This solemn Festival is celebrated on the first and second days of the seventh month, Tishri, which is the first month in the Jewish civil calendar. The Festival is called in the Holy Scriptures (Num. xxix, 1) "Yom Teruah" (Day of Blowing the Horn), and the solemn tone of the *shofar* (ram's horn) reminds man that he should remember God and return to the path of duty. (See par. 11, p. 146.)

In Talmudic literature, "Rosh Hashanah" is also known as "Yom Hazikaron" (Day of Memorial), and as "Yom Haddin" (Day of Judgment). On this day, our sages of old tell us, the Ruler of Life sits on the world's throne and investigates the behavior of man; and He allots to each one his destiny for the coming year, whether for life or for death, for happiness or for woe.

On this solemn day, therefore, every Jew must look upon his behavior during the year that has passed. He must recognize that God, the stern Judge of the World, searches our hearts and reads every thought therein, and he must resolve to begin a new life with higher ideals and purposes. The Jew must renew his trust in God, the Ruler of our Destiny, and must express his gratitude to Him, as he looks back upon the past year with its experiences of joy and sorrow.

II. THE MONTH OF ELLUL

1. The forty days, from "Rosh Hodesh" (New Moon) of the month of Ellul until after "Yom Kippur" (Day of Atonement), are days of good will; for, although throughout the whole year the Holy One, blessed be He, accepts the repentance of those who turn unto Him with a perfect heart, nevertheless these forty days are more appropriate for repentance, inasmuch as they are days of mercy.

2. It is customary to sound the *shofar* (ram's horn) daily after the morning service, during the whole month of Ellul, beginning with the second day of "Rosh Hodesh," except on the Sabbath and on the day before "Rosh Hashanah" (New Year) when it is not blown in order to make a distinction between the voluntary sounding of the *shofar* (during the whole month) and the mandatory sounding (on "Rosh Hashanah"). The reason for sounding the *shofar* during this month is to stir the people to repentance. Every day, after the morning and evening prayers, beginning with the second day of "Rosh Hodesh" until "Shemini Atzeret," it is customary to recite the Psalm (xxvii) "Ledavid, adonai ori" (Of David, the Lord is my light).

3. Beginning with the Sunday before "Rosh Hashanah," we rise early and attend the service known as "Selihot" (supplications for forgiveness). If "Rosh Hashanah" occurs on Monday or Tuesday, we begin saying the "Selihot" on the Sunday of the preceding week. When rising early, we wash our hands and say the benediction "Al netilat yasayim" (concerning the washing of the hands), and the benediction of the Torah. After the "Selihot," we wash our hands again without saying the benediction.

4. On the day before "Rosh Hashanah," it is customary with some people to fast until after the "Minhah" (afternoon) service, at which time they partake of some food, in order not to inaugurate the Festival while fasting.

5. We should bathe and have our hair cut on the day before "Rosh Hashanah" in honor of the Festival. The hair should be cut in the afternoon. We should also put on our Sabbath clothes on "Rosh Hashanah."

6. On the day before "Rosh Hashanah," it is customary to go through the ceremony of annulling vows, by saying the prescribed formula as is given in the Prayer Book. One who does not understand the Aramaic, the language in which the formula is written, should say it in the vernacular.

III. LAWS CONCERNING ROSH HASHANAH (NEW YEAR)

1. In the *kaddish*, recited from "Rosh Hashanah" through "Yom Kippur" (Day of Atonement), we repeat the word "Leela," thus, "Leela, leela" (though He be high above), without adding the letter *vav* (uleela). But as there must be exactly twenty-eight words in the *kaddish*, we contract the preposition *min* (from, or above) into the prefix *mi*, making it read "mikkal" instead of "min kal"; thus making it a total of twenty-eight words.

2. During the whole of the rest of the year, we say in the "Shemoneh esreh" (silent prayer) "Hael hakkadosh" (the holy God), and "Melekh oheb tzedakah umishepat" (King who lovest righteousness and judgment); but from "Rosh Hashanah" until after "Yom Kippur," we say instead, "Hammelekh hakkadosh" (the Holy King), and, "Hammelekh hammishepat" (the King of judgment), because on these days, the Holy One makes His sovereignty manifest through His judgment of the world.

3. In the "Maarib" (evening) service on Friday night, in the benediction "Magen abot" (He was a shield, etc.), we also say, "Hammelekh hakkadosh" instead of "Hael hakkadosh."

4. After the "Maarib" service on the first night of "Rosh Hashanah," it is customary to exchange greetings by saying "Leshanah tobah tikateb vetihatem" (be thou inscribed and sealed for a happy year), and to a woman it is said in the feminine form of the Hebrew language, "tikatebi vetihatemi"; but these greetings are not exchanged in the daytime.

5. At the evening meal it is customary to make the auguries for a good year: we dip in honey a portion of the *hallah* (white bread) over which we have said the "Hamotzi" (who bringeth forth bread), and after eating a piece the size of an olive, we say: "May it be Thy will, O Lord our God, to renew unto us a happy and pleasant year"; after this we dip a piece of sweet apple in honey over which we say the benediction "Bore peri haetz" (who createth the fruit of the tree), and after eating it, we again say: "May it be Thy will, O Lord our God, to renew unto us a happy and pleasant year."

6. On "Rosh Hashanah," when saying, "Our Father, our King,

we have sinned before Thee," we do not beat our breasts (the seat of sin) as we do on a weekday or on "Yom Kippur," because sins are not to be confessed on a Festival day.

7. When the Scrolls of the Law are taken from the Holy Ark, we say the thirteen attributes ("Adonai, adonai, el rahum vehanun"), and "Ribono shel olam" (Master of the universe). In some communities neither of the above is recited on the Sabbath.

8. The *shofar* should be sounded as follows: The *Teruah* is the blowing of nine short sounds; the *Shebarim* is of three sounds in succession, each being as long as the three short sounds of *Teruah*, so that the *Shebarim* also is equal to nine sounds. One should be very careful not to prolong the blowing of the *Shebarim* until each one equals nine short sounds, for in such an event the precept would not be fulfilled. The *Tekiah* is a simple sound. The *Shebarim* and *Teruah*, when they follow one another, should be sounded in one breath; the prompter should therefore announce them at the same time, together, "Shebarim-teruah."

9. No *shofar* is blown on the Sabbath.

10. When the one who sounds the *shofar* pronounces the benedictions, the congregation should not respond, "Barukh hu ubarukh shemo" (blessed be He and blessed be His name), but merely listen attentively and after each benediction respond "Amen." (See par. 7, p. 50.) From there on it is forbidden to make any interruption till after the *Tekiot* (*shofar*-blowing) during the "Shemoneh esreh" (silent prayer).

11. After the sounding of the *shofar* during the repetition of the "Shemoneh esreh," people generally recite, "Yehi ratzon" (may it be Thy will), as it is printed in the prayer-books. Care should be taken not to pronounce the names of the angels given there. In many communities this prayer is not recited at all, and this procedure is more proper. The principal reason for blowing the *shofar* is to stir the people to a full-hearted repentance. As Maimonides, of blessed memory, said: "Although the blowing of the *shofar* is a scriptural command, yet there is a hint involved, saying, 'Awake ye that are sleepy and ponder your deeds; remember your Creator, and

go back to Him in penitence. Be not of those who miss reality in their hunt after shadows, and waste their years in seeking after vain things that can neither profit nor deliver; look after your souls, and consider your deeds; let everyone of you forsake his evil ways and thoughts and return to God that He may have mercy on you.'"

12. At the repetition of the "Shemoneh esreh" when the *hazan* says, "Vaanahnu koreim" (and we bow), the congregation says it with him, and all bow but they are not to fall on their faces except on the Day of Atonement where the "Abodah" (the order of the Temple service) is read. The *hazan* kneels and prostrates himself, but he is not allowed to leave his place during the repetition of the "Shemoneh esreh"; he therefore stands at a slight distance from the desk, so that he may be able to bow and prostrate himself without moving from his place, and those who stand near him assist him to rise, that he may not be compelled to move his feet. The *hazan* should not blow the *shofar* during the repetition of the "Shemoneh esreh," unless he is confident that in so doing he will not become confused in his prayers.

13. Concerning the "Tekiot" during the repetition of the "Shemoneh esreh" and at the conclusion of the prayers, different customs prevail, and each community should abide by its customs.

14. After the "Minhah" (afternoon) service on the first day of "Rosh Hashanah," we go to a stream which contains fish, and if there is no stream containing fish, we may go to any river or to a well, and we say the verses: "Mi el kamokha" (who is a God like unto Thee), according to the order of the "Tashlikh" given in the prayer books. We then shake the ends of our robes, to symbolize the casting away of our sins. If the first day of "Rosh Hashanah" occurs on a Sabbath, we perform the "Tashlikh"-ceremony on the second day.

15. At the synagogue, it is our duty to avoid the company of our friends so that we do not indulge in light conversation; for we should devote our spare time to the study of the Torah, recite the Psalms, or read books of instruction, because this is a day holy to our Lord.

16. The two days of "Rosh Hashanah" are considered as one

continuous day, and are of the same degree of holiness. Therefore the authorities differ as to whether the benediction "Sheheheyanu" (who kept us in life) should be said on the second day when reciting the *kiddush*, or when lighting the candles, or when blowing the *shofar*. For some contend that since both days are one continuous holiness, and we have already said "Sheheheyanu" on the first day, we need not say it again on the second. Therefore, it is customary to lay a new fruit on the table or put on a new garment, in order that the benediction "Sheheheyanu," said in the *kiddush* or when the candles are lighted, should apply also to the new fruit or the new garment. Yet even if this is not done, "Sheheheyanu" should be said. The one who blows the *shofar* on the second day, should, if possible, put on a new garment; if, however, the first day of "Rosh Hashanah" occurs on a Sabbath when the *shofar* is not sounded, he need not put on a new garment, inasmuch as he has not yet said "Sheheheyanu" for the *shofar*.

IV. THE TEN DAYS OF REPENTANCE

1. The ten days of repentance, from the first day of "Rosh Hashanah" through "Yom Kippur," as indicated by its name, are set aside for penitence. During this time everybody is duty bound to search into his deeds, and to turn away from all evil actions. One should also devote more time than usual to the study of the Torah, the performance of the precepts, and the distribution of charity. Above all, every man should make amends for all the wrongs he has committed against his neighbor, for which there is no atonement unless he makes restitution to his neighbor and conciliates him so that he may obtain forgiveness.

2. During these days of repentance, it is proper for everyone to be more scrupulous than on other days by rigidly adhering to the Law of God, just as we pray to God, blessed be His name, that he deal with us with loving-kindness.

3. It is the custom not to perform any marriages during these days of repentance.

4. On the Sabbath during the ten days of repentance, when

"Shubah Yisrael" (Return, O Israel) from the Book of Hosea (xiv, 2) is read for the "haftorah," an eminent person should be called up for the "maftir."

2. YOM KIPPUR (DAY OF ATONEMENT)

Yom Kippur (Day of Atonement), observed on the tenth day of Tishri was, by Divine command, set aside as a day "of atonement and affliction of the soul." The Law of God was explicit concerning this Solemn Day (Lev. xxiii, 27–32): "Howbeit on the tenth day of the seventh month is the day of atonement; there shall be a holy convocation unto you, and ye shall afflict your souls . . . And ye shall do no manner of work in that same day; for it is a day of atonement, to make atonement for you before the Lord your God. For whatsoever soul it be that shall not be afflicted in that same day, he shall be cut off from his people. And whatsoever soul it be that doeth any manner of work in that same day, that soul will I destroy from among his people. . . . It shall be unto you a sabbath of solemn rest, and ye shall afflict your souls; in the ninth day of the month at even, from even unto even, shall ye keep the sabbath."

In accordance with this Divine Command, *Yom Kippur* has been set aside by the Jews as a day of self-retrospection. We fast and abstain from other worldly pleasures, and pray to God that He forgive our sins which we have committed against Him. We humble ourselves before God and sincerely repent, promising solemnly to better our ways in the future. If the Almighty, who knows our thoughts, sees that our repentance is sincere, He grants us pardon. (See "Sin and Repentance," pp. 141–143.)

However, sins committed against our fellow-men are not forgiven by Him. Such sins will be forgiven by the Almighty only when we conciliate the person we have wronged.

Yom Kippur thus gives expression to the most sublime teachings of the Jewish religion:

1. Sin is merely a weakness of man, always subject to his control,

if he will but earnestly strive to overcome it, and not the work of some evil power that has plotted man's downfall since the days of Adam and Eve.

2. As a child of God, man is always certain that his Father will receive him in favor and forgive his sins, as soon as he returns solemnly to Him.

3. No priest and no mediator is necessary to obtain forgiveness of sins; man himself can obtain such forgiveness from his Creator by solemnly repenting of his misdeeds, and vowing to begin a new life of virtue and goodness.

4. We must be reconciled with our neighbors before we ask God's pardon.

I. THE DAY BEFORE YOM KIPPUR

1. On the day before "Yom Kippur," in the forenoon, we perform the ceremony of *kapparot*. Men select roosters and the women select hens. Each takes the fowl in his or her right hand, recites "Bene adam" (children of man), and then swings the fowl above the head three times, each time reciting, "Zeh *or* zot kapparati" (this is in my stead). He who swings it above the head of another, should say, "Zeh *or* zot kapparatkha" (this is instead of thee), but he must first swing it above his own head. By no means should we imagine that the fowl atones for us, but we should bear in mind that whatever is done to the fowl should properly be done to us because of our iniquities, and we should lament because of our sins, and the Holy One, blessed be He, in His mercy, will accept our repentance. Some people are accustomed to give the redemption fowl to the poor, but it is best to redeem the fowl with money to be given to the poor.

2. Neither "Mizemor letodah" (A Psalm of thanksgiving), nor "Tahanun" (petition for grace), nor "Lamenatzeah" (For the chief musician), nor "Abinu malkenu" (our Father our King) is recited on the day before "Yom Kippur." But when "Yom Kippur" falls on the Sabbath, then "Abinu Malkenu" is recited in the "Shaharit" (morning) service on the day before "Yom Kippur."

3. It is a religious duty to feast sumptuously on the day before

"Yom Kippur," and to the person who complies with this precept it is counted as a virtue, as if he had fasted on that day also. It is proper to eat fish at the first meal.

4. "Yom Kippur" does not atone for transgressions committed against our fellowmen unless we conciliate them. We should therefore return to others what may lawfully belong to them and gain their pardon. If we have sinned against others, even if only by means of words, we are also obliged to conciliate those against whom we have sinned, and it it our duty to go personally to them. If, however, it is difficult for us to do so, or if we understand that they will be easily reconciled through another, we may conciliate them through a mediator. The person whose forgiveness is sought should not cruelly refuse, but grant forgiveness willingly and wholeheartedly, for such is the characteristic of an Israelite. Even if he has been grievously wronged, he should not seek vengeance, nor bear a grudge against the one that wronged him. On the contrary, if the offended does not come to him to sue for forgiveness, the offended person should present himself to the offender in order that the latter may beg his pardon. If a person harbors enmity in his heart, his prayers will not be accepted on "Yom Kippur," but all sins of the one who forbears retaliation will be forgiven.

5. It is customary to put on the Sabbath garments when we go to the synagogue to pray the "Minhah" (afternoon) service before "Yom Kippur." Before reciting "Elohai netzor" (O my God, guard), at the end of "Shemoneh esreh" (silent prayer) of "Minhah," we say "Yiheyu leratzon" (let the words of my mouth), and then we recite "Al het" (confession), beginning with "Elohenu velohe abotenu tabo lephanekha" (our God and God of our fathers, let our prayers come before Thee), to "Vehalayim raim" (and sore diseases), when we repeat the verse "Yiheyu leratzon."

6. "Al het" (the confession) should be recited while standing and in a bowed attitude as when saying "Modim" (we give thanks). When we mention the sin committed we should beat our breasts, as if to say: "You were the cause of my sins." "Al het" should be recited by all alike, according to the version given in the Prayerbooks.

7. "Abinu malkenu" (our Father our King) is not recited after "Minhah," whether "Yom Kippur" occurs on a weekday or on the Sabbath.

8. Towards nightfall we eat the final meal before the fast, at which is is customary to dip in honey the piece of *hallah* (white bread) over which the "Hamotzi" has been pronounced, as we do on "Rosh Hashanah." Only food which is easy to digest should be served at this meal, such as the flesh of fowl; spicy foods should be avoided. It it not customary to serve fish on this occasion. It is important that this meal be concluded while it is yet day, a short time before twilight. If we finish the meal long before sunset and we intend to eat or drink after that, we must either expressly say so, or bear it in mind, before reciting the Grace after meals.

9. It is a religious duty to honor this holy day of "Yom Kippur" with clean apparel and with lights; hence, in the synagogue as well as in the house, beautiful covers are spread and many lights are lit. When lighting the candles at home, we pronounce the benedictions: "Lehadlik ner shel yom hakkippurim" (to kindle the light of the Day of Atonement), and "Sheheheyanu" (who kept us in life). If "Yom Kippur" occurs on the Sabbath, we say the first benediction: "Lehadlik ner shel shabbat veshel yom hakkippurim" (to kindle the light of the Sabbath and of the Day of Atonement).

10. Pious men generally put on a *kittel* (white robe), which is the garment of the dead, for this serves to humble the arrogant hearts of men. Women wear clean white dresses in honor of the day; but they abstain from wearing any jewelry or ornaments, because of the awe of the judgment.

(Note: Originally, the white garments worn by pious Jews in the synagogue of old, did not serve as reminders of the grave. On the contrary, they were symbolic of the festal character of the days appointed for life's spiritual renewal. The Jerusalem Talmud (Rosh Hashanah i, 3) remarks: "When men are summoned before a mortal ruler to defend themselves against a charge lodged against them, they appear downcast and dressed in black like mourners, being uncertain of their verdict. The children of Israel appear before God, on the Day of Judgment, dressed in white as if going to a feast, because they are confident that their Father will pardon and not condemn." White stood for purity, innocence, confidence and hope.)

11. It is customary with some fathers and mothers to bless their children before going to the synagogue on "Yom Kippur" eve.

12. We put on the *talit* (fringed garment) for the evening service. But we must be careful to put it on while it is yet day, and say the benediction thereon. If, however, we have delayed in putting it on until twilight, we must not say the benediction (because the precept of *tzitzit* (fringes) is to be performed during the daytime only and not at night).

II. YOM KIPPUR EVE

1. Before saying "Kol nidre" (all vows), the most venerable of the congregation takes a *sefer torah* (Scroll of the Law), and walks with it around the *hazan's* (reader's) platform, while the people embrace it and kiss it, and plead for pardon and forgiveness for having lessened its dignity by disobeying its precepts. They must then resolve that henceforth they will be guided by its precepts. The verse "Or zarua latzaddik" (light is sown for the righteous) is repeated many times. Two respected men of the congregation each with a *sefer torah* in his hand, stand near the *hazan*, at his right and at his left, and the three say together, "Biyeshibah shel maalah" (by the authority of the Court of High), after which the *hazan* recites "Kol nidre" while chanting the inspiring traditional melody, and all worshipers say it in an undertone together with the *hazan*. It is proper to begin saying "Kol nidre" while it is yet day, and continue it until nighttime. After the *hazan* has said "Barkhu" (bless ye) and the congregation responded "Barukh" (blessed be, etc.), the Scrolls are returned to the Holy Ark and the two men near the *hazan* return to their respective places. On Sabbath they may return to their places when the congregation begins reciting, "Mizemor shir leyom hashabbat" (A Psalm, a Song for the Sabbath Day).

2. When the *hazan* says the benediction "Sheheheyanu" (who kept us in life), it should be his intention to exempt the congregation from saying it. Nevertheless, it is proper for each worshiper to

say this benediction in an undertone with the *hazan*, but the worshiper should hasten to conclude it before the *hazan*, so that he may respond "Amen." Women and men who have already said "Sheheheyanu" when lighting the candles, need not repeat it at the synagogue.

3. On "Yom Kippur," both in the evening and during the day, "Barukh shem kebod malkhuto leolam vaed" (Blessed be His name, whose glorious kingdom is forever and ever) should be said in a loud voice.

III. LAWS CONCERNING YOM KIPPUR

1. It is forbidden to eat, drink, wash, massage, wear shoes, or to have sexual intercourse on "Yom Kippur." It is forbidden also that any sort of manual labor be performed, nor should one carry from one domain to another. In this respect, all laws effective on the Sabbath must be observed on "Yom Kippur." Inasmuch as it is necessary to add from the profane to the sacred, all of the above are forbidden on the day before "Yom Kippur" while it is yet day, a short time before twilight, and beyond the conclusion of "Yom Kippur" until a short time after the stars become visible.

2. One who is ill, even though not critically so, may wash in the usual manner. A bride, within thirty days of her wedding day, may wash her face on "Yom Kippur."

3. Anointing or massaging even a part of the body is forbidden on "Yom Kippur." However, if one is ill, even though not critically so, one may anoint or massage oneself.

4. Only leather shoes, or shoes covered with leather, are forbidden on "Yom Kippur," but shoes made of other material may be worn. If, however, a person has to walk in a muddy or wet place, and feels much distressed to walk there without shoes on, he may wear shoes or slippers without heels, and if the shoes have heels, he should change them around by putting the right shoe on the left foot, and the left one on the right foot. But these must be removed at the entrance to the synagogue. One should take care not to touch them with bare hands, so that one may not be required to wash one's hands.

5. One who is even slightly indisposed, or one who has a bruised foot, or a woman within thirty days of her confinement, may wear leather shoes on "Yom Kippur."

6. Regarding the profanation of "Yom Kippur" for a person who is critically ill, or for a woman in her confinement, we must be governed by the same laws that govern the Sabbath. (See Part Two, Chapter I, Sections XII–XIII, pp. 103–105.) If one considers himself too ill to fast—whether or not his opinion contradicts that of physicians—he should not fast, for in this case, a sufferer is considered the best judge of his own condition.

7. When food is to be given to a pregnant woman, to a woman in confinement, or to a sick person, it is placed before them, and they are told: "If you are sure that you may possibly be in danger unless you eat as much as you may require, then you may eat until you feel satisfied. If, however, it is possible for you to eat less than the required quantity at one time, then act as follows: Eat at one time no more than the quantity of two-thirds of an egg and rest somewhat, then eat the same quantity again and rest, and continue thus." When drinking, they should be told to take less than a mouthful at one time, and rest before drinking again.

8. All those who are to be given food because they are in danger, may be given forbidden food, in the event permitted food is lacking.

9. If the mind of the ill person is composed, he should say a benediction before and after eating, but he should not say the *kiddush*. In the Grace after meals, he should include "Yaaleh veyabo" (May it come up, etc.), and if it is a Sabbath, he should also include "Retzeh" (accept); but if he has omitted saying either, he is not required to repeat the Grace.

10. Children less than nine years old should not be permitted to fast even a part of the day, because it may affect their health. Children fully nine years old and in good health, should be trained to fast gradually. They may at first be taught to abstain from food for a few hours beyond their regular eating time. In abstaining from wearing shoes, washing, and anointing, children should be trained even before they are fully nine years old.

11. On "Yom Kippur" memorial services for the dead are said. It

is customary for those whose father and mother are alive to leave the synagogue while the memorial prayers are recited. Anyone whose father or mother has passed away during that year also leaves the synagogue during the memorial services.

12. The time to begin the "Neilah" (concluding) service is when the sun is reddening the tops of the trees, so that it may be concluded when the stars become visible. When the "Neilah" is prolonged into the night, after the stars have become visible, we may say "Hatmenu" (seal us), but instead of saying, "Hayyom yiphneh" (the day is nearly past), which would appear as a falsehood, the congregation should say, "Hayyom panah, hashemesh ba uphanah" (the day has passed, the sun has set and is gone). But the *hazan* recites *birkat kohanim* (the priestly benediction), and "Sim shalom" (bestow peace) even if it is already night.

13. When the "Neilah" service is concluded, we say "Abinu malkenu" (our Father, our King), even if it is a Sabbath and still day. We then say once, "Shema yisrael" (hear, O Israel); three times, "Barukh shem kebod malkhuto leolan vaed" (blessed be His name whose glorious kingdom is forever and ever); and seven times, "Adonai hu haelohim" (the Lord, He is God). The *hazan* then chants the whole *kaddish* in a joyful tone, after which the *shofar* is sounded once, as it was when the Torah was given on Sinai, and as it was sounded on the "Yom Kippur" of the Jubilee year. The *shofar* may be sounded even at twilight while the stars are not yet visible, even on a Sabbath, but it should not be sounded in the daytime. After the sounding of the *shofar*, all say three times, "Leshanah habaah birushalayim" (for the ensuing year in Jerusalem).

14. After the stars become visible, we pray the "Maarib" (evening) service, and we include in its "Shemoneh esreh" (silent prayer), "Attah honantanu" (Thou hast bestowed upon us). If it is Saturday night, we recite "Veyitten lekha" (and God give thee), but we omit "Vihi noam" (may the pleasantness), and "Veattah kadosh" (and Thou art holy). Friendly greetings are then exchanged with merriment and joy as on a Festival, and the ceremony of the sanctification of the moon is performed. (See pp. 166–167.)

15. We do not begin the *habdalah* on "Yom Kippur" night with

"Hinneh el yeshuati" (behold the God of my salvation), but we say the benedictions over a goblet of wine, over the light, and "Hammabdil" (who hath made a distinction); no benediction is pronounced over the spices. If it is Saturday night, we say the *habdalah* as we do on the conclusion of an ordinary Sabbath.

16. On the conclusion of "Yom Kippur," there is feasting, drinking and rejoicing.

17. Immediately upon the conclusion of "Yom Kippur," the erection of a *sukkah* is begun.

18. On the day after "Yom Kippur," we rise early to go to the synagogue to pray. No one is allowed to fast, not even on the occasion of a *jahrzeit*, on the days that elapse between "Yom Kippur" and "Sukkot." We also omit the "Tahanun" (petition for grace) on these days.

CHAPTER IV

MINOR FESTIVALS

I. HANUKKAH

1. During the existence of the Second Temple, the Greeks enacted drastic decrees against the Israelites in order to destroy their religion, forbidding them to engage in the study of the Torah or in the practice of the precepts. They robbed them of their property, violated their daughters, and entered the Temple, desecrating and polluting its sanctity. Then God took pity on the oppressed Israelites: He enabled the sons of the Hasmonian High Priest to defeat the Greeks, and thus saved the Israelites from their hands. The kingdom of Israel was again established under the rule of one of the High Priests and lasted for more than two hundred years, until the destruction of the Second Temple. On the twenty-fifth day of the month of Kislev, the Jews upon entering the Temple after their victory, found only a small bottle of the pure oil sealed with the seal of the High Priest. This oil was sufficient to last but one day, but when they lit the *menorah* (candelabra) with it, it lasted for eight days until they had time to pound olives and extract from them the pure oil they needed. For this reason, the wise men of those days decreed that these eight days which begin on the twenty-fifth day of Kislev, be set aside as days of rejoicing and of praise. Every night, during these eight days, lights are lit towards evening in a conspicuous place to bear witness to the miracle. These days are called *Hanukkah* (dedication) to commemorate the joyful dedication of the Temple won back from the enemies who had polluted

it. On *Hanukkah* every Jew should re-tell amid feasting the miracles that were wrought for our fathers. The feasting must be accompanied by songs and praises. Charity, too, should be liberally dispensed on *Hanukkah*, especially to those who are poor and are engaged in studying the Torah.

2. Fasting is not permissible on *Hanukkah*, but it is permitted to fast on the day before and on the day after *Hanukkah*.

3. It is permissible to do all kinds of work during the eight days of *Hanukkah*, although it is customary for women to abstain from doing work while the *Hanukkah* lamp is burning.

4. While all kinds of oil are valid for the *Hanukkah* lights, olive oil is preferable. If this cannot be obtained, other oil which gives a clear and bright flame should be selected, or else wax candles may be used as their light is also clear. There should not be two candles stuck together, for these then resemble a torch.

5. An endeavor should be made to procure a beautiful metal candlestick, and if it can be afforded, a silver candlestick, in order that the precept may be performed in the handsomest manner.

6. On the first evening one candle is lit; on the second evening, two candles; and thus one more is added each evening until the eighth when all eight candles are lit.

7. The lights should be placed in an even row; one should not be higher than the other; and there should be sufficient space between the lights, so that one flame may not merge with another and resemble a torch. There should also be sufficient space between the wax candles, so that one may not heat another, thus spoiling its appearance by causing the wax to drip.

8. The time to light the *Hanukkah* lamp is immediately after nightfall, when the stars become visible. It is forbidden to do anything, even to study the Torah, before lighting the *Hanukkah* lamp, but the "Maarib" (evening) prayer should be said before lighting it. Candles for the *Hanukkah* lamp must be large enough to burn at least half an hour. We must assemble the entire household for the occasion of lighting the candles, as it were to spread the news of the miracle. If we have failed to light the lamp immediately upon the appearance of the stars, we may do so afterwards and say the

benedictions as long as the household is awake, but if they are asleep and the miracle can no longer be "published," we should light the *Hanukkah* lamp without saying the benedictions.

9. The order of lighting the *Hanukkah* lamp is as follows: On the first evening, the candle to be lit is placed at the right end of the *Hanukkah* lamp; and on every succeeding evening, one is added towards the left. The newly-added candles must be lit first, immediately after the benedictions are pronounced, then the lighting of the rest of the candles is continued towards the right.

10. On the first evening, whoever lights the *Hanukkah* lamp recites three benedictions: "Sheasah nissim" (who hath wrought miracles); "Vetzivanu lehadlik ner shel hanukkah" (and hath commanded us to light the *Hanukkah* lamp); and "Sheheheyanu" (who kept us in life). On the other evenings, the benediction "Sheheheyanu" is not recited. Immediately after the benedictions are pronounced, the candle that has been added that evening is lit, and while lighting the rest of the candles, "Hanerot halalu" (these lights) is recited.

11. It is forbidden for any one to make any use of the light shed by the *Hanukkah* candles, during the half hour which the lights must burn to comply with the law. Hence, it is customary to place the "shamesh" (the servile candle with which the lamp was lit) near the *Hanukkah* lights, so that in the event we make use of the light for any purpose, we may do so by the light of the "shamesh." The "shamesh" should be placed slightly higher than the other lights, in order that it may be obvious that it is not one of the required number of candles lit for *Hanukkah*.

12. Women, as well, must observe the precept of lighting the *Hanukkah* lamp, because they, too, were benefited by the miracles of *Hanukkah*. A woman may light the *Hanukkah* lamp and exempt the entire household. Even children, provided they are old enough to by trained and tutored, must be taught to light the *Hanukkah* lamp.

13. On Friday, the *Hanukkah* lamp must be lit before the Sabbath candles. It is necessary that the *Hanukkah* candles be large enough to keep burning for no less than thirty minutes after the

appearance of the stars, as otherwise the benedictions pronounced over them are without validity.

14. On Saturday night, the *Hanukkah* lamp must be lit before the *habdalah* ceremony is performed. At the synagogue, it is lit before "Veyitten lekha" (and may God give thee) is said.

15. During the eight days of *Hanukkah*, we include "Al hannissim" (for the miracles) in the "Shemoneh esreh" (silent prayer) and in the Grace after meals.

16. During the eight days of *Hanukkah*, we recite the entire "Hallel." We do not say "Tahanun" (petition for grace), nor "Lamenatzeah" (for the chief musician), nor "Tzidekatekha tzedek" (Thy righteousness), during *Hanukkah*.

17. Each day of *Hanukkah*, we call up three male-adults to say the benedictions over the reading of the portion of the Torah wherein is recorded the sacrifices brought by the *nesiim* (princes), contained in the *Sidrah* (weekly portion) "Naso" (Num. vi).

II. THE FOUR PARSHIYOT (EXTRA SABBATHS)

1. The Sabbath before the New Moon of the month of Adar (the one close to the month of Nisan), is called "Pareshat Shekalim," and for the *maftir* we read that portion of the Torah which contains the precept concerning the giving of half a *shekel* for the Temple (Ex. xxx, 11–16). On the first of Adar, the people were called upon to donate half a *shekel* towards the purchase of necessary sacrifices for the Temple, during the year. (See par. 5, p. 163.) If the New Moon of Adar occurs on a Sabbath, then this Sabbath is "Pershat Shekalim."

2. The Sabbath before *Purim* is "Pareshat Zakor," and we read for the *maftir* (Deut. xxv, 17–19): "Zakor et asher asah lekha amalek" (remember what Amalek hath done to thee), because Haman was of the descendants of Amalek.

3. The Sabbath before the New Moon of Nisan, is "Pareshat Hahodesh," and we read for the *maftir* (Ex. xii, 2–20): "Hahodesh hazzeh lakhem rosh hadashim" (this month shall be unto you the beginning of months); thus, Nisan, by the command of God, was designated as the first month of the religious year. If the New Moon

of Nisan occurs on the Sabbath, then this Sabbath is "Pareshat Hahodesh."

4. The Sabbath before "Pareshat Hahodesh" is "Pareshat Parah," and we read for the *maftir* the portion of the Torah (Num. xix, 1–22) containing the precept of the *parah adummah* (the red cow). (See, Month of Nisan, page 121, above.) In ancient times this reading served as a reminder to those who had become polluted by contact with a dead body, that they must purify themselves by having the ashes of the *parah adummah* sprinkled upon them, so that they might sacrifice the paschal lamb the day before Passover.

III. PURIM

Purim is celebrated on the fourteenth day of the month of Adar, and commemorates the rescue of the Jews of Persia from the destruction plotted against them by Haman, the wicked prime minister of Ahasuerus (Xerxes), King of Persia.

Purim means *lots,* and refers to the lots cast at Haman's order to decide on what day the Jews of Persia were to be killed. The lots were turned against Haman by Esther, the queen, and her cousin Mordecai, and the day became a day of victory and joy for the Jew, and of woe and doom for his enemies.

The feast of *Purim* has always been celebrated by joyous banquets and the sending of presents to friends and neighbors and gifts to the poor. The Book of Esther is read in the synagogue and is always accompanied by expressions of good humor. It has always been more a popular festival than a solemn day of thanksgiving.

This festival teaches us ever to have faith in God, the Guardian of Israel, and ever to remember the needy in the midst of joy.

THE READING OF THE MEGILLAH

1. As soon as the month of Adar arrives, we begin our merrymaking and rejoicing.

2. In the days of Mordecai and Esther, the Jews gathered on the thirteenth day of the month of Adar to defend themselves against and take revenge upon their enemies. They had to ask for mercy from the Holy One, blessed be His name, that He might help them;

and we find that when the Israelites were at war, they fasted so that the Lord might help them. Therefore, all the Israelites have taken it upon themselves to fast on the thirteenth day of Adar. This is known as the Fast of Esther. The fast is to remind us that the Holy One hears the prayer of everyone who fasts and returns to Him with all his heart, as He heard the prayers of our forefathers then.

3. *Purim* is the fourteenth day of Adar. If *Purim* occurs on a Sunday, the fast is observed on Thursday.

4. In honor of the *Megillah* (Scroll *or* Book of Esther), we should put on our best clothes in the evening, and upon our return home from the synagogue we must find the lights lit and the table set in token of the evening festivities. In the evening, after the "Shemoneh esreh" (silent prayer), the whole *kaddish* is said, including "Titkabbel" (may the prayers and supplications). Then the *Megillah* is read, after which "Veattah kadosh" (and Thou art holy) is recited. Then the whole *kaddish* is said, omitting "Titkabbel." If it is Saturday night, we say "Vihi noam" (let the pleasantness) and "Veattah kadosh," after which we recide the whole *kaddish*, omitting "Titkabbel" and "Veyitten lekha" (and may God give thee). The *habdalah* is then recited over a goblet of wine, and thereafter we say "Alenu" (it is our duty).

5. Before the reading of the *Megillah* in the evening, it is customary for every Jew to donate half the unit coin current in the country, to commemorate the half-*shekel* the Jews were accustomed to give for the buying of the public sacrifices during the existence of the Temple at Jerusalem. These contributions are known as "Mahatzit hashekel" (half a *shekel*). The general practice is for every person to give three half-*shekels,* because in the *Sidrah* (portion of the week) *Ki Tissa* (Ex. xxx, 11–16), where the donating of the half-*shekel* has been ordained, the word "Terumah" (offering) is mentioned three times. This money is then distributed among the poor.

6. In the "Shemoneh esreh" of the evening, morning, and afternoon services, as well as in the Grace after meals, we include "Al hannissim" (we thank Thee also for the miracles).

7. Everyone, man, woman, and child, is obliged to hear the *Megil-*

lah read both in the evening and in the daytime. Hence, maidens, too, should go to the synagogue. Those unable to go to the synagogue, should hear the *Megillah* read at home. Very young children should not be taken to the synagogue, less they disrupt the service.

8. At night it is forbidden to read the *Megillah* before the stars become visible, however distressed by hunger one may be. But, if necessary, one may have some light refreshments before the *Megillah* is read, in order to alleviate somewhat the weakening effect of the fast.

9. The best way of observing the precept is to hear the *Megillah* read in the synagogue.

10. It is the prevailing custom among the children of Israel, that, when reading the *Megillah* for the congregation, the reader does not read it out of a *Megillah* that is rolled together, but he spreads it out and folds it, folio upon folio, like a letter, because the *Megillah* is designated as *iggeret* (letter) of *Purim* in the Book of Esther (ix, 29).

11. The one who reads the *Megillah*, whether at night or in the daytime, pronounces three benedictions before the reading: "Al mikra megillah" (concerning the reading of the *Megillah*); "Sheasah nissim" (who hath wrought miracles), and "Sheheheyanu" (who hath kept us in life). When these benedictions are pronounced by the reader, the listeners should not respond "Barukh hu ubarukh shemo" (blessed be He and blessed be His name) after mentioning "Adonai" (Lord), but they should listen attentively and after each benediction respond "Amen." (See par. 7, p. 50.) Upon the conclusion of the reading of the *Megillah*, the reader rolls it completely together, places it before him, and recites the benediction "Harab et ribenu" (who doth plead our cause).

12. When reading the *Megillah*, the reader should do so with the intention of exempting all the listeners from reading it, and the listeners should bear in mind that they are thus fulfilling their obligation. Therefore, they should listen to every word, for should they fail to hear even one word, their obligation would not be fulfilled. The reader is required to cease reading altogther while there is

tumult and confusion at the mention of "Haman," and he must wait until quiet is restored.

13. After the "Shemoneh esreh" (silent prayer) of the morning services, half-*kaddish* is said, and three persons are called up to say the benedictions over the portion of the Torah (Ex. xvii, 8 ff.), "Vayabo amalek" (and Amalek came), after which half-*kaddish* is said. The Scroll of the Law is replaced in the Holy Ark, and then the *Megillah* is read. When the reader concludes "Hael hammoshia" (O God, the Saviour), the congregation reads "Shoshanat yaacob" (the lily of Jacob), "Ashre" (happy are they), and "Uba letzion" (and a redeemer shall come); then the whole *kiddish* is said, including "Titkabbel" (may the prayers and supplications). The *tephilin* should not be taken off before the *Megillah* is read.

SENDING OF PORTIONS—GIFTS TO THE NEEDY—PURIM SEUDAH (FEAST)

1. On *Purim*, it is the duty of everybody to send no less than two gifts to one of his friends, no matter whether this friend is rich or poor. The more gifts one sends, the more meritorious is the act. Nevertheless, to give as much charity to the needy as possible, is held to be more praiseworthy than to make a great feast and to send any number of gifts to our friends. There is no greater joy and no more glorious deed before the Holy One, blessed be He, than the gladdening of the hearts of those in need.

2. Strictly speaking, these gifts given as "portions" must be gifts of food which need no preparation, such as boiled meats and fish, confectionery, fruits and wines. But the custom now prevails to include in the *shaloah-manot*-gift such items as books, wearing apparel, and other useful articles.

3. Everybody, even the poorest Jew who is himself dependent upon charitable contributions, is obliged to give at least one gift each to two poor persons. No discrimination should be shown in distributing the *Purim* monies; whoever is willing to accept charity must be allowed to participate. If one lives in a community where there are no people willing to accept charity, one must either keep the *Purim* money until one meets poor persons who will accept it, or send it to charitable institutions.

4. Women, too, must send gifts to their friends and contribute charity on this day. Women should send gifts to women, and men to men, but as regards charity to the needy, women may help men, and men may help women.

5. *Purim* must be celebrated by feasting, drinking, and making merry. On the night of the fourteenth of Adar, there must also be fasting and rejoicing. Nevertheless, the obligation of feasting on *Purim* is not fulfilled by the feast that we make at night, as it is a religious duty to make the feast principally in the daytime, generally in the afternoon. Portions (shaloah manot) to our friends and charity to the poor, should also be sent in the daytime. When *Purim* occurs on Friday, the feast is held in the morning, in honor of the Sabbath. No labor may be done on *Purim*, unless it is done for us by a non-Jew; it is permissible to attend to business, to write letters of friendship, to make a note of debts due, and to do anything needful that does not require much attention. Especially is it permissible to write something for the sake of a religious duty. It is permissible to perform even hard labor for the requirements of *Purim*.

7. The fifteenth day of the month of Adar is known as "Shushan Purim." On this day we do not say "Tahanun" (petition for grace), nor "El erekh appayim" (O God, Thou art long-suffering), nor "Lamenatzeah" (for the chief musician). On this day it is also forbidden to hold a funeral address or to fast. It is customary to make more festive meals than usual and to rejoice also on "Shushan Purim," but no "Al hannissim" (we thank Thee for the miracles) is said.

IV. ROSH HODESH (NEW MOON)

1. It is a religious duty to feast sumptuously on "Rosh Hodesh" (New Moon). If "Rosh Hodesh" falls on the Sabbath, an extra dish should be prepared in its honor.

2. It is permissible to do work on "Rosh Hodesh," although tradition has made "Rosh Hodesh" a semi holliday for women, and they abstain from sewing and other work which can be postponed.

3. At the morning prayers, after the *Hazan* repeats the "Shemoneh

esreh" (silent prayer), half-*hallel* is said, followed by the recitation
of the whole *kaddish*. A Scroll of the Law is taken out, and four
male adults are called to pronounce the benedictions over reading
the portion of the Torah which deals with "Rosh Hodesh" (Num.
xxviii, 1 ff.). After this half-*kaddish* is said; then we say "Ashre"
(happy are they) and "Uba letzion" (and a redeemer shall come),
and after that half-*kaddish* again. The *tephilin* are then removed,
and the "Musaph" (additional) service for "Rosh Hodesh" is read.

4. On "Rosh Hodesh" it is forbidden either to fast, or to deliver
a funeral eulogy, or to say the services for the dead.

5. The moon must be consecrated each month, not before it is
actually night, that is, when its light is reflected upon the ground
and one may enjoy its loveliness. If the moon is obscured by a cloud,
it should not be consecrated unless the cloud is light and filmy. If
we have begun the benediction and a cloud then obscured the moon,
we should conclude it. If, however, we know beforehand that we
shall be unable to conclude the benediction before the moon is
obscured, we must not begin it.

6. The moon should be consecrated under the open skies and not
under a roof. In case of emergency, it may be consecrated in the
house through a window.

7. The religious duty is best fulfilled if the consecration occurs
on the conclusion of the Sabbath, provided that it falls within ten
days since the New Moon.

The moon should be consecrated when at least three days have
elapsed since the New Moon and not more than fourteen full days,
eighteen hours and twenty-two minutes.

8. It is a religious duty to consecrate the moon in the midst of a
multitude, for "In the multitude of people is the King's glory"
(Prov. xiv, 28).

9. The moon should not be consecrated before "Tisheah Beab"
(the ninth day of the month of Ab), nor when one is in mourning.
If, however, the days of mourning will not end within ten days after
the New Moon, one may consecrate it during the mourning days.
On a fast day, it should not be consecrated before some food has
been eaten. Nevertheless, on the conclusion of the Day of Atone-

ment, when we leave the synagogue full of joy because our sins have been forgiven, we consecrate it before tasting any food.

10. The moon should not be consecrated on a Friday night, nor on the night of a Festival, unless in an emergency when the time for the consecration will have passed on the conclusion of the Sabbath.

11. A blind person is permitted to consecrate the moon.

V. LAG BAOMER

On the thirty-third day of counting the *Omer,* we observe a kind of semi-holiday. See page 131, concerning this minor festival.

VI. HAMISHAH ASAR BISHEBAT

On the fifteenth day of the month of Shebat, is the "New Year of Trees." On this day no *tahanun* (petition for grace) is said. It is generally celebrated by partaking of a variety of fruits, especially Palestinian fruits.

CHAPTER V

THE FOUR FAST DAYS

I. THE PUBLIC FAST DAYS

1. It is a religious duty imposed upon us by the Prophets, that we fast on those days on which sorrowful events occurred to our forefathers. The object of the fast is to impel us toward repentance. Therefore, on fast days, it is our sacred duty to be mindful of this purpose, and to search out our evil deeds and to repent, for the principal thing is not the fast itself, but it is the preparation for repentance.

2. These are the four public fast days: (1) The third day of the month of Tishri; (2) the tenth day of the month of Tebet; (3) the sevententh day of the month of Tammuz; and (4) the ninth day of the month of Ab.

3. The third day of Tishri is a fast day which commemorates the murder of Gedaliah, the son of Ahikam. After the destruction of the First Temple by the Babylonians, King Nebuchadnezzar left a small number of farmers in the land of Israel, and appointed Gedaliah as their governor. Because Gedaliah was assassinated, the remnant of Jews left in Palestine were either exiled or slain by the Babylonians. Thus the last ray of hope of Israel was dimmed.

4. The tenth of Tebet is observed as a fast day, because on that day Nebuchadnezzar, the king of Babylon, approached the city of Jerusalem and laid siege to it, and this marked the beginning of the destruction of Jerusalem and the Temple.

5. The seventeenth day of Tammuz is observed as a fast day,

169

because five sorrowful events occurred on this day: (a) The tablets on which the Ten Commandments were inscribed, were broken by Moses when he descended from Mount Sinai, as is told in the Holy Scriptures (Ex. xxxii, 19). (b) The regular daily sacrifices in the Temple were abolished. (c) The Romans made a breach in the wall surrounding Jerusalem during the existence of the Second Temple. (Although during the destruction of the First Temple, the Babylonians breached the wall on the ninth of Tammuz, the destruction of the Second Temple is regarded as the more severe disaster.) (d) Apsotomos burned a Scroll of the Law. (e) Through the wickedness of some Jews, an idol was placed in the Temple of God, and this caused the destruction of the Temple and the exile of Israel.

6. A public fast day is observed on the ninth of Ab, to commemorate four tragic events: (a) When the Israelites were in the wilderness, Moses sent twelve scouts to explore Canaan, the land of their promise. On the ninth day of Ab, the scouts returned with discouraging reports, and all Israel believed the evil reports and wept in vain. God thereupon decreed that they should not enter the promised land. (b) The First as well as the Second Temple were destroyed. (c) The site of the Temple was ploughed over with ploughshares by the Roman Procurator T. Annius Rufus, and the prophecy was thus fulfilled (Jer. xxvi, 18): "Zion shall be ploughed into a field." (d) The city of Bethar was conquered by the Roman legions during the Bar Kokhba revolution.

7. If any of these four fast days occurs on the Sabbath, it is postponed until after the Sabbath. When the tenth of Tebet occurs on Friday, the fast is observed and completed that day.

8. If one does not sleep regularly during any of the nights preceding the first three fast days, one may have food during the night until the break of day. If, however, one does sleep regularly, one is not allowed to drink or eat upon awakening, unless one so intended before going to sleep. One who is accustomed to drink something after his sleep, need not determine to do so before going to sleep. But on the ninth of Ab, we must eat nothing from the time the sun sets on the preceding afternoon. On the first three fast days, it is

permissible to wash, to anoint, and to wear leather shoes, but on the Ninth of Ab, all these are forbidden.

9. On a public fast day, it is forbidden to rinse one's mouth with water in the morning.

II. THE INTERVAL BETWEEN THE SEVENTEENTH DAY OF TAMMUZ AND THE NINTH OF AB

1. The three weeks, between the seventeenth day of Tammuz and the ninth day of Ab, are a period of mourning. During these days no marriage may be performed, but a betrothal may take place until the New Moon of Ab, even if it be accompanied by a feast. After the New Moon of Ab, a betrothal may take place, but it is forbidden to make a feast, and only preserves and the like may be served.

2. It is the custom not to say the benediction "Sheheheyanu" (who kept us in life) during these days. Therefore one should neither purchase nor put on a new garment, as that would necessitate the saying of "Sheheheyanu."

3. It is also customary not to have the hair cut during these days.

4. From the first to the ninth day of Ab, joy and merriment should be avoided as much as possible. No new structure should be erected either for pleasure or for business. If one has made a contract with a non-Jew to decorate one's house, one should make every effort to induce the non-Jew to allow a postponement, even if one has to pay a small financial penalty. If, however, the work cannot be postponed, it may be done. The moon should not be consecrated till the Ninth of Ab.

5. During the first nine days of Ab, we must abstain from eating meat and drinking wine. It is forbidden to partake of food cooked with meat or with meat-fat; even the flesh of poultry is forbidden, except to a person to whom dairy meals are harmful. Of course, none of these prohibitions apply in the case of an invalid who might be endangered by them. At a feast held in honor of the performance of a precept, such as a circumcision, the redemption of the first-born, or the conclusion of a Talmudic treatise, meat and wine may be served not only to one's immediate family and to those directly

concerned in the performance of the precept, but also to ten invited guests, provided that these guests would have been expected to come to one's feast had it occurred at any other time. Such a feast is permissible even on the day before the Ninth of Ab before noon, but not after that time. Concerning the goblet of wine for the *habdalah* recited on the conclusion of the Sabbath, if there is a minor who is able to drink the greater part of the goblet, it should be given to him; otherwise he who recites the *habdalah* may drink it himself.

6. Of course, wine and meat are permissible on the Sabbath that occurs during those nine days.

7. During the nine days, it is not permissible to bathe even in cold water except for medicinal reasons, in which case it is permitted to bathe even in warm water.

8. If the New Moon of Ab occurs on a Friday, one who is accustomed to bathe every Friday is permitted to bathe then even in warm water, but he is not allowed to bathe in warm water on the Friday before "Shabbat Hazon" (when we read for the *haftorah* the first chapter of Isaiah, beginning with the word "hazon," the vision of); he may then wash only his hands and face and bathe his feet.

9. One should not walk for pleasure on the day before the Ninth of Ab. In the afternoon, one may study only the subjects permitted on the Ninth of Ab. (See Section that follows.)

10. The *tahanun* (petition for grace) is omitted in the "Minhah" (afternoon) service on the day before the Ninth of Ab.

III. THE NINTH OF AB

1. In the evening, upon entering the synagogue, we remove our shoes. The Holy Ark is unveiled, and but one light is lit in front of the *hazan* (reader). The "Maarib" (evening) prayers are said in a low voice, with a weeping intonation, as in mourning. "Nahem" (comfort) is not included in the "Shemoneh esreh" (silent prayer) until the morrow in the "Minhah" service. After the "Shemoneh esreh," the entire *kaddish* is said, including "Titkabbel" (may the

prayers and supplications). The worshipers are seated either on low stools or on the floor, and only a few lights are lit, sufficient only to enable them to read "Ekhah" (Lamentations) and "Kinnot" (special lamentations). "Ekhah" and "Kinnot" are chanted in measured plaintive traditional tones. After the "Kinnot" "Veattah kadosh" (and Thou art holy) is recited, and then the entire *kaddish* without "Titkabbel." On the morrow, in the morning service, "Titkabbel" is again omitted, and it is said only in the "Minhah" service.

2. In the morning, one puts on neither the *tephilin* nor the big *talit* (fringed garment), but the small fringed garment should be worn as usual, without saying the benediction thereon. The worshipers arrive at the synagogue a little earlier than usual. No light at all should be lit for the prayers, and the prayers are said in a low weeping voice. "Mizemor letodah" (A Psalm of thanksgiving) is said. The *hazan*, in the repetition of the "Shemoneh esreh," says "Anenu" (answer us) between "Goel yisrael" (the Redeemer of Israel) and "Rephaenu" (heal us, O Lord), as on every other public fast day, but he does not say "Birkat kohanim" (the blessing of the Priests); after the "Shemoneh esreh," he says half-*kaddish*. Neither *tahanun* (petition for grace) nor "El erekh appayim" (O God who art long-suffering) is said. A Scroll of the law is taken out, and the section (Deut. iv, 24): "Ki tolid banim" (when thou wilt beget children) is read for three persons, and after this half-*kaddish* is said. Then we read the *haftoroh* (Jer. viii, 13): "Asoph asiphem" (I will surely destroy them), in the tone of "Ekhah." The Scroll is then replaced in the Ark. The worshipers, seated on the ground, say "Kinnot," the reading of which should be prolonged until close to noon. Thereafter we say "Ashre" (happy are they), omitting "Lamenatzeah" (For the chief musician), and we say "Uba letzion" (a redeemer shall come to Zion), omitting the verse "Vaani zot beriti" (and as for Me, this is My covenant). Then "Veattah kadosh" (and Thou art holy) is followed by the saying of the whole *kaddish* with "Titkabbel" omitted; after which we say "Alenu" (it is our duty to praise), and then the mourner's *kaddish*. The "Yom" (hymn of the day) is not recited.

3. A person who is ill, although not critically so, is not bound to complete the fast, but should abstain from food only for a few hours. This rule applies especially to one who is naturally weak. They who are compelled to eat on the Ninth of Ab, however, should eat no more than is necessary to preserve their health.

4. Bathing is forbidden, whether in hot or cold water.

5. Anointing for pleasure's sake is forbidden, but it is permissible when necessary for health.

6. It is forbidden to wear shoes only if they are made of leather, or are trimmed with leather. However, there are exceptions to this prohibition: anyone who walks among non-Jews may wear leather shoes so that he will not be exposed to ridicule; and any one who walks a considerable distance, may wear shoes, provided that on nearing a town he removes them. One who rides in a vehicle is forbidden to wear shoes.

7. At the "Minhah" service, we put on the *talit* and the *tephilin*, with the appropriate benedictions, and say the "Yom" (hymn of the day) and all other portions omitted in the morning service. We then say "Ashre" (happy are they), and the half-*kaddish*. The Torah and the *maftir* are then read as on any other public fast day. The Scroll is afterwards replaced in the Ark, and the *hazan* says half-*kaddish*. After this we read the "Shemoneh esreh," and in the benediction "Velirushalayim irkha" (and to Jerusalem Thy city), we say "Nahem" (comfort Thou). The *hazan* recites "Birkat kohanim" (the blessings of the Priests) in the repetition of the "Shemoneh esreh," and, concluding the "Shemoneh esreh," he recites the whole *kaddish*, including "Titkabbel." We then remove the *tephilin*, and we pray "Maarib" (evening) service. It is customary to sanctify the moon, if it is visible.

IV. THE NINTH OF AB OCCURRING ON SATURDAY OR SUNDAY

1. If the Ninth of Ab occurs on Sunday, or if it occurs on Saturday and is postponed to Sunday, we may eat meat and drink wine during the Sabbath. Even at the third meal after "Minhah" we may eat everything, provided we do not feast in a company, but eat our

meal with our family, in which case we may say Grace with a quorum of three. We must finish our meal while it is still daytime, as eating, drinking or bathing are forbidden in the twilight. We should not remove our shoes until after "Barkhu" is said. The *hazan* should remove his shoes before saying "Vehu rahum" (and He being merciful).

2. We say "Ab harahamim" (may the Father of mercies), and we may hold Memorial Services in the morning, but in the "Minhah" service, "Tzidekatkha tzedek" (Thy righteousness) is not said.

3. We do not say "Lamenatzah" (to the chief musician) before "Maarib," nor "Vihi noam" (and let the pleasantness), nor "Veyitten lekha" (may God give unto thee).

4. When we see the candle-light at dark, we should say the benediction "Bore meore haesh" (who createth the light of the fire), and in the "Shemoneh esreh" we say "Attah honantanu" (Thou hast favored us). The *habdalah* should not be recited until the conclusion of the Ninth of Ab, when we say it over a goblet of wine; but we do not say the benedictions over the spices and over the light, even if we have neglected to say the latter benediction on Saturday night. If we have forgotten to say "Attah honantanu," we need not repeat the "Shemoneh esreh," because the *habdalah* will be recited over a cup of wine when the fast is over. We are not allowed to taste any food before the *habdalah*, and if we find it necessary to do work before the *habdalah*, we should recite "Hamabdil ben kodesh lehol" (who maketh a distinction between the holy and the profane), omitting the Divine Name and the Royal attributes.

5. When the Ninth of Ab occurs on the Sabbath and is postponed to Sunday, it is nevertheless forbidden to eat meat or drink wine on the night after the fast.

V. COMMEMORATING THE DESTRUCTION OF THE TEMPLE

1. After the destruction of the Temple, our sages decreed that on every occasion of rejoicing we must commemorate the destruction of the Temple, as it is written (Ps. cxxxvii, 5): "If I forget

thee, O Jerusalem. . . . If I prefer not Jerusalem above my chief joy."

2. At the writing of a betrothal contract (tenaim), after it has been read, we shatter an earthen vessel, commemorative of the destruction, but it is proper that a broken vessel be used for that purpose. For the same reason, the bridegroom breaks a glass vessel under the nuptial canopy.

PART THREE

OUR DUTIES TOWARDS OUR FELLOWMEN

CHAPTER I

CHARITY–LOANS

As has been pointed out before (see pp. 24–25), belief in the Unity of God is the quintessence of the Jewish Creed. The primary duty of every Jew is to believe in the existence of One God, the Creator of all existing things. Yet mere belief in God and His Unity does not suffice. Love of God is the quintessence of Jewish Life. And this love must be translated into deeds, for the Jewish religion is based on action, not on mere belief. In fact, there is no express command in the Holy Scriptures which orders the Jews to *believe* in God. All we are told is to *know* God as He is manifested by His works, and to follow His ways and to adopt His attributes by being forbearing, kind, and merciful.

Because we are all the children of one Father, there is imposed upon the community and upon every individual, according to his means, the duty of providing for the needy; the protection of the helpless, the widow, and the fatherless; the safety and shelter of the stranger and homeless; the care of the sick; and the burial of the dead. According to our great teacher Hillel the Elder, who lived in the first century before the common era, this duty toward our fellow-men is considered the foundation of the entire Jewish religion (Babli, Shabbat 31a): "What is hateful to thee, don't do to another; this is the basis of the entire Jewish Law, while the rest is a mere commentary thereon. Go and complete its study."

Moreover, according to the religious concept of the Jew, God is the real Owner of the world, and we, the inhabitants of the earth, are merely His trustees. Whatever we possess is simply entrusted to us by His graciousness with the charge of providing for the needy. If we withhold our share from them, we rob them of what by Divine Law belongs to them, and we abuse our trust.

1. CHARITY

1. It is a religious duty to give charity to the poor, as the Almighty commanded (Deut. xv, 8): "Thou shalt surely open thy hand unto him." If we see a poor man ask for help and we shut our eyes and disregard his supplications and refuse to give him relief, we transgress God's command, for He ordained (Deut. xv, 7): "Thou shalt not harden thy heart nor shut thy hand from thy needy brother." Let no man think to himself, saying: "Why should I diminish my wealth by giving it to the poor?" For he must be mindful that the wealth really belongs not to him, but that it was simply given to him as a trust with which to execute the will of the One who has entrusted this fund to him. And this (charity-giving) is man's real portion which he has saved from all his toil in this world.

2. Every man must contribute to charity according to his means. Even if a person can give but very little, yet he should not abstain from giving it, for the little he gives is equally as worthy as the large contributions of the wealthy. But he who has barely sufficient for his own needs, is not obligated to give any charity, for his own sustenence takes precedence over another's.

3. The poor of all nations must be fed and clothed together with the poor of Israel.

4. He who gives alms to the poor with an unfriendly mien and downcast face, even if he give as much as a thousand pieces of gold, his deed it without merit, for it is marred by ill-will. Charity must be given freely with a full heart.

5. We must not turn away empty-handed anyone who comes to us for help, even if all we are able to give is a morsel of bread. If we have nothing in our possession to give him, then let us at least give him kind words. We must neither rebuke nor speak harshly to the poor, for their hearts are broken and humbled. Woe unto him who has put the poor to disgrace and ridicule. We must be like

a parent to the poor and show them mercy by deed as well as by words.

6. A promise made to give charity is in the nature of a vow. Therefore if we say: "We shall give a certain sum of money as charity," we must do so without delay.

7. He who urges others to give charity and causes them to practice it, earns a greater reward than the one who gives.

8. The highest merit in giving charity is attained by the person who comes to the aid of those who have not reached the stage of actual poverty. Such aid may be in the form of a substantial gift, or by a loan, or by assistance in obtaining employment.

9. It is meritorious to make charitable contributions in secrecy, and if possible, in such a way that the giver himself is not aware to whom he is giving it, and the recipient does not know from whom he is receiving it. No man should ever boast of the charitable contributions he makes. But if a man consecrates a certain article for charitable purposes, it is permissible that his name be engraved on it that it may serve as a memorial.

10. We must take special care in the treatment of a poor scholar who studies the Law of God, and to offer one's gifts to him in a manner that accords with his dignity. If he is unwilling to accept money in the form of charity, some profitable business transaction should be arranged for him, or if he is capable of conducting a business, money should be lent to him for that purpose.

11. A person should at all times suffer hardship rather than become dependent on men. And thus did our Sages, of blessed memory, command (Babli, Shabbat 118a): "Rather make thy Sabbath a weekday (as regards festive meals) than be dependent on men." Even if an honored sage should become poor, he should find some occupation, even of a menial kind, rather than become dependent on men.

12. Whoever accepts charity without need and by deceit, shall live to become dependent on the charity of his fellow-men. On the other hand, one who is actually in need of charity, either because he is sick, or old, or in pain, and who refuses to accept it on account

of pride, is guilty of bloodshed and forfeits his own life, and he has nothing for his suffering but sins and transgressions. He, however, who is in need of charity, and suffers distress and hardship, not because of pride but because he does not wish to become a burden on the public, shall live to acquire the means of supporting others.

II. LOANS

1. By the command of the Almighty (Deut. xv, 7–8) we must lend money to the poor. As regards loans, a poor man who is a relative takes precedence over others, and the poor of one's own city take precedence over the poor of another city. The religious act of lending money to the poor, is greater than the one of giving charity to the poor.

2. It is a religious duty to lend money even to a rich man, if he is in need of a loan, and also to speak kind words to him and to advise him with advantage to his position.

3. It is forbidden to lend money even to a scholar, without witnesses, unless it is secured by a pledge. The best course is to have a note drawn up referring to the loan.

4. It is forbidden by Divine Law to exact payment from the borrower when it is known that he is unable to pay. It is prohibited even to confront him lest he be put to shame when he is unable to repay, and concerning this, it is written (Ex. xxii, 24): "Thou shalt not be to him as a creditor."

5. Just as the lender is forbidden to oppress the borrower, so is the latter forbidden to withhold his neighbor's money, by telling him to come again, when he has the money, as it is written (Prov. iii, 28): "Say not unto thy neighbor, 'Go, and come again.'"

6. A borrower is forbidden to lend the money he has borrowed lest it be lost and he himself be unable to repay the debt. Should he do so, he would be considered an evil-doer, as it is written (Ps. xxxvii, 21): "The wicked borroweth, and payeth not." The Sages have commanded (Abot ii, 17): "Let thy neighbor's property be as dear unto thee as thine own." If the lender knows that the borrower is a man with little or no consideration for the property of others,

he should not lend him the money, lest he be compelled thereafter to exact repayment, and so transgress the precept: "Thou shalt not be to him as a creditor."

7. He who lends money on a pledge, must avoid making use of the pledge, as such use might be considered interest. If he lends money to a poor man on the security of something such as a ploughshare or an axe, which can be hired out at a good price and will only be slightly worn by use, he may do so without asking the owner's permission, but he should deduct the proceeds from the debt, as it may be assumed that the borrower would agree to it.

8. A person should avoid whenever possible becoming a trustee for another or acting as his guarantor.

9. It is forbidden to keep a paid note in one's possession, as it is said (Job xi, 14): "And let not unrighteousness dwell in thy tent."

10. It is necessary for one to be scrupulous in guarding a bailment, but even more scrupulous in guarding a pledged article.

11. If one lends money to a neighbor on a pledge, with the condition that if he does not repay the loan at a certain time, he shall forfeit the pledge, then the lender must take care to tell the borrower when the loan is made: "If you do not redeem the pledge by such and such a time, I shall acquire title to it from the present time."

12. If a man owes money to another, and if the latter says to him: "I am sure that you owe me nothing," then the debt is considered as cancelled and the borrower need not repay the loan.

III. INTEREST ON LOANS

1. The Law of God forbids the taking of any interest on loans made to persons in need, as such interest is considered unlawful gain. The Holy Scriptures read (Deut. xxiii, 20): "Thou shalt not lend upon interest to thy brother: interest of money, interest of victuals, interest of anything that is lent upon interest." This prohibition against taking interest is repeated several times in the Holy Scriptures. Our Talmudic sages tell us (Mishnah, Baba Mezia v, 11) that all parties concerned in a loan involving interest—the lender, the borrower, the surety, the witnesses and even the scribe—are guilty of violating the Divine Law.

2. It has been man's nature to long for the acquisition of wealth, and of all the illegal means of acquiring wealth, the taking of interest has appeared not only most feasible but also most easily dissembled. In robbery or fraud, the victim usually tries to defend himself, and the perpetrator is often himself inhibited by shame or fear. When a person takes interest for the loan of money, however, he usually finds the borrower actually or seemingly grateful, so that the lender may easily convince himself that far from committing a crime, he is, on the contrary, performing a kind and meritorious deed. Hence it is very easy for a man to be caught in the forbidden snare of interest-taking. And it is precisely for this reason that our Holy Torah is very strict about this prohibition and includes many specific prohibitory laws regarding it. He who lends on interest, transgresses six prohibitory laws and will not rise at the resurrection of the dead; as it is written (Ezek. xviii, 13): "He hath given forth upon interest, and hath taken increase; shall he then live? he shall not live." The borrower transgresses three prohibitory laws; the scribe, the witnesses, and the broker who negotiated the loan, as well as any one instrumental in bringing about the loan—even if only by saying, "So-and-so is willing to lend," or, "So-and-so is anxious to borrow"—all these transgress one prohibitory law.

3. He who has transgressed and has taken interest, is bound to return it.

4. Even though no rate of interest is fixed at the time of the loan or extension of credit, if, when the time of payment arrives, the debtor offers to pay the lender something for postponing the time of payment, this also is considered usurious and is forbidden.

5. Even if the borrower, of his own free will, returns to the lender more than he has borrowed when the loan becomes due, and even if he does not call the excess payment interest, the transaction is forbidden.

6. Even if the borrower, when paying the interest, declares it to be a gift, the lender must not accept it. If, nevertheless, the lender has accepted the interest but later repents and wishes to make restitution, and if the borrower refuses to accept it, he is then permitted to retain it.

7. The lender should be careful not to derive any benefit through the borrower without his knowledge while the loan remains unpaid, even if it be something to which the borrower would not have objected had the loan not been made. If the lender derives any benefit without the sanction of the borrower, it is considered as extortion for it presumes upon the dependency of the borrower. However, even with the borrower's knowledge, the lender may enjoy only that which the borrower would have granted even if the loan had not been made, provided it be not of a public nature.

8. If the borrower had not been accustomed to greet the lender before the loan was made, he must not do so afterwards. All kinds of attention by the borrower on account of the loan, even by word of mouth, are forbidden. The lender, too, must avoid gaining any benefit from the borrower even through mere words, as for example, if he should say to the borrower: "Let me know if so-and-so should come from such-and-such a place." Even though he does not trouble him more than to speak a few words, if he has not been accustomed to ask such a favor from him previously, he may not ask it now, because under the circumstances it would constitute a form of usury and is forbidden.

CHAPTER II

BUSINESS TRANSACTIONS

I. BARGAIN AND SALE

1. We must take extreme care not to deceive one another. If anyone deceives his neighbor, whether as a seller deceiving a buyer, or as a buyer deceiving a seller, he transgresses a prohibitory law, for it is written (Lev. xxv, 14): "And if ye sell aught to your neighbor or buy of your neighbor's hand, ye shall not wrong one another." According to our Talmudic Sages (Shabbat 31a), this is the first question that a man is asked when brought to judgment before the Heavenly Court: "Hast thou (while on earth) been dealing honestly?"

2. Just as deception is forbidden in buying and selling, so is it forbidden in hiring, in working on contract, and in money changing.

3. If a person deals honestly, he cannot be guilty of deception. Thus, if one has been cheated and has overpaid for an article of merchandise, and if he wishes to resell it, he may offer it to a buyer honestly by stating what he has paid for it and what profit he wishes to derive from its resale, since, in so doing, he does not deceive the buyer as to the intrinsic value of the commodity but merely bases the price on the price he himself has paid. A seller who has himself been deceived may not on that account deceive another.

4. A seller is forbidden to falsify the appearance of any commodity to make it seem better or other than it really is.

5. It is likewise forbidden to mix inferior commodities with those of good quality and to sell the whole as if it were of good quality, as for example, the adulteration of foods or liquors.

6. A shopkeeper is permitted to distribute parched grain and nuts to children in order to induce them to buy from him. He may also sell below the market price so that people may prefer to buy from him, and the other tradesmen may not prevent him from doing so.

7. He who gives a short measure or weight, even to a non-Jew, transgresses a prohibitory command of the Divine Law, for it is written (Lev. xix, 35): "Ye shall do no unrighteousness in judgment, in meteyard, in weight, or in measure."

8. On the contrary, it is necessary to measure and to weigh generously. This means that one should give somewhat more than the exact quantity demanded, as it is written (Deut. xxv, 15): "A perfect and just weight shalt thou have"; by "just" is meant, "give him a little of yours."

9. It is necessary to measure according to the custom of the community, and not to deviate from it. Where it is the custom to give a "heaped" measure, one must not give a "level" measure even if it is done with the consent of the buyer who does not pay the full price; and where it is the custom to give a "level" measure, one must not give a "heaped" measure even if the seller consents because the buyer gives more money. For the Torah has laid down strict rules prohibiting incorrect measures, lest a stumbling block for others arise from it, for an onlooker may notice that the measure is in this wise and be under the impression that such is the rule of the community, and in like manner will he measure to another person who is also ignorant of the custom of the place, and thus unwittingly deceive him.

10. A person who keeps in his house or in his shop short measures, even if he does not use them, transgresses a prohibitory law, for it is written (Deut. xxv, 13–14): "Thou shalt not have in thy bag diverse weights, a great and a small. Thou shalt not have in thy house diverse measures, a great and a small." It is forbidden to make any use of such measures anywhere, lest someone else use them unknowingly for measuring purposes. If, however, it is the rule of the community that only measures stamped with a certain well-known mark may be used, and if a given short measure is not

so marked and cannot therefore be used even by mistake, then it may be kept.

11. It is forbidden to rent or buy a piece of property, real or personal, which has already been offered to another at a price fixed and agreed upon by both parties, even though the transaction has not been completed. If, however, the prospective buyer and seller have not yet agreed upon the price, one may intervene and offer to rent or buy.

12. Anyone delegated as an agent to purchase real property or chattels, who then makes the purchase in his own name with his own money, may keep the property, though he is an impostor. But if he has made the purchase in his own name with the principal's money, he may not keep the property even if he returns the money.

13. If a transaction has been agreed upon and the price has been declared acceptable by both buyer and seller, whether or not any money has been paid as deposit or any mark has been placed on the commodity involved, the word of both is binding on both, and neither buyer nor seller may retract. If either retracts, he is held guilty of dishonesty, for an Israelite must abide by his word, as it is written (Zeph. iii, 13): "The remnant of Israel shall not do iniquity, nor speak lies."

14. A person is considered lacking in honesty if, having promised a small gift to another who thereafter depends on the receipt of it, he retracts his promise. If, however, he promises to give a large gift and then retracts, he is not considered as one lacking in honesty, as it is not reasonable for the one to whom the promise has been made to depend upon it. Nevertheless, even in the latter case, the promise must be made in good faith and not with the intention of retracting it. The above rule refers only to a promise made to a rich man, but if the promise has been made to a poor man, whether the promised gift be large or small, the promise is considered as a vow and must not be retracted. Even an unspoken promise to a poor man, such as the mere determination to give a gift to him, must be fulfilled.

II. BORROWING AND HIRING

1. He who borrows or hires anything from his neighbor, is not allowed to lend it or hire it out to another without the consent of the owner. Even in the case of books, the lending of which is considered meritorious, the borrower may not lend them to another, nor may he take it for granted that the owner would approve even if the reading of such books constitutes a religious duty, for the trustworthiness of the ultimate borrower must be determined by no one but the owner. The borrower of a book may, however, allow another person to use it for study in the former's house, on the condition that he studies by himself and not together with someone else. If it is known that the owner of the article is accustomed to trust the third party in such matters, then the borrower may lend and the hirer may hire out to such party.

2. It is a religious duty to pay the wages of a hired workman at the proper time, and he who delays such payment is guilty of transgressing a Divine Law, for it is written (Deut. xxiv, 15): "In the same day thou shalt give him his hire, neither shall the sun go down upon it." It is also a religious duty to pay for the hire of an animal or of utensils at the proper time. And what is the proper time? A workman, whether he be hired by the day, week, month, or year, who finishes his work during the day is entitled to payment before the end of that day, and if he finishes his work in the evening, he is entitled to payment before the end of that night.

3. The employer who postpones payment because he has not the money to pay the workman or because the workman failed to demand his wages, is not considered a transgressor. Nevertheless, a scrupulous employer should if necessary borrow the money rather than delay payment of wages.

4. If a hired workman, through negligence or otherwise, spoils or destroys the article on which he has worked, it is the religious duty of the employer to waive his legal rights and release the workman from liability. If the workman is poor and without food, it is the employer's duty to give him his wages. Charity and justice must be

practiced to an even greater extent than is specifically required by law.

5. Just as the employer is cautioned not to rob a workman of his wages and not to delay payment, so is the workman warned not to cheat his employer by idling away his time. He must do all he is able to do, so that his wages may be justly earned.

III. ARTICLES LOST AND FOUND

1. It is our duty upon finding an article that has been lost by an Israelite, to restore it to the owner, for it is written (Deut. xxii, 1): "Thou shalt surely bring them back unto thy brother." And if the property of our neighbor is threatened with destruction, it is our duty to save it, for this also is included in the precept of restoring a lost article to the owner.

2. The finder of a lost article may be forced by law to restore it to its rightful owner, provided the latter can properly identify it. Where the finder is required by the law of the land to restore the article to its owner, he must restore it under all circumstances.

3. Any one who finds an article, whether or not it bears a special mark of identification, in such a manner or in such a place that it may be presumed to have been left there temporarily by its owner, is forbidden to touch it. This would apply for example to an axe left by the side of a fence, or to a coat or hat left in a public place.

4. If a man, who is aged and respected, finds a common article, of such a nature that, even if it were his own, he would not take it home because it would be below his dignity to do so, he is not bound to do so.

IV. BAILMENTS

1. Nowadays, when one places money on deposit with anyone, we may take it for granted that the depositor tacitly agrees to the use of the money for regular business purpose. Money so deposited, therefore, assumes the character of a loan unless it is specifically designated otherwise by the depositor, or tacitly designated as not to be used, as, for example, by sealing it in a package or tying it with a special knot.

2. A person with whom an article has been deposited, is not allowed to make personal use of it, even if the article is in nowise spoiled by such use, because he who borrows an article without the owner's knowledge, is classed as a robber.

3. It is the duty of the bailee to guard the article deposited with him, in what is generally regarded as the safest manner possible. Even if the bailee himself does not usually take pains in guarding his own property, he must nevertheless take special care in guarding property entrusted to him.

4. The bailee is forbidden to entrust to the care of others the articles deposited with him, even if others are more trustworthy and of greater integrity than himself, unless the depositor has been accustomed to deposit such property with them.

5. The bailee must not return the article deposited with him to any member of the depositor's household, other than his wife, without his knowledge. This rule of law applies not only to bailees but to borrowers as well.

V. PLEADING AND TESTIMONY

1. When a controversy arises between two persons, they should do everything possible to compromise the matter between them, in order to avoid the humiliation of a law-suit.

2. If it is impossible for them to reach a compromise, and they are forced to go to court, they should have recourse to a Jewish tribunal.

3. If the subject in dispute is a debt, the debtor must not seek to force a compromise which results in his payment of less than he owes, as in so doing, he does not discharge his debt before the Judgment of Heaven, however he may succeed in blinding the judgment of his fellowmen. To discharge his obligation he must pay the claimant all that is rightfully due him.

4. One of the litigants is forbidden to present his case before the judge in the absence of his opponent. For that reason, neither litigant should appear before the judge without the other, lest he be suspected of unethical conduct.

5. Just as the judge who takes a bribe, even to acquit the inno-

cent, transgresses a Divine Law, so does he who gives the bribe transgress a Divine Law (Lev. xix, 14): "Thou shalt not put a stumbling block before the blind."

6. When the people of a community appoint a judge, they must first ascertain whether he possesses the following seven qualifications: wisdom in the Torah, humility, fear of God, hate of money even of his own, love of truth, love of his fellowman, and the esteem and respect of his fellowman based on his past conduct. Whosoever appoints a judge unfit for his position, transgresses the Divine Law, which says (Deut. i, 17): "Ye shall not respect persons in judgment," meaning thereby: "Ye shall not favor anyone by saying, 'So and so is wealthy, so and so is my relative, I will have him appointed as judge.'" It is forbidden to rise in the presence of any judge whose appointment has been bought by means of silver and gold, and it is likewise prohibited to show him any mark of respect.

7. If one is summoned by one's neighbor to testify on his behalf at a court of law, and if one is qualified to do so, he is obliged to appear as a witness, whether or not there are other witnesses besides himself. If he refuses to testify, he will be answerable to the Heavenly Court. A person is forbidden to testify in a matter of which he has no personal knowledge, even if his intended testimony is based on what a reliable person has told him.

8. Should a witness, who is obliged by law to testify, accept a reward for testifying, his testimony is null and void. A witness may accept compensation to cover travel expenses or loss of time or income occasioned by his appearance at the court. One who is asked to witness a transaction regarding which he will be required to testify subsequently, may be paid to the extent that he has been inconvenienced.

9. Any witness who derives any benefit from the matter involved in his testimony, or who has any personal interest in it, no matter how remote it may be, is unfit to testify.

10. One should abstain as much as possible from taking an oath, even if it be a true one.

11. If a litigant is aware that his opponent, who is obliged to take

an oath, will swear falsely, he must come to terms with him in the best way possible, so as not to let him swear falsely.

12. A witness may testify to any remembered fact, however long ago it may have taken place, and may, if necessary, refer to records of his or others to refresh his memory. He is permitted to be reminded of the facts by another person or another witness, but not by one of the litigants, unless the litigant brings the facts to his attention through a third party.

13. A witness who is related to one of the litigants or to one of the judges, or to another witness in the case—even if the relationship be on the wife's side—may in certain cases be declared unfit to testify. In such cases, it is immaterial in whose favor the witness would have testified; the mere fact of relationship excludes him by the decree of the Torah. Therefore if a witness is, or has been so related, he must so inform the judges that they may decide whether he may testify according to law.

CHAPTER III

INJURIES

I. THEFT AND ROBBERY

By divine right we may consider as our own whatever we produce, acquire, or turn into use by the just work and skill of our hands. On the sacredness of the right of property, rests the security of life, home, and the welfare and progress of society. The violation of it is a crime against God and man.

The Divine Law forbids taking unlawful possession of anyone's property directly by theft or robbery, or by misappropriation through deceit or extortion, or by withholding what is due to him, or by taking unfair advantage of his helplessness or ignorance. In brief, it forbids any dishonest dealing with our fellowmen.

LAWS CONCERNING THEFT AND ROBBERY

1. It is forbidden to steal an article even of trivial value from a Jew or a non-Jew.

2. It is also forbidden to steal anything from one's neighbor with the intention of returning it, even if only to annoy or tease him.

3. The robber or thief is ordered by a Divine Command to restore what he has stolen, if it is in its original state and has not been altered, as it is written (Lev. v, 23): "Then he shall restore that which he took by robbery." Restitution in money is not acceptable, unless the stolen goods have been lost or irretrievably altered or disposed of, in which case it is the obligation of the thief or robber to pay back what the goods were worth at the time they were stolen.

If the rightful owner is no longer alive, restitution must be made to his heirs.

4. He who robs the public—for example, a dishonest shopkeeper, or a public official who favors some at the expense of others, or one who takes usury from the public—cannot easily effect repentance by making restitution. To those whom they can identify among their victims they must return what they have taken. The rest of their unlawful gain should be given to supply a public need.

5. It is a serious sin to buy stolen goods from a thief, for in so doing one encourages the thief to steal again.

6. It is forbidden to derive any benefit from stolen property while it remains in the possession of the thief.

7. It is therefore forbidden to accept any benefit from a known thief or robber, or from anyone whose property is presumed to have been acquired by theft or robbery. Even the poor are forbidden to accept charity from such a person.

8. He who takes someone else's coat or hat by mistake—for example, from a cloak-room at a restaurant—should return it unused even if he has left his own there and cannot recover it. If a person receives something which is not his—as, for example, a garment from a laundry or cleaner's—he must return it unused even if one of his own garments has not been returned. If, however, through oversight, the article should remain in his possession a long time, he may presume that the rightful owner has made inquiries about it and has been reimbursed for it by the shopkeeper who was at fault, and therefore he may in good conscience make use of it.

9. It is forbidden to derive any benefit from another's property without his knowledge and consent, even if one is sure that the owner would not object but even be pleased by such use of his property. Therefore one may not take flowers from the garden, even of a friend, without his consent.

10. Next to God and home, our country claims our deepest love and devotion. It offers us shelter and protection, and gives us the freedom and safety we enjoy. Therefore we owe it allegiance; we must respect and obey its law; we must live and strive for its welfare and glory; and, whenever called upon, be ready to defend with

our lives its honor and liberty. The law of the government is law, and in all civil matters supersedes the Jewish law.

II. DAMAGE TO PROPERTY

1. It is strictly forbidden to damage another person's property either directly or indirectly, even with the intention of making reparation, just as it is forbidden to steal or rob, even with the intention of making restitution.

2. He who sustains loss through property damage may not recover his loss at the expense of another. But he may in an effort to forestall damage to his own property take such actions as may be necessary even if it involves injury to others. Thus, if one's property is menaced by flood, one may dam a stream which then might overflow into another's fields; but if the water has already overflowed into one's property, one must not then try to turn its course away at another's expense.

3. It is a serious offense to surrender by deed or word the person or the property of another into the hands of a heathen, whether it be by slander or betrayal; and whoever acts as an informer will have no share in the world to come. It is forbidden to inform even against an evil-doer, who has transgressed the Law, and so cause him to suffer either in his person or in his property. If, however, a man who has been betrayed cannot prove his innocence without informing against the betrayer, he is permitted to do so.

4. A person is forbidden to do anything even on his own premises which may annoy or cause damage to his neighbor. Thus, if his home and his neighbor's home are in a common court, he must avoid placing anything nearer than three hand-breadths distance from his neighbor's wall lest it cause damage to his property. Hence a drain pipe that carries off the water from the roof, must be at least three hand-breadths away from a neighbor's wall.

III. PHYSICAL INJURY

1. An Israelite is forbidden to strike his fellow-man. He who merely raises his hand against another with the intention of striking him, is called *rasha* (wicked). In ancient days, one who smote his

fellow-man was excommunicated and could not be counted as one of a quorum of ten in the performance of sacred duties, until he was released by the *Bet Din* (court) upon his agreement to abide by their decision.

2. It is forbidden to strike a disobedient servant.

3. We are accountable for every injury caused by our carelessness or recklessness. Hence, one must not throw broken glass, or anything else, in any place where it may cause harm to anybody.

4. One must not disturb one's neighbor unnecessarily even by something done in one's own home, as by hammering, when one's neighbor is ill.

5. One must not terrify one's fellowman even in jest, as by a sudden scream or by appearing suddenly before him in the dark.

6. The person who injures his neighbor in any way—whether he has paid for the injury or not—cannot obtain forgiveness in heaven until he has begged forgiveness of the injured party. The latter should be ready to forgive the wrong done him, and not be cruel in refusing his pardon.

7. It is obligatory upon every Jew to do everything in his power to protect his fellowman against injury. If he cannot himself come to the rescue, it is his duty to engage others to do so. If the one who is assisted can afford it, he must repay the money thus expended on his account; but even when it is known that he cannot afford such repayment, one must not shirk one's duty on that account, but save him at one's own expense. If one abstains from doing so, one is guilty of transgressing the Divine Command (Lev. xix, 16): "Neither shalt thou stand idly by the blood of thy neighbor." Should one discover an evil conspiracy against his fellowman and yet fail to warn him, one is likewise guilty. Even if one can save a man only by paying his enemies, one must do so. Our Talmudic sages tell us (Mishnah, Sanhedrin iv, 5): "He who saves one life in Israel, is considered as if he had preserved the whole world."

8. It is a religious duty to remove anything which might prove dangerous to human life or limb. It is not permissible, therefore, to raise a vicious dog or to allow a broken ladder to stand on one's premises.

IV. TALEBEARING–SLANDER–VENGEANCE–BEARING A GRUDGE

1. Man's honor is his most precious possession, and the Divine Law therefore warns us against slander which tends to deprive a man of his good name. The spreading of false or defamatory reports is forbidden by the Law of God.

2. The Divine Command reads (Lev. xix, 16): "Thou shalt not go up and down as a talebearer among thy people." He who indulges in idle gossip of any sort is a talebearer, whether the gossip he spreads is true or false. Even if no one is actually hurt by what he says, the mere fact that he goes from one to another to spread gossip is a violation of the Divine Command, and constitutes the crime of talebearing.

3. The spreading of idle gossip, however, is less grievous a sin than the spreading of slander, which consists in issuing or repeating any report, true or false, with the malicious intent of subjecting anyone to ridicult or contempt. To the slanderer, the words of the Psalmist apply (Ps. xii, 4): "May the Lord cut off all flattering lips, the tongue that speaketh proud things."

4. Not only is it forbidden to speak slanderously of any one, but it is forbidden to listen to the slanderer or in any way to invite another to speak in a slanderous manner about any one. On the contrary, it is our duty to defend any one whose reputation is unjustly attacked, and to judge charitably the motives and actions of everyone. He who listens to slanderous reports is considered more guilty than the person telling them, because he encourages the sinner by listening.

5. If one maliciously invents untruths about a person, then one is guilty not only of the grave sin of slander but of defamation of character as well.

6. How far does the prohibition against slander extend? A man asks of his fellow-man: "Where can I find fire?" And the reply is: "Fire can be found in the house of so-and-so, where there is plenty of meat and fish, and where they are always cooking something." This also constitutes slander.

7. There are certain "shades of slander." For instance, the mere

hint, by silence, that a person is of doubtful character, a shrug or gesture, or a seemingly innocuous phrase, like, "If I were to tell you," or "I'd rather not say"; or a jest that conceals slander with laughter or an innocent smile; or a calculated slanderous "slip of the tongue"; or a question asked in pretended ignorance of the facts. All these are slander.

8. He who takes vengeance upon his fellow man violates the Divine Command (Lev. xix, 18): "Thou shalt not take vengeance." Vengeance may take many forms, but even in its mildest form it is not permissible. Thus, if one refuses to lend something to one's neighbor in retaliation for a similar refusal on his part, one is guilty of the sin of taking vengeance.

9. There is but one good way to take vengeance upon one's enemies: to act in so virtuous and righteous a manner that the excellence of one's qualities and reputation may prove grievous to them. If, however, one stoops to the contemptible acts of revenge, one's enemies rejoice over one's disgrace and shame and the true vengeance is theirs.

10. He who bears a grudge against his fellow man violates a Divine Command, for it is written (Lev. xix, 18): "Thou shalt not bear any grudge against the children of thy people." Bearing a grudge is often the consequence of unsatisfied revenge. For example, in the case cited above, if one accedes to the request of his neighbor who has refused him a similar request, but accedes with ill-grace, reminding his neighbor of the past unpleasantness, he is acting as one who bears a grudge, and violates the Law of God.

V. WRONG DONE BY MEANS OF WORDS

1. Just as it is forbidden to do wrong by means of dishonest buying and selling, so is it forbidden to do so by means of words. The latter crime is even more serious, because no amends can be made and because the wrong is directed not against one's possessions but against one's person. He who cries to God on account of wrong done to him by means of words, is answered immediately.

2. Words spoken with the intention of injuring anyone's feelings are sinful, as, for example, words designed to remind a penitent man

of his former deeds, or idle words that send a man on a fool's errand or raise false hopes or unwarranted fears in him.

3. A word used as an approbrious nickname for the purpose of insulting any one is sinful even if the person to whom the word is applied is unaware of the insult and does not seem to mind it.

4. Words meant to deceive any human being, even an idolater, are sinful. This applies to false-labelling of goods or foods as well as to "harmless" lies. A half truth is also forbidden; for example, if one sells an article, which is imperfect, at its real value, and in saying that it is worth its price, withholds the fact of its imperfection, one is guilty of using words to deceive.

5. Words should not be used in vain. Thus, a person should not invite anyone to dine with him, if he knows in advance that his invitation will not be accepted. Nor should a person make an attempt to present another with a gift, when he is certain that the gift will be refused. Nothing should be spoken with the tongue, that is not also spoken with the heart. Thus all flattery, sham, and hypocrisy are sinful.

PART FOUR

OUR DUTIES TOWARDS OURSELVES

CHAPTER I

PERSONAL BEHAVIOR

The Almighty commanded us (Lev. xix, 1): "Be ye holy, for holy am I, the Lord your God." This concept of holiness is the fundamental principle of all moral duty, which we owe to ourselves. This Divine Command enjoins us to strive for the utmost purity of life, and thus come nearer to our Father in Heaven, the highest ideal of perfection.

The chief duties which the Jewish religion imposes upon us are Fear of God and Love of God. As has been stated before (see p. 25), Love of God is love of obedience; our Love for Him must be translated into action by obedience to His precepts. Fear of God will necessarily result in the prevention of moral turpitude. When we think of Him as the great Lord and Master, in whose hands are our destinies, whose will we all must obey, we stand in awe and reverence before Him. Fear of God will save us from pride. Dread of His displeasure will keep us from doing wrong and from behaving immorally even when not seen by human eyes.

We should refrain from indulgence in intemperate habits of eating and drinking or in our sensual pleasures. Only by remaining within the limits of God's Law is there blessing in our enjoyments. When overstepping these, we sink to the level of the animals. We should, therefore, observe moderation in all things and soberness on all occasions.

God, the Most High and Holy One, is greatest in His condescension. He comes down to man to help him in all his needs. He delights in humbleness. He hates the proud and the haughty and

203

dwells with those who are humble of heart. We must humble ourselves before Him, confess our weakness and sin before Him, and implore His aid in every good endeavor.

We must guard against conceit and overbearing pride, as well as against vanity which endeavors to excite admiration by outward appearance without regard to inner worth. We must strive for simplicity and modesty in all things.

We should also be kind and polite in our relations with out fellow men and omit offensive words. We must keep our friends and companions in high esteem and never betray their trust. Those that are beneath us in station we must treat with fairness and friendliness, those above us with respect.

Anger and passion lead to quarrels, ill-will and hatred, revengefulness and malice, and often end in blood shed. Therefore it becomes our duty to curb our passions and restrain our evil dispositions; and to foster the spirit of amiability and mildness toward every man. We must learn to exercise self-control, and not give way to ill-temper, but show gentleness and patience in the most trying conditions of life.

We must especially guard against envy. This selfish passion causes us to feel pain when we see others in the possession of what we would like to have. We begrudge it to them, and even hate them for it. We must overcome such feelings and learn to look with a friendly eye upon the happiness of others, and be satisfied with our own lot. We must cherish the virtue of contentment coupled with good-will towards others.

We must also shun avarice, that passionate desire for money which makes the hoarding of wealth the sole aim of life and causes man to forget the higher purposes of existence.

Idleness is the chief source of mischief and sin. A noble occupation dignifies man as a useful member of society.

I. DRESS AND DEPORTMENT

1. A person must be modest in all his ways; and he should never say to himself: "Lo, I am alone in my inner chamber and in the dark; who can see me?" For the glory of the Almighty fills the

universe, and darkness and light are alike to Him; and modesty and shame cause a man to humble himself before Him, blessed be His name.

2. We must also show modesty and decorum in our dress and appearance. We should avoid wearing costly garments, for this is inducive to pride; nor should we wear clothes that are too common or soiled, in order that we may not be despised by people. Our clothing should be neat and of moderate price.

3. We are not allowed to walk four cubits or to utter a single word of holiness with uncovered head. Also small boys must be trained to have their heads covered in order that the fear of God may be upon them.

II. MORAL LAWS

1. Men differ widely in temperament: Some are chronically angry, others of a placid disposition; some are too haughty and others too humble; some are sensuous and others ascetic; some are greedy, others generous, still others shiftless and without ambition; some are avaricious and others spendthrifts; some are naturally gay and others melancholy; some cruel, others kind and gentle. There are no two things in nature exactly similar, and there are no two human beings exactly similar.

2. One should in all things adopt the middle course, the happy mean, and not the extreme. One should desire only those things that are actually needed for a healthy existence, and not luxuries. Neither should one spend lavishly and unnecessarily, nor be too tight-fisted, but should spend and give according to one's means. One should neither be too jocular and gay, nor too morose and melancholy; but should strive at all times to be happy, friendly, amiable, satisfied, and pleasant. The person who adopts the middle course in life is considered wise and pleasing in the sight of the Almighty.

3. Pride, even in the slightest degree, is a grave vice. Every Jew must be humble in spirit, and treat every person with fairness, friendliness and respect.

4. Anger is an extreme vice in the eyes of our law-makers. Many

follies and heinous crimes have been committed in moments of anger. A person should therefore make every attempt to control himself even when a rightful cause for anger exists.

5. Silence is a great virtue. One should speak only of matters appertaining to wisdom, learning, and the necessities of life, and even then one should not talk too much about these.

6. It is the nature of man to follow his friends and imitate them in their actions. It is therefore necessary that one always seek the association of the righteous and learn to follow them, so that one's character may be ennobled thereby, and shun the corrupting company of the wicked and the vulgar.

7. Every Jew is bound by the Divine Command to love his neighbor as he loves himself, as it is written (Lev. xix, 18): "And thou shalt love thy neighbor as thyself." He is therefore bound to have the same regard for his neighbor's honor and property as for his own.

8. He who hates his neighbor in his heart violates God's Law, for it is written (Lev. xix, 17): "Thou shalt not hate thy neighbor in thine heart." Thus, when one is wronged, one must not let the injury fester, but seek out the wrongdoer and speak openly to him in an effort to reach a mutual understanding and forgiveness.

9. If one sees another about to commit a sin, it is one's duty to convince him that he is doing wrong, for it is written (Lev. xix, 17): "Thou shalt surely rebuke him." But one must do so privately, and with gentleness, so that he may understand that one is trying to help and instruct him. If, however, one is certain that one's words will be spoken in vain and that the sinner will not heed, one must say nothing; on the contrary, one is actually forbidden to rebuke him.

10. It is a sin to insult anyone, either by word or by deed, especially in public. Our Talmudic sages tell us (Baba Mezia 58b): "He who insults his fellow-man in public, will have no share in the world to come." One must therefore refrain from calling anyone by an insulting name, or from narrating in a person's presence anything of which he feels ashamed.

11. If, having been wronged by another, one neither rebukes,

nor hates, nor bears a grievance against him, but forgives him with one's whole heart, such a one shall be highly rewarded by Heaven.

12. One must be especially careful to speak kindly to orphans, widows, and to all other persons in suffering and distress. One must not vex them even with words, because their souls are downcast.

13. Every person must conduct himself in such a manner as to avoid suspicion; for it is a man's duty to please humanity as well as Heaven.

14. It is a saintly virtue not to accept gifts; for we must have confidence in the Almighty that He will sufficiently supply our needs; as it is written (Prov. xv, 27): "But he that hateth gifts shall live."

15. It is the duty of every person to guard his property against all loss. He who wilfully breaks a utensil, or tears a garment, or destroys articles of food or drink, or throws away needlessly or spoils anything that can be enjoyed by man, is guilty of violating a Divine Command.

III. OATHS AND VOWS

1. One should avoid taking an oath. If, however, one does make a promise under oath, one must abide by it under any circumstance.

2. One should avoid making a vow, even for the purpose of giving charity. If one desires to donate something not yet in one's possession, one should wait until one has it to give, and make no vow concerning it. If one has to make a charitable contribution in common with others in answer to a general appeal, one must expressly state that no vow is being made. Also at *yizkor* (Memorial Service), when it is usual to donate charity, one must clearly say: "I am making no vow." If, however, one is in great distress, one is permitted to make a vow.

3. If a person resolves to fix a certain time for the daily study of the Torah or to observe a certain Divine Command, and he fears that he might relax thereafter in fulfilling it, or if he fears that, incited by passion, he might violate a prohibition or be prevented from observing a Divine Command, he is permitted to fortify his resolution by making a vow or by taking an oath. If, when making

a resolution, he makes a simple declaration, without using the word "vow" or "oath," it is nevertheless considered as a vow and he is obliged to keep it.

4. He who makes a vow in order to improve his conduct, deserves credit. For instance, if a man is a glutton, and he vows to abstain from eating meat for a certain time; or if he is intemperate, and he vows to abstain from drinking wine or any other intoxicating liquor; or if he has become conscious and proud of his good looks, and he vows to become a Nazirite—all of such vows are considered as being made for the worship of the Almighty. Nevertheless, a person should not accustom himself to make vows even of this nature, and should strive to conquer his shortcomings without making any vows.

5. A vow is not effective unless it is made with intention and uttered with the lips. If a vow is made in error, that is, if a person uttered with his lips a vow that he had no intention of making, or if he merely thought of making a vow, but he did not utter it with his lips, it is not considered a vow.

6. There is a procedure by which a vow may be annulled. One must go before three men versed in the Torah at least one of whom must be sufficiently expert in the laws concerning vows to know in what manner, if any, a particular vow may be annulled. If the vow can be annulled, these three men may absolve one from it.

7. The oath or vow of a male child who reaches the age of twelve years and one day, or of a female child of eleven years and one day, is valid and binding if the child understood in whose name the vow or oath has been made.

8. A father may annul certain vows of his daughter until she reaches the age of twelve years and six months, if she is unmarried, and a husband may annul certain vows of his wife, whether or not she is present, by saying three times: "It is invalid," or any other expression which clearly indicates that he abrogates the vow. The annulment must be declared before the end of the day on which the vow was made. Thus, if the vow was made during the night, it may be declared void at any time during the whole of that night

and the following day; if it was made during the day at any time before sunset, it may be declared void only before the stars become visible.

9. The father and the husband can annul only those vows which involve physical deprivations, such as vows made to abstain from bathing, washing, using ornaments or cosmetics or rouge, and the like.

IV. ENCHANTMENT AND SUPERSTITION

1. The Lord our God commanded us in His Law (Lev. xix, 25): "Neither shall ye use enchantment nor observe times." Thus, it is forbidden to believe in personal omens as harbingers of good or ill luck, as this is included in the prohibition against practicing enchantment. There are many who violate this commandment—for example, those who consider it ill-luck for bread to drop from their mouths, or for a cane to fall from their hands, or for their sons to call them from behind, or for a raven to croak at them, or for a deer or a black cat to cross their path, or for a snake to pass on their right or a fox on their left; or those who, on hearing the chirping of a bird, say, "May it mean this and not that," or, "now we know it is good to do this, but it is bad to do that"; and those who, when asked to repay a loan, say: "I pray you, leave me alone now, because it is early in the morning, and I do not wish to begin the day by making payments"; or, "It is the close of the Sabbath, and I do not wish to begin the week by making payments," or, "It is New Moon, and I do not wish to begin the month by making payments." All these are guilty of practicing enchantment and their superstitions must be rejected unconditionally by Jews. Belief in superstition savors of witchcraft and disbelief in God.

2. The prohibition against "observing times," forbids one to believe in horoscopes, to speak of one day or month or year as being lucky or unlucky for certain enterprises.

3. One must not knock on a wooden object and say "knock on wood," in order to ward off the effects of an "ayin hara" (evil eye). This, too, is a foolish superstition and is classed as enchantment.

4. One must not consult a wizard, a witch, or a soothsayer, or gypsies, or fortune-tellers, or cards, or tea-leaves, because in so doing one denies the Almighty's control over human destinies.

5. It goes without saying that no Jew should turn to Christian Science for salvation when suffering pain, believing that this will relieve his suffering. Salvation can come only from our Father in heaven who is the Healer of all diseases. In Him alone must we put our trust even when we consult a physician, and if we look for help from any other being or power, we are guilty of the very serious sin of idol-worship. One cannot believe in Christian Science and be really a Jew at the same time.

V. PHYSICAL WELL-BEING

1. It is the command of the Almighty that one must keep one's body healthy and strong. One should therefore shun anything which tends to injure the body, and strive to acquire habits that help develop the body to its full vigor.

2. One should therefore adopt the happy mean, eating neither too little nor too much. Excessive eating can be as harmful as malnutrition.

3. When a person is young his digestive system is strong; therefore he is in greater need of regular meals than the middle-aged person. The aged man, because of his weakness, requires light food, little in quantity and rich in quality to sustain his strength.

4. On hot days the digestive system is weak, therefore less food should be consumed than on cool days. And the medical scientists have suggested that in the summer a person should eat only two-thirds of the amount he eats in the winter.

5. It is a known rule in medical science that before eating, a person should take some exercise, by walking or by working, until the body becomes warm. While eating, he should be seated or recline on his left side; and after the meal, he should not move about too much, so that the food may not reach the stomach before it is well digested and cause him harm, but he should walk a little and then rest.

6. A person should eat only when he has a natural desire for

food, and not an unnatural one. A natural desire for food is called "hunger," and occurs when the stomach is empty; an unnatural desire is a longing for a particular kind of food, and is called "appetite." In general, a healthy, strong person should eat twice a day, and the feeble and the aged should eat little at a time several times during the day, because excessive eating weakens the stomach. It is best to omit one meal during the weak, in order that the stomach may have a rest from its work and its digestive power may thus be strengthened.

7. It is advisable that every person should become accustomed to have breakfast in the morning.

8. Since the digestive process begins with the grinding of the food with the teeth and by mixing it with the juice of the saliva, therefore one should not swallow any food without masticating it well, so as not to overtax the stomach.

9. Water is the natural drink for a person and is healthful for his body. If it is clean and pure, it is helpful in that it preserves the moisture of the body and hastens the expulsion of worthless matter. One should select cool water for drinking, because it satisfies the thirst and helps the digestion more than water which is not cold. But the water should not be too cold, because it quenches the natural warmth of the body; especially when a man is tired and weary, he should be very careful not to drink very cold water.

10. A person should eat only when he is hungry, and drink when he is thirsty, and should not neglect the call of nature even for one moment.

11. Weariness in a moderate degree is good for the physical health, but weariness to an excess, as well as inactivity, are injurious to the body. In the hot season, a little exercise will suffice, but in the cold season, more is required. A fat person needs more exercise than a lean one.

12. He who desires to preserve his health, must learn about his psychological responses and control them; joy, worry, anger, and fright are psychological actions. A wise man must always be satisfied with his portion during the time of his vain existence and should not grieve over a world that does not belong to him. He

should not look for superfluities, and he should be in good spirits and joyous to a moderate extent at all times.

13. A person should endeavor to dwell where the air is pure and clear, on elevated ground, and in a house of ample proportions.

14. The air best for the physical well-being is that of even temperature, neither too hot nor too cold. Therefore precautions should be taken not to heat the house too much in the winter time as many senseless people do, because excessive heat occasions many illnesses. A house should be heated just enough so that the cold may not be felt.

VI. CRUELTY TO ANIMALS

There is a certain sacredness attached to the life of every creature, and it must therefore be treated with regard.

While we are permitted by Divine Law to kill an animal for the nourishment of our body, we are by no means allowed to take the life of an animal for mere sport or pleasure in the shedding of its blood, nor to torment it. No life, not even of the lowliest creature, should be wantonly destroyed and wasted, for God alone is the Author of life.

God entrusted the domestic animals into our care, and we should not abuse them nor treat them cruelly. The Talmud tells us (Berakot 40a) that we must first feed our domestic animals before we sit down to enjoy our own meals.

LAWS CONCERNING CRUELTY TO ANIMALS

1. The Law of God forbids the infliction of needless pain upon any living creature. On the contrary, it is our duty to relieve any living creature of pain, whether it is ownerless or not.

2. When horses drawing a cart come to a rough road or to a steep hill, so that they cannot draw the cart without help, it is a religious duty to help them, even when they belong to a non-Jew lest the owner smite them to force them to draw more than their strength permits.

3. It is forbidden to tie the legs of a beast or the wings of fowl in such manner as to inflict pain.

4. It is also forbidden to set a bird on eggs that are not of her species, for this is cruelty to animals.

VII. UNLOADING AND RELOADING

1. If we meet someone on the road with his beast of burden lying beneath its load, it is our duty to assist him in unloading the animal, as the Lord God commanded us (Ex. xxiii, 5): "Thou shalt surely help with him." After we have helped unload the animal, we must not depart, leaving our neighbor in distress, but we must help replace the load upon the animal, as it is written (Deut. xxii, 4): "Thou shalt surely help him to lift them up again."

2. If after all this, the beast should fall again, we are obliged to repeat our assistance even if it be a hundred times. For this reason, we must accompany him the distance of a parasang, as he might need our help again, unless he expressly tells us that he no longer needs us.

3. We must unload the animal gratuitously, but we are not obliged to load without compensation; we should also be paid for accompanying him.

4. If a company travel together in vehicles, and one of the vehicles breaks down so that it is necessary to delay a little in order to repair the damage, the rest of the company are not permitted to abandon him with his broken vehicle, unless the delay be prolonged beyond a reasonable time.

PART FIVE

OUR DUTIES TOWARDS OUR FAMILIES

CHAPTER I

FAMILY LIFE

I. MARRIAGE

1. It is the duty of every man to take unto himself a wife and it is the express command of the Almighty that he marry not a daughter of the heathen peoples (Deut. vii, 3): "Neither shalt thou make marriage with them: thy daughter thou shalt not give unto his son, nor his daughter shalt thou take unto thy son." Intermarriage was forbidden lest it introduce into the life of the Jew ideals and cultures directly opposed to the teachings of God.

2. A man should ever be careful to treat his wife with respect, for it is only for the wife's sake that a man's house is blessed with wealth; and thus were our Talmudic sages wont to say (Baba Mezia 59a): "Treat your wives honorably in order that you may be blessed with wealth."

3. It is customary for a groom and a bride to fast on their wedding day, because their sins are atoned on that day, and in the "Shemoneh esreh" (silent prayer) of the "Minhah" (afternoon) service, they include "Anenu" (O answer us), the same as on any other fast day.

4. It is a religious duty to do everything in our power to make the groom and the bride happy.

II. CIRCUMCISION

1. The Almighty concluded a covenant with Abraham and his descendants, appointing them as keepers and propagators of his truth and justice for all generations. As a sign of this covenant, the

rite of circumcision was instituted by which each male child in Israel is consecrated to the service of the God of Abraham.

2. The Lord God commanded us that every father must circumcise his son, or appoint someone else to circumcise him. Immediately after the circumcision, the father pronounces the following benediction: "Blessed art Thou, O Lord our God, King of the universe, who hath sanctified us by His commandments and hath commanded us to bring him into the covenant of our father Abraham." The father should be particular in choosing a *mohel* (circumciser) and a *sandek* (god-father) who should be the best and most righteous men it is possible to select.

3. All those present at the ceremony of circumcision remain standing, excepting the *sandek*, who holds the baby while seated. When the father concludes the benediction, those assembled say: "Just as he has been initiated into the covenant, so may he be initiated into the study of the Torah, to his nuptial canopy, and to the performance of good deeds."

4. It is essential that the *mohel* should be versed in the laws regarding circumcision, and he should examine the infant to ascertain if he is healthy.

5. Extreme care should be taken not to circumcise an infant who is ailing, as the fulfillment of all Divine Ordinances must be postponed if there is danger to human life. Moreover, the circumcision can be performed later than the time prescribed by law, but the life of a human being once sacrificed can never be restored. If a circumcision has been postponed, it cannot be performed on the Sabbath or on a Festival.

6. The circumcision should take place on the eighth day of the infant's birth, even if it occurs on the Sabbath or a Festival.

7. If an infant is born at twilight, or close to it, then the learned should be consulted as to the proper time for the circumcision.

8. It is customary to make a feast on the day of the circumcision. He who can afford to make a feast but economizes and serves only coffee and sweets, is not doing the proper thing. It is customary also to make a feast consisting of fruits and beverages on the Friday

evening preceding the day of circumcision; and this, too, is considered as a feast in honor of the performance of a precept.

III. PIDEYON HABBEN (REDEMPTION OF THE FIRST-BORN)

By the Law of God (Num. xviii, 15–18), all first-born males of men as well as of animals, belonged to God. The first-born males were to devote themselves to the active service of God, while the first-born *kosher* animals were to be given to the priest. The first-born asses were redeemed or repurchased by a lamb. The first-born sons may formally be redeemed or repurchased from the *Kohen* (priest) by paying five *shekels*—approximately three dollars. In this religious ceremony of redemption, known as "Pideyon habben" (redemption of the first-born), a *Kohen*, a descendant of the priestly family of Aaron, redeems the child at the father's request, by receiving five *shekels* as redemption money. This ceremony is generally accompanied by an elaborate feast to which at least ten male-adult persons are invited.

LAWS CONCERNING THE PIDEYON HABBEN

1. The father must redeem his son, who is the mother's first-born, from the *Kohen* by giving him either cash or something else of the value of five *shekels*.

2. If the father has told one *Kohen* that he would redeem the son from him, he is forbidden to retract; nevertheless, if he does retract and redeems him from another *Kohen*, the redemption is valid.

3. The first-born should not be redeemed before he is fully thirty days old, and on the thirty-first day he is redeemed immediately so as not to delay the performance of a precept. The redemption may not take place on the Sababth, or on a Festivval, or on a fast day, but it may take place on the Intermediate Days of a Festival. It is customary to make the redemption in the daytime. Nevertheless, if the thirty-first day has passed and the infant has not been redeemed, or if that day falls on a Sabbath, or on a Festival, or a fast

day, the redemption should take place immediately on the following night and should not be delayed until the following day.

4. Only the first-born of the mother must be redeemed but not of the father. If a man who has never before been married, marries a woman who has had children by another husband, their son is not to be redeemed.

5. Again, the child must be actually the first-born. If the mother has given birth to a daughter before the birth of the son, he requires no redemption.

6. The ceremony of redemption should take place in the manner provided for in the Prayer Books.

7. If the father is away, in another town or place, he may redeem his son from a *Kohen* wherever he is, by saying to the *Kohen*: "I have a first-born son to redeem," whereupon the *Kohen* inquires: "What wouldst thou rather," etc.

8. To comply with the law, the father should choose a poor *Kohen* who is learned in the Law and God-fearing. Both he and the *Kohen* should resolve that the redemption money should not be returned; but the father may give the redemption money to the *Kohen* in the nature of a temporary gift with the condition that it be returned to him.

9. If for any reason a first-born son has not been redeemed, he is obliged to redeem himself when he is grown up, at which time he should say the benediction: "Who hath sanctified us by His commandments, and hath commanded us concerning the redemption of the first-born," and also the benediction "Sheheheyanu" (who hath kept us in life).

10. Priests and Levites are exempt from the redemption of their first-born sons. Even the daughters of a priest (Kohen) or Levite who are married to an Israelite are exempt from redeeming their first-born sons.

IV. TRAINING CHILDREN

Just as children have duties towards their parents, so parents have duties also towards their children. They are obliged to provide for their physical needs and offer them shelter and protection as long as they are unable to take care of themselves. They are enjoined to educate them and develop all their intellectual and mental faculties; thereby making good, honest, wise and useful members of society. They must bring them up by precept and example, in the fear of God, in the knowledge of God's laws, and with love for their fellow man.

Parents owe it to their children to lead a virtuous and religious life and they should give them an example of modesty and simplicity in their home life; of rectitude, kindness and fairness in their social relations, and of humble devotion and piety in their relation to God. They must refrain from any act that lessens their honor, and from conduct that is not honorable.

Children of wicked parents inherit their bad name and evil inclinations and are easily influenced by their bad example. Thus an evil-doer brings punishment upon his children and children's children. On the other hand, the piety and good deeds of parents will work blessings upon the children for many generations to come. God will remember their merits, and their memory will serve as a power for good even to an undeserving posterity, so that the seeds of virtue shall bear fruit.

LAWS CONCERNING TRAINING OF CHILDREN

1. It is the duty of every father to train his children in the fulfillment of the commandments of God. Each child should be educated in these precepts in accordance with his or her intelligence. Children should be guarded against committing any forbidden act. The father should take special care in training his children to tell the truth at all times, and to shun swearing.

2. The time for training a child in the performance of the positive commandments depends upon the ability and the understanding of each child. Thus, as soon as the child understands the significance of the Sabbath, it becomes the child's duty to hear the *kiddush* and the *habdalah*. The time to train a child to observe the negative commandments, is when he or she can be expected to understand a simple prohibition. It is proper to train a child to respond "Amen" at the synagogue. The children should be trained, as early as pos-

sible, to be respectful in the synagogue; but it is best not to take very young children there who may tend to run about and cause confusion.

3. It is forbidden to give a child, even under the age of nine, to carry anything on the Sabbath, even for the purpose of fulfilling a precept, such as taking a prayer book to the synagogue, or the like.

4. A parent should not threaten a child with future punishment. A child who misbehaves should be either punished immediately, or forgiven, or the fault should be ignored.

5. Every father is duty bound to teach the Torah to his son, as it is said (Deut. xi, 19): "And ye shall teach them to your children to speak of them." And he is even obliged to teach his grandchildren, for it is written (Deut. iv, 9): "And thou shalt make them known to thy children's children."

6. A child, upon first beginning to talk, should be taught to recite the verse: "The Torah Moses had commanded us," etc., and, "Hear, O Israel, the Lord our God, the Lord is one."

V. BAR MITZVAH

1. The thirteenth birthday of a Jewish boy is known as "Bar Mitzvah Day." On this day of confirmation, the boy assumes the obligation of observing all the commandments incumbent upon all Jews. From that day on, the boy is considered a full-fledged member of the Jewish community. He is qualified to participate as one of ten male adults in a *minyan*, the minimum congregational quorum required for holding communal or synagogue worship. (See p. 22.)

2. When a boy becomes *Bar Mitzvah*, he is called up to say the benediction over the reading of the Torah for the first time. When he concludes the second benediction, the father should say: "Barukh sheptarany meansho shelazah" (Blessed be He who released me from the responsibility of this child). It is a religious duty for the father to prepare a feast in honor of the day upon which his son becomes *Bar Mitzvah*.

VI. HONORING ONE'S FATHER AND MOTHER

Next to God, our parents have the highest claim to our love and gratitude. They are our greatest benefactors and truest friends on earth. We are what they have made us, for they have given us life, watched over our helpless infancy, provided for our physical needs, and guided our intellectual and moral development. Thus the parents are to the child in the place of God. Messengers of His benign providence, they manifest that divine love which delights in doing good without regard to recognition. He who honors his parents honors God in whose place they stand, and he who dishonors them dishonors God also. The Talmud (Kiddushin 30b) says: "Three beings share in man's life: The father, the mother, and God. If you honor and reverence father and mother—God says—you also honor Me. If you displease and cause them grief, you also grieve Me."

As our parents advance in years and grow feeble and helpless, it becomes our duty to afford them every possible assistance and comfort in return for what they have done for us in former days. We must bear with their weaknesses and do all we can to render their old age peaceful and pleasant. If we render old age a period of blessing for our parents, our children will also honor us when we shall have grown old.

LAWS CONCERNING HONORING PARENTS

1. We must be very particular in fulfilling the Divine Command that we must honor and fear our fathers and mothers. According to the Talmudic sages (Kiddushin 30b), the fifth of the Ten Commandments: "Honor thy father and thy mother, that thy days may be long upon the land which the Lord thy God giveth thee," requires that we honor and fear them even as much as we must honor and fear the Almighty. The Almighty is anxious, so to speak, that we honor our parents, because our parents and He share in man's creation, the parents provide the material, and the Almighty the spiritual part of the human being.

2. One shows fear of parents in many ways: for example, one

should not occupy the seats generally occupied by them, even when they are not present; one should neither contradict them nor approve of what they say, as if to imply equality.

3. One shows honor to one's parents by cheerfully providing them with food, clothing and all else that they need. Children who provide their parents with the finest luxuries, but do so with ill grace, incur Divine punishment.

4. Children should arouse their parents from their sleep only in the interests of the parent and never for their own sake or advantage. Thus it is the duty of children to arouse their father for the purpose of attending services at the synagogue or for the performance of any religious duty, as all are equally bound to honor the Almighty.

5. Children should protect their parents. If a child has done something at his mother's bidding of which the father later seems to disapprove; and if the father should ask in anger, "Who told you to do this?", the child should rather incur the father's anger than implicate the mother by telling the truth.

6. Children must rise and remain standing in the presence of their father and their mother.

7. Parents must be honored even after their death.

8. When a child sees his father transgress a Divine Law, he must not say to him: "You have transgressed the command of the Law," but should rather ask in the form of a question: "Father, is it not written thus and thus in the Torah?" so that the father may correct himself without being put to shame.

9. Children must not hearken to their parents when they tell them to transgress a Divine Law, because both children and parents are equally obliged to honor the Almighty and fear Him.

10. It is the duty of both men and women to honor their parents.

11. If children put their father or mother to shame, even if only by a look or by a word, they are included among those whom the Almighty has cursed, as it is written in the Holy Scriptures (Deut. xxvii, 16): "Cursed be he who lightly esteems his father or his mother."

12. Parents are forbidden to place an unbearable yoke upon their

children, and they must not be too exacting with them in matters relating to the honor due them, so that their children may not stumble into sin. The parents are obliged rather to overlook their children's shortcomings and to forgive them without reservation.

13. Parents are forbidden to chastise their grown-up children. The word "grown-up" in this regard refers not to age but to maturity. If there is reason to believe that a child will resent chastisement, and express that resentment either by word of mouth or by deed, it is absolutely forbidden to chastise the child. Instead, the child must be reasoned with. Parents who beat their grown-up children deserve to be excommunicated, because they transgress the Divine Command (Lev. xix, 14): "Thou shalt not put a stumbling block before the blind," for they are apt to bring sin and punishment upon their children.

14. Children must honor and respect their step-mother during their father's life-time, and their step-father during their mother's life-time. And it is highly proper that children honor their step-mother and their step-father even after the death of their own parents.

15. One is bound to honor one's elder brother, even if he be one's half-brother. One must also honor one's grandparents and one's father-in-law and mother-in-law.

16. Children best honor their parents by honorable conduct, so that the parents may feel that they have bestowed their kindness upon good and worthy children. Therefore children who truly desire to honor their father and mother, should devote their time to the study of the Torah and do the biddings of our Lord God, by performing good deeds. Children who do not walk in the right path, bring a reproach and disgrace upon their parents. Therefore, parents who are desirous of being compassionate with their children, should themselves be good, so that their children may learn from them and act likewise. Thereby the parents bring honor upon themselves through their children.

CHAPTER II

MOURNING

The Jewish religion conceives of life on earth merely as a preparatory period for the life to come in the hereafter. The human lifetime is vain unless it is utilized for the purpose of accumulating good deeds, the reward for which will be reaped in the world to come. In the words of our great Sages (Mishnah, Abot iv, 21): "This world is like an antechamber of the world to come; prepare thyself in the antechamber that thou mayest be admitted into the reception hall."

According to Judaism, life is no mere empty struggle or dream that ends with death. Human beings do not exist and perish like cattle. They have a soul, a very portion of the throne of the Almighty, which was sent down from heaven to dwell in the body that it may perform the will of the Almighty, and then receive its reward in the world of everlasting bliss.

Death, as the Jew conceives of it, does not terminate life. Only the material body returns to dust, but the soul, which is a portion from God, returns to heaven when it rids itself of the body. For the soul, life begins anew, after the body's death, in the world to come. There people receive their rewards and punishments in accordance with their merits and deeds during the body's span of life on earth.

Life is therefore a sacred thing, and must not be spent merely in bodily pleasures, but must be devoted chiefly to carrying out the will of the Almighty. Death, according to this conception, is really the ultimate goal of life, when the soul, freed from its material encasement, becomes pure and holy, soaring to its origin in the high heavens. Death is therefore more sacred than life.

In recognition of the sacredness of life, the Jew must perform every deed in sanctity. Every act must be done for the sake of Him who gave us life. To show that death is the holy goal of a sacred life, the Jew, from time immemorial, laid down many rules of law concerning the dying person, the treatment of the dead, and mourning. It is the sacred duty of every Jew to become acquainted with these laws.

I. VISITING THE SICK

1. It is the duty of every Jew to help provide a cure for the sick. If a sick man is poor and helpless, we must help to secure him all necessities.

2. It is our duty to visit a sick person as often as possible. Extreme care must be taken not to be troublesome to the invalid.

3. The essential reason for the religious duty of visiting one who is ill is to ascertain his needs, pray for him, and cheer him.

4. When talking to a sick person, judgment and tact must be used, so as not to discourage him nor yet give him false hope of a speedy recovery, for, if the invalid is given false hope, he will abstain from praying for mercy from Heaven. If he is critically ill, he should be advised to concern himself with his affairs, and state whether he is indebted to others, or others to him. He should be made to understand that to divulge such information cannot hasten his death or delay his recovery.

5. Our sages tell us that the Almighty takes no delight in a person who bequeathes all his property to strangers, even though it be for charity. It is sinful to disinherit one's natural heirs however badly they have behaved. One may not bequeath a larger portion to one child than to another, although one child may seem more worthy. The pious must refuse to witness a will, or to give counsel in making a will in which the natural heirs are disinherited.

6. When a person is gravely sick, he should be advised to make confession. He should be told tactfully: "Fear not that evil will ensue because of your confession, for many are they who have confessed and become well again, and there have also been many who neglected to confess and died. On the contrary, as a reward for making confession, a cure may be granted and your life prolonged. Moreover, all those who make confession of their sins have a share in the world to come." If the invalid is unable to confess by

word of mouth, he should make a mental confession; and if he is able to speak but little, he should say this very short confession: "May my death be an atonement for all my sins." The invalid should also be reminded to ask the pardon of all those whom he has wronged during his life-time.

7. A brief form of confession is as follows:

"I acknowledge unto Thee, O Lord, my God and God of my fathers, that both my cure and death depend on Thy will. May it be Thy will to heal me. Yet if Thou hast decreed that I should die of this disease, may my death expiate all my sins, iniquities, and transgressions which I have committed before Thee. Grant me a portion in Gan Eden, which is reserved for the righteous."

If the invalid desires to make a lengthy confession, he may adopt the one recited on the Day of Atonement.

II. WHEN A PERSON IS DYING

1. Life is the gift of the Almighty, and Only He, the Giver of Life, can take His gift back and deprive a living being of life. Nothing should therefore be done to accelerate death. For this reason, we are forbidden to touch or move the body of a dying person, lest his death he hastened. Even if the patient is suffering a painful and slow death, and is causing great suffering to his loved ones, it is nevertheless forbidden to hasten death even in an indirect manner.

2. From the moment a person is in the grip of death, he must not be left alone to die. Those present at the time of the soul's departure should be extremely careful not to engage in idle or frivolous conversation.

3. It is forbidden to partake of any food in the room where the deceased lies, unless a partition is erected. It is likewise forbidden to pronounce any benediction there.

4. The corpse should not be handled on the Sabbath, even if it is for the purpose of performing some religious duty.

III. THE RENDING OF THE GARMENTS

1. It is an established custom in Israel to make a rent in one's garments for the loss of one's next of kin for whom one is required

to observe mourning. (See "Seven Days of Mourning" page 234.) This ceremony must be performed while standing; if it is performed while the mourner is seated, the obligation is not fulfilled, and it must be repeated in the proper fashion. It is best to tear the clothes when one's sorrow is still most intense before the coffin is closed.

2. The mode of rending the garments for one's father or mother, differs in many respects from the mode obtaining for other relatives. For the latter only a rent of the size of a hand-breadth should be made in the external garment only, but for a father or a mother all garments must be rent, with the exception of the shirt and the overcoat.

3. According to custom, the rent should be made on the right side of the garment for all relatives, except for a father or a mother which is made on the left side of the garment. Nevertheless, an error in this regard does not invalidate the fulfillment of the duty.

4. For all relatives one may either rend the garment with one's hand or with an instrument, but for one's father or mother it must be done by hand. It is customary for one of the brotherhood to cut the garment slightly with a knife, whereupon the mourner takes hold of the garment where it is cut and rends it. Those present must see to it that the rent be made lengthwise and not crosswise.

5. If the deceased is one's father or mother, one must make a rent every time one changes one's garments during the seven days of mourning, but one need not do so for any other relative.

6. Every mourner should honor the Sabbath by wearing clothes other than those in which a rent was made, but not those especially set aside for the Sabbath. If the mourner has no other weekday clothes than those that contain the sign of mourning, the mourner must turn the rent inside, so that it is invisible, because public mourning is forbidden on the Sabbath.

7. Unless the deceased is one's father or mother, the rent may be basted together after the seven days of mourning, and completely sewed up after thirty days. In the case of mourning for a father or a mother, the rent may be basted after thirty days and never completely sewed up.

8. If one does not learn of a relative's death until after thirty days,

one need not rend one's garments, but if it is the death of one's father or mother one must rend the garments one is wearing at the time but not the garments which one may change thereafter.

9. The intervention of a Festival cancels all rules of mourning to be observed during the first thirty days even as regards the rending of the garments. Therefore, one mourning the loss of a relative may completely sew up the rent after the *Minhah* (afternoon) service on the day before the Festival, and baste the rent together when mourning the loss of a father or a mother.

IV. AN ONAN

1. Any person who loses by death one of his next of kin for whom he is bound to observe mourning (see p. 234), is termed *onan* from the time of the death until after the interment. An *onan* should not eat in the room where the dead is lying, nor eat an elaborate meal, nor eat meat nor drink wine.

2. An *onan* is exempt from observing all precepts, because of the honor due the dead. However, he must observe all the prohibitory laws. If he desires to partake of bread, he must wash his hands but without saying the benediction; nor should he say the "Hamotzi" (who bringeth forth bread), nor Grace after meals.

3. Even if the *onan* happens to be in another city, he must observe all rules relating to an *onan*, unless there are also some relatives in the place where the dead lies, who are required to observe the rules of mourning.

4. As a sign of mourning, the mourner should not remove his shoes before the interment takes place. He is permitted to leave the house if need be to make provisions for the funeral.

5. An *onan* is not permitted to sit on a chair, sleep in a bed, bathe, anoint himself with oil, participate in joyous celebrations, greet friends, cut the hair, study the Torah, or do any manner of work for profit.

6. If death occurs on the Sabbath, on which the law prohibits burying the dead, the mourner is not subject to the laws relating to an *onan*, and he must observe all precepts, but he is not allowed to study the Torah. If the dead be his father or his mother, he may

say the *kaddish* if there are no other mourners. If there are other mourners, he should not say the *kaddish* before the burial.

7. If death occurs on the Sabbath towards evening, the mourner should read the "Shema" without its benedictions. He should not pray the "Maarib" (evening service), nor perform the *habdalah* ceremony, and he is permitted to eat without saying the *habdalah*. After the interment, he is permitted to say the *habdalah* over a cup of wine, without the benedictions over the light and the spices, until Tuesday.

8. One who becomes an *onan* at the termination of a Festival, may recite the *habdalah* after the interment only if it occurs on the day after the Festival, as the proper time for the *habdalah* ceremony after a Festival is only until the end of the day following the Festival.

9. On the eve of the fourteenth day of the month of Nisan, an *onan* should employ an agent to make the search for unleavened bread, but he himself should recite the formula, "Kal hamira" (all leaven).

V. THE SHROUDS AND PURIFICATION OF THE BODY

1. A human being, made in the image of God, deserves respect even when the body is dead. The corpse must be prepared for burial in accordance with the time-honored customs of the Jewish people. Therefore the men who prepare the shrouds and wash the body of a dead person must be familiar with these laws and customs. They must follow the rules as laid down by our Sages of old as contained in the Jewish Code of Law.

VI. ACCOMPANYING THE DEAD; THE FUNERAL

1. It is not allowed to let the body of the dead remain over night, unless it be in honor of the dead, as to procure a coffin, shrouds, or to await the arrival of relatives.

2. As regards all relatives, it is praiseworthy to bring them to their eternal rest as soon as possible, but not so with one's parents.

3. It is the duty of every man and woman to accompany the dead

during the funeral procession for a distance of at least four cubits (about six feet). One who sees a coffin pass by and fails to join the procession is likened to the one who mocks and sneers at the poor, and deserves to be excommunicated.

4. Our Sages of old tell us (Talmud, Shabbat 105b; Zohar, Ahare) that the Holy One, blessed be He, counts the tears shed for the death of a virtuous man, and He stores them up in His treasury; and that the merit of shedding such tears is so great that the children of the person who sheds them will not die when young.

5. Neither burial services nor the *kaddish* are recited at the cemetery at night.

6. Burial services should not be said for a deceased infant less than thirty days old.

VII. SUICIDE AND THE WICKED

1. There is none more wicked than the one who has committed suicide, as it is written (Gen. ix, 5): "And surely your blood of your lives will I require." For the sake of one individual was the world created, to indicate that he who destroys one's soul is considered as though he had destroyed the whole world. Therefore one should neither rend one's garments, nor mourn, nor should a eulogy be pronounced for one who has committed suicide. But, for the sake of his relatives, such a one should be dressed in shrouds, properly washed and buried.

2. Without proof to the contrary, a man is not presumed to be wicked. If therefore a man is discovered choked to death, or hanging, the act of killing should, as far as possible, be considered as murder and not as suicide.

3. If a minor has committed suicide, it is considered that he had done the deed unwittingly. If an adult has committed suicide either through madness or through fear of suffering terrible torture, as was the case with King Saul who feared the inhuman cruelty of the Philistines, he should likewise be treated as though he had died a natural death.

4. All rules concerning an *onan* and mourning should not be observed for the death of apostates and informers.

5. Relatives must observe all rules of mourning for one who has been executed either in accordance with the law of the land or otherwise, even if he were an apostate. For death caused by the hand of man acts as an atonement for sins.

VIII. DEFILEMENT OF A KOHEN (PRIEST)

1. The *Kohen* (Priest) who had been chosen by the Almighty to attend to the Holy Temple and to sacrifice offerings, was enjoined to be holy, and to shun contact with anything that defiles the body. He was therefore commanded by the Law of God not to defile himself by coming in contact with a dead body.

2. A *Kohen* must not enter a house where a dead body is found, even if the house is very large. He is even forbidden to enter a house where a person is dying, as death may occur at any moment and thus cause his defilement.

3. A *Kohen* is forbidden to approach within four cubits of a corpse or a grave. This is only true when the body lies in its permanent place, but if it lies there only temporarily, as during the funeral procession or funeral services, he need keep away only a distance of four hand-breadths.

4. It is a *Kohen's* religious duty to defile himself upon the death of the following relatives: his wife to whom he is legally married, his father or mother, his son or daughter, and his brother or unmarried sister if they are the children of his father. He must not defile himself for an infant who has lived less than thirty days. On the Sabbath, when burial is forbidden, the *Kohen* must not defile himself even for these, even if it is for the purpose of guarding the body. But concerning all things necessary for burial, he is in duty bound to defile himself. Even if all the burial preparations were made by the holy brotherhood and he himself does not attend to them at all, he is permitted to remain in the room, for it may be necessary for him to obtain something that may be needed. He may defile himself by contact with these dead relatives only until the grave is closed, but not thereafter.

5. A *Kohen* may not defile himself for any of the relatives for whom he need not observe mourning. (See following Section.)

6. A *Kohen* should not defile himself by contact with a dead relative who lost a limb or was killed.

IX. SHIBEAH (*SEVEN DAYS OF MOURNING*)

1. Our sages of old have divided the period of mourning, in accordance with the Biblical Law, into three stages of varying intensity. The first period, known as *Shibeah* (seven), refers to the first seven days of mourning. The laws pertaining to these seven days are most strict. The second period, known as *Sheloshim* (thirty), relates to the first thirty days after a death. The third period embraces the twelve months from the time a death occurs.

The Jewish law distinguishes between mourning to be observed for one's parent and that to be observed for all other next of kin. In the former case, the laws and regulations of mourning are much more severe.

2. One is obliged to observe the rite of mourning on the death of the following next of kin: one's father; mother; son; daughter; brother, or sister, whether from father's side or mother's side; wife or husband.

3. For the death of a child that did not live fully thirty days, the rite of mourning need not be observed.

4. The period of mourning begins as soon as the dead is buried and the grave is filled with earth.

5. During one's seven days of mourning, one may not perform any work, bathe, anoint oneself, massage, wear leather footwear, have sexual intercourse, study the Torah, offer greetings, wear freshly washed garments, cut the hair, or be present at any festivity. On the first day, the mourner is also forbidden to put on the *tephilin.*

6. During the first three days of mourning, a mourner should not perform any work, even if he is a poor man who relies on charity. But from the fourth day on, if the mourner is a poor man and has nothing to eat, he may work privately at home. Our sages say: "May poverty overtake the mourner's neighbors who force him to do work," for it is their duty to provide for the poor, especially during the days of mourning.

7. Just as the mourner is forbidden to do work during the seven

days of mourning, so is he forbidden to transact business. If, however, he may sustain a great loss by not working or doing business, he should consult a competent Rabbi.

8. He is allowed to send someone to collect a debt, if he fears that he will be unable to collect it thereafter.

9. Such writing as is allowable during *Hol Hammoed* (Intermediate Days of a Festival) is also permissible to a mourner (see p. 119), if it cannot be done through another.

10. Domestic occupations are not included in the work which a mourner may not perform. Thus a woman in mourning is allowed to bake, cook, and to attend to all her necessary domestic duties.

11. A mourner may wash his hands and face and bathe his feet only in cold water, but he is not allowed to bathe his whole body during the first thirty days.

12. A person of delicate constitution who would suffer in health by abstaining from bathing, is permitted to bathe.

13. Anointing and massaging are permissible for medicinal or hygienic purposes only.

14. Shoes made of leather may not be worn by a mourner during the seven days.

15. A woman within thirty days of her confinement, and a person who is suffering from sore feet are permitted to wear leather shoes during the first seven days of mourning.

16. A mourner may not be called up to the reading of the Torah during the seven days, even if he is the only *Kohen* in the synagogue.

17. During the first three days of mourning, the mourner should neither greet nor be greeted by any one. If others, through ignorance, offer a greeting, the mourner is not allowed to respond to their greetings but should inform them that he is a mourner. After the third day and until the seventh, the mourner must not greet others, but may respond to the uncalled for greetings of others.

18. During the seven days of mourning, the mourner is not allowed to sit on a chair or upon cushions or pillows. An invalid or an old man is permitted to put a small cushion on the prescribed low bench or stool. One is not compelled to sit, but may walk about or stand, but must be seated when others offer condolences.

19. The wearing of freshly washed garments, even a shirt, is

forbidden during the seven days, even if it is in honor of the Sabbath.

20. A mourner may change his soiled clothes even on a weekday during the seven days, if the fresh clothes have already been worn by some one else.

21. A mourner is not permitted to laugh or rejoice during the seven days of mourning.

22. During the seven days of mourning, a mourner must not leave his house except on matters of great urgency.

23. The mourner may not leave his house to go to the synagogue, except on the Sabbath. But if it is impossible for him to gather ten male adults in his house to make up a quorum, and there is a *Minyan* (quorum) in his neighborhood, he may go there to pray.

X. THIRTY DAYS AND TWELVE MONTHS

1. During one's thirty days of mourning, one is forbidden to wear Sabbath clothes even on the Sabbath. One is forbidden, of course, to put on new clothes. One who mourns for a parent is forbidden, according to custom, to put on new clothes during the entire year. If, however, one is compelled to buy new clothes, one should not put them on until another has first worn them for two or three days.

2. A mourner is not allowed to cut his hair or shave during the thirty days of mourning. If he mourns for a parent, he is not permitted to cut his hair the entire twelve months, unless his hair is a burden to him, or if he goes among people of different beliefs who would look upon him with disdain because of his hair.

3. It is customary for a mourner to change his place at the synagogue during the first thirty days of mourning for his next of kin, and during the first twelve months of mourning for his parent. The new place should be at least four cubits (about six feet) distant from his accustomed seat and further removed from the Holy Ark.

4. One is forbidden during the first thirty days of mourning for one's next of kin, and during the first twelve months of mourning the death of a parent, to join in any celebration, even of a religious duty, such as a circumcision, the redemption of the first-born, or a

wedding. The mourner may, however, participate in a religious feast celebrated at the mourner's house, provided it is not a wedding feast.

5. During the first thirty days of mourning for one's next of kin, and the twelve months of mourning for one's parent, one is not permitted to invite others to say Grace, or to join with others in saying Grace; neither should he send or receive gifts.

6. During the first thirty days of mourning for one's next of kin, and the twelve months of mourning for one's parent, the mourner may not enter a house where a wedding feast is being celebrated, even if it is merely for the purpose of hearing the benedictions. After the first thirty days, however, the mourner may act as best man in escorting the bridegroom under the nuptial canopy, and on that occasion may put on Sabbath clothes.

7. After the first thirty days of mourning, even for one's father, a mourner who officiates either as godfather or as circumciser, is permitted to put on his Sabbath garments and wear them until after the circumcision, and he may also join in the feast.

8. A mourner is permitted to serve as waiter at a wedding, and may, in his own house, eat whatever is sent him from the feast.

XI. THE MEAL OF CONDOLENCE

1. The first meal on the first day of mourning, must not consist of the mourner's own food. It is therefore a religious duty devolving upon the mourner's neighbors to supply the food for the first meal, which is known as the "Meal of condolence." The reason for this rule of law is obvious. A person in dire distress is in need of friendly neighbors and their consolation.

2. If the mourner's first meal after burial is delayed until nightfall, it may, inasmuch as the first day has passed, be then made of the mourner's own food. A mourner living a lone life without neighbors to contribute food for the meal of condolence, should therefore fast until nightfall; nevertheless, a person unable to fast, is not obliged to suffer, but is allowed to eat of his own food.

3. To women in mourning, the meal of condolence should be supplied by women and not by men.

4. If the burial has taken place at night and the mourner desires

to eat during that night, he is forbidden to eat of his own food, but he should be provided with food for the meal of condolence. Should he not desire to eat during the night, he is forbidden to eat the first meal of his own food the following day, since the first day of mourning is not over until sunset.

5. A married woman is not allowed to take the first meal of her husband's food, for inasmuch as it devolves upon him to support her, it is considered as her own food.

6. If the burial takes place on a Friday after three o'clock in the afternoon, the mourner should not be served with a meal of condolence in deference to the Sabbath. The mourner should abstain from eating until the evening.

7. If the burial takes place on a Festival, the meal of condolence is not served to the mourner; but if it takes place on the Intermediate Days of a Festival, a meal of condolence should be served.

8. The meal of condolence must be served to one who has received "timely" news (see Section that follows), but not on "delayed" news. If the mourner has received "timely" news on the Sabbath, he may eat the first meal of his own food, and no meal of condolence should be served to him even on the Sunday thereafter.

XII. "TIMELY" AND "DELAYED" NEWS

1. If one has heard of the death of his next of kin, for whom he is required to observe the rites of mourning, within thirty days, even on the thirtieth day, the tidings are "timely" and he should rend his garments and observe the seven days of mourning, counting them from the day on which he has received the news. He should also observe the thirty days of mourning counting them from the same day. The day when the news reaches him is governed by the same rules as obtain on the day of burial. The thirty-day period which is considered as "timely" is to be counted from the day of the interment and not from the day of death.

2. If the news has reached him after thirty days, the tidings are "delayed," and he need not observe the rite of mourning for more than one hour, and it makes no difference whether he has received the tidings by day or by night. One hour's mourning is sufficient in

that event even for one's parent, with the exception that it is the mourner's duty to observe the usual mourning of twelve months for one's parent, even if the tidings of the death were "delayed." The twelve months of mourning are to be counted from the day of death, and if the tidings have reached him after the twelve months, he need not observe any kind of mourning for more than one hour.

3. No mourning ritual is to be observed upon receiving "delayed" tidings, other than the removing of his shoes, or sitting on a low bench for one hour.

4. One who has received "timely" news on the Sabbath, should count the Sabbath as one day, and at the termination of the Sabbath he should rend his garments and observe six days of mourning thereafter.

5. If one has received "timely" news on a Sabbath or a Festival, but this news will become "delayed" after the Sabbath or the Festival, one should observe all the rules of mourning in private, and at the conclusion of the Sabbath or the Festival, one should observe one hour's mourning as though the news were "delayed."

6. If one received "timely" tidings on the Sabbath which is the eve of a Festival, inasmuch as he must observe mourning in privacy, the Festival annuls the seven days of mourning.

7. He who receives "delayed" tidings on a Sabbath or a Festival should not observe any mourning even in privacy, but at the conclusion of the Sabbath or the Festival he should observe one hour's mourning.

8. If after a Festival one has received news of a death that occurred before the Festival, the Festival does not annul the mourning. Therefore if the news has reached him within thirty days after the burial, he must observe the seven and the thirty days of mourning.

9. It is improper to inform any one of his relative's death. Concerning such a news-bearer, it is said (Prov. X, 18): "He that uttereth a report is a fool." As long as a person is ignorant of his relative's death, he may be invited to any joyful gathering.

10. If one inquires concerning the welfare of a relative who has died, he should not be told that the relative is alive, for it is written

(Ex. XXIII, 7): "Keep thee far from a false matter," but he should be answered ambiguously.

11. It is customary to inform sons of the death of their father or mother in order that they should say *kaddish*.

XIII. THE MOURNER'S KADDISH

1. Many stories have been told by our Sages of old to the effect that because of the son's saying *kaddish* for his departed father or mother, the dead are saved from judgment. It is therefore customary for a mourner to say *kaddish* and to be called up to *maftir* and to act as Reader before the congregation.

2. The mourner's *kaddish* has no special reference to the dead. But great importance has been attached to the reciting of the *kaddish* for several reasons. First, the son, by reciting the *kaddish* is instrumental in calling forth the most important congregational utterance: "Amen, yehe shemeh rabba meborakh lealam ulealme almaya" (Amen, let His great name be blessed for ever and to all eternity). The parent's memory is honored by this public participation of his child in honoring God through the voice of the assembled people. The Talmudic authorities speak often of the importance of this utterance.

Secondly, the *kaddish* is Messianic; it points toward the establishment of the Kingdom of God, after the Resurrection. Indirectly, then, the *kaddish* contains the assurance of immortality, and hope for the day when the reign of death shall be over, and life eternal be established. Thirdly, the *kaddish* is a touching expression of reverential submission to the Divine Will. At the very moment when death has laid its cold hand on the mourner's heart, he stands forth to pronounce before the congregation the greatness and holiness of God. "The Lord gave and the Lord hath taken, blessed be the name of the Lord" (Job i, 21).

3. It is customary to say *kaddish* no longer than eleven months after the parent's death, in order not to make the departed appear as evildoers, for the wicked are judged by the Heavenly Court during the first twelve months. The Jewish religion teaches that, with the exception of a very few, no soul suffers eternal perdition,

but the maximum period during which the wicked suffer punishment is twelve months.

4. A daughter should not say *kaddish* in the synagogue.

5. Although the saying of *kaddish* is helpful to the departed parents, it is far more important that they obtain Divine Grace through their children who walk in the paths of righteousness. A man should therefore charge his children to adhere to a certain precept. Its fulfillment shall stand him in better stead than the saying of *kaddish*. This is especially useful to one who has only daughters.

6. If there is no mourner for a father or a mother present in the synagogue, any one who has neither father nor mother should recite the mourner's *kaddish* whenever necessary, in memory of the departed in Israel.

XIV. COMFORTING THE MOURNERS

1. It is an important religious duty to visit mourners and to comfort them. The comforters are not allowed to open the conversation before the mourner has first commenced to speak, and if they perceive that the mourner wishes them to withdraw, they must do so.

2. The comforter must not say to the mourner: "What can you do? It is impossible to alter the decree of the Creator, blessed be He." Such an expression is akin to blasphemy, implying that were it possible for him to change it, he would do so. A man must accept in love the decree of the Almighty.

3. The mourners should mourn in the place where the death took place. It is a religious duty to pray there with a *Minyan* (a quorum of ten male adults) in the morning and in the evening, even if there is no mourner present. If there is a mourner present, he is to be counted in the *Minyan*.

4. A candle or lamp should be kept burning for the departed soul during the seven days of mourning, especially when the prayers are offered.

5. If a mourner is present, no *Hallel* is to be recited in the house where a death occurred, during the first seven days of mourning. *Hallel* should be recited, however, if the services are held in the

house where the death occurred when there is no mourner present, or if it is held in the house of the mourner, where the death did not occur.

XV. WHEN MOURNER MAY MARRY

1. During the first seven days of mourning, a mourner is not permitted to marry. It is permissible to arrange a betrothal without a feast, even during the first seven days of mourning.

2. If one's wife has died, one is not permitted to remarry until three Festivals have elapsed. Rosh Hashanah, Yom Kippur, and Shemini Atzeret are not considered Festivals in this respect. If, however, the widower has young children and has no one to look after them, he need not wait for the three Festivals to pass; but even then, it is proper for him to wait until after the first thirty days of mourning. A woman whose husband has died must wait ninety days before remarriage.

XVI. EXCESSIVE GRIEF IS FORBIDDEN

1. It is strictly forbidden to grieve excessively over the dead. We must acknowledge that the Lord God is righteous in all His ways. Our Sages say that the Holy One, blessed be He, says: "You are not permitted to be more compassionate than I am."

2. If a member of a family has passed away, the entire family should evince sorrow, and if one of a society has passed away, all the members of the society should evince sorrow.

3. He who does not mourn in accordance with the regulations laid down by our Sages is considered heartless.

XVII. PART OF A MOURNING DAY

1. Our Sages say: "A part of a day is considered as the entire day." Therefore on the seventh day of mourning, after the time when the comforters have been wont to come, the mourner is permitted to do all those things that were forbidden him during the seven days.

2. With reference to the thirtieth day of mourning, the Sages also say that a part of a day is considered as an entire day. Therefore immediately after sunrise on the thirtieth day, the mourner is ab-

solved from observing the laws pertaining to the thirty days of mourning. If the thirtieth day occurs on the Sabbath, the mourner is permitted to bathe in warm water on Friday in honor of the Sabbath; he may put on the Sabbath garments, and he may resume his original seat in the synagogue, but he may not cut his hair.

3. The rule that "a part of a day is considered as the entire day," does not apply to the twelve months of mourning for one's parent. On the contrary, it is customary to add the Jahrzeit (anniversary of death) day to the twelve months of mourning, even if it occurs on the Sabbath. During a leap year, when an additional month is added to the Jewish calendar, mourning need not be observed for the loss of a parent longer than twelve months; and inasmuch as the twelve months expired before the Jahrzeit day, the mourner is not required to resume mourning on the Jahrzeit day.

XVIII. MOURNING ON THE SABBATH OR FESTIVAL

1. On the Sabbath that occurs during the first seven days of mourning, all the rules regulating the mourner's private life must be observed, such as the prohibition against sexual intercourse and bathing. No rites of mourning, however, are to be observed in public. Therefore before the recital of "Mizmor shir leyom hashabbat" (A psalm, a hymn for the Sabbath), the mourner may put on his shoes, sit on a regular chair, and put on another garment in place of the one bearing the mark of mourning. (See p. 230, par. 6.)

2. If the mourner is called up to pronounce the benedictions over the reading of the Torah, he must go up, because his refusal would indicate public observance of mourning.

3. The Sabbath day is included in the total of the first seven days of mourning. Even if he received "timely" tidings of the death of a relative on the Sabbath when he did not begin mourning, the Sabbath is counted as one of the seven days, and he should rend his garments at the conclusion of the Sabbath.

4. If a burial takes place, or "timely" news is received on a Festival itself or during the Intermediate Days of a Festival (Hol Hammoed), no rites of mourning are to be observed in public until after the conclusion of the Festival, but all the rules regulating the mourner's private life must be observed.

5. At the conclusion of the Festival, the mourner should begin to count six days of mourning, because the last day of the Festival is counted as one of the seven days.

6. The Festival days, including the Intermediate Days of the Festival, are included in the total of the thirty days of mourning. One should therefore count the thirty days from the day on which the burial took place.

XIX. A FESTIVAL ANNULS THE MOURNING PERIOD

1. If the burial takes place before a Festival, and the mourner has observed some rites of mourning before the beginning of the Festival, the Festival annuls the seven-day mourning period, for it is considered as though he had observed the entire seven-day period of mourning. The first day of the Festival is counted as the eighth day of mourning from which time he has to complete the thirty-day period of mourning.

2. If the mourner either inadvertently or intentionally has neglected to observe some rites of mourning before the Festival, or if he has been unable to observe them because the burial took place at the approach of night, he is not exempt from observing the seven-day mourning period, as the Festival in this case does not annul it; and the mourner is subject to the same law as applies to one who buries his dead on a Festival.

3. If the mourner has observed the seven-day mourning period before a Festival, even if the seventh day occurs on the day before the Festival, the thirty-day mourning period is annulled by the intervention of the Festival. The mourner may bathe and have his hair cut towards nightfall. If the seventh day occurs on the day before Passover, all of the above may be done immediately after midday.

4. The intervention of a Festival does not annul the thirty-day mourning period as regards the restriction against cutting the hair, if the mourning is observed for the loss of a parent.

5. If a mourner has observed the rite of mourning for a short time before the Passover, he is considered as having mourned for a full seven days, which together with the eight days of Passover makes a total of fifteen days, and he need mourn only fifteen more days to complete the thirty-day period. If he has observed mourn-

ing for a short time before Shabuot (Pentecost), this is reckoned as though he had observed mourning for seven full days, and the first day of Shabuot is also reckoned as seven days, while the second day of Shabuot constitutes the fifteenth day of mourning, and only fifteen more days are needed to complete the thirty-day period. Similarly, time spent in mourning before Sukkot (Feast of Tabernacles) is counted as seven days, which together with the seven days of Sukkot are reckoned as fourteen days, the Festival of Shemini Atzeret counts also as seven days, making it a total of twenty-one days; Simehat Torah counts for one day, so we have twenty-two days; and only eight more days are needed to complete the thirty-day period.

6. Rosh Hashanah and Yom Kippur are considered as Festivals with regard to the annulment of the seven days and the thirty days of mourning. Thus, any time spent in mourning before Rosh Hashanah annuls the seven days of mourning, while Yom Kippur annuls the thirty-day period. Any time spent in mourning before Yom Kippur annuls the seven days, while Sukkot annuls the thirty-day period.

XX. DEDICATION OF TOMBSTONE

1. It is an ancient custom in Israel, dating from the days of our ancestor Jacob, to set up a tombstone at the head of the grave in honor of the departed.

2. In some communities the custom prevails not to put up a tombstone until twelve months after death.

XXI. JAHRZEIT (ANNIVERSARY OF DEATH)

1. It is a religious duty of every person to observe the anniversary of the death of one's father or mother, by fasting, in order that one may be impelled to self-criticism and repentance. By doing this, one obtains Divine Grace for one's father or mother in heaven.

2. The anniversary should always be observed on the day the death occurred. However, if there was an interval of several days between the day of death and the burial, then the first year the Jahrzeit should be observed on the day the burial took place, but in subsequent years it is always observed on the day of death.

3. On a day when *tahanun* (petition for grace) is not recited (see pp. 32–34), no fasting should be observed. The following do not fast: the father, the *sandek* (god-father), and the *mohel* (circumciser) on the day of circumcision; the father and the *Kohen* on the day a *pideyon habben* (redemption of the first-born) takes place; and a bridegroom and a bride during the seven days of rejoicing in honor of the wedding. But it is not permissible to partake of the meal served at a *siyum* (completion of a Talmudic treatise) on the day of Jahrzeit. On the days when no fasting is to be observed, one should devote time to the study of the Torah and to the performance of good deeds.

4. If one is not certain of the date of one's parent's death, one should select the approximate date, and should always observe that day as Jahrzeit.

5. If one has been unable to say *kaddish* on the Jahrzeit day, as for instance if he has been on a journey, then he may say *kaddish* at the *maarib* (evening) service following the day of the Jahrzeit.

6. It is customary to kindle a light on the eve of the Jahrzeit, which is kept burning for twenty-four hours. This practice is linked with the thought expressed by King Solomon (Prov. xx, 27): "The spirit of man is the lamp of the Lord."

XXII. YIZKOR (MEMORIAL SERVICE)

1. It is the custom to recite *yizkor* (memorial prayers) for the departed four times during the year: on Yom Kippur (Day of Atonement); on the eighth day of Sukkot, known as Shemini Atzeret; on the last day of Passover; and on the second day of Shabuot (Pentecost). We donate to charitable institutions, while saying *yizkor*, for the souls of the departed.

2. If one is unable to attend the services at the synagogue, one may recite the Memorial Service at home.

3. *Yizkor* is not said during the first twelve months after the death of one's father or mother.

4. It is customary for those whose father and mother are alive to leave the synagogue while the Memorial Prayers are recited. Anyone whose father or mother has passed away during that year also leaves the synagogue during the Memorial Service.